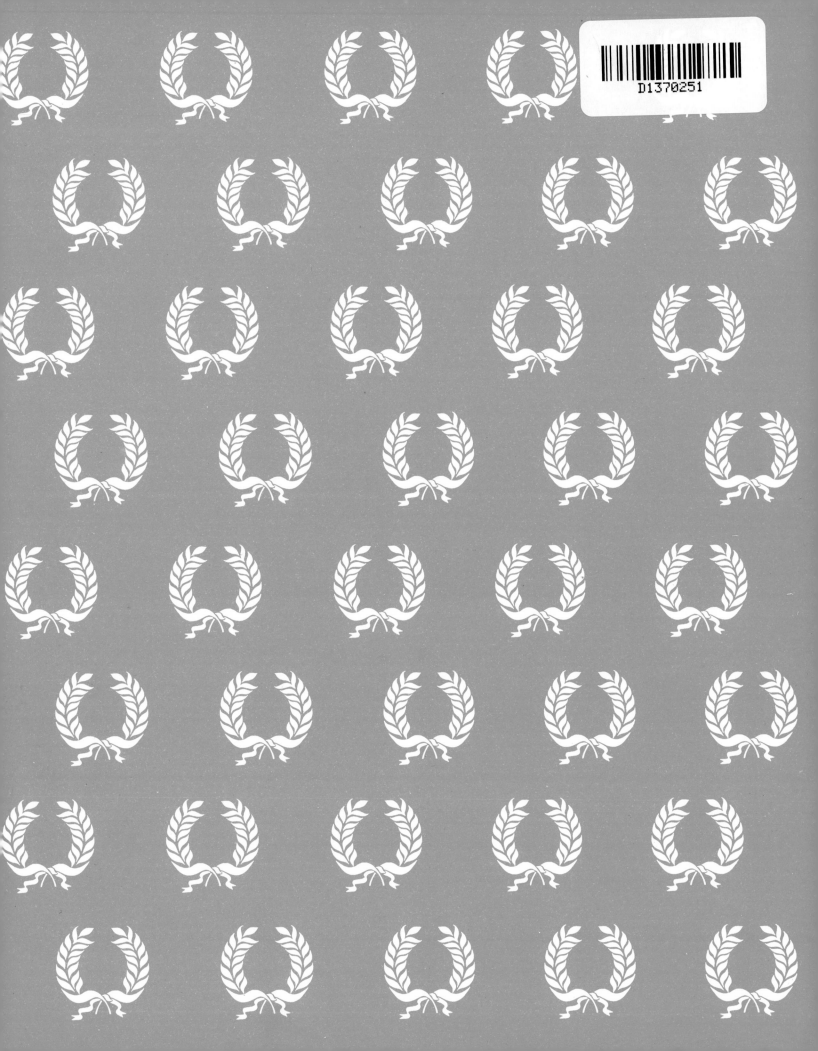

I Wonder Why

Romans Wore Togas

and Other Questions About Ancient Rome

Fiona Macdonald

KINGFISHER

NEW YORK

KINGFISHER
Larousse Kingfisher Chambers Inc.
95 Madison Avenue
New York, New York 10016

First edition 1997
10 9 8 7 6 5   HB - 5TR/0600/TIM/HBM/128MA
Copyright © Kingfisher Publications Plc

LIBRARY OF CONGRESS CATALOGING-IN-PUBLICATION DATA
Macdonald, Fiona.
I wonder why Romans wore togas and other questions about
ancient Rome / Fiona Macdonald
     p.   cm.—(I wonder why)
     Includes index.
Summary: Questions and answers introduce the
clothing, food, language, religion, and other aspects
of daily life in ancient Rome.
1. Rome—Civilization—Juvenile literature.
2. Rome—History—Empire. 30 B.C.–476 A.D.
—Juvenile literature. 3. Rome—Social life
and customs—Juvenile literature.
[1. Rome—Civilization—Miscellanea.
2. Question and answers.]
I. Title. II. Series: I wonder why (New York, N. Y.)
DG78.M23 1997
937'.06—dc20 96-34547 CIP AC

ISBN 0-7534-5057-7
Printed in China

Series designer: David West Children's Books
Author: Fiona Macdonald
Consultant: Dr. Paul Roberts
Cover Illustration: Nicki Palin
Cartoons: Tony Kenyon (B.L. Kearley)

CONTENTS

Who were the Romans?

The Romans were people who lived in Rome more than 2,000 years ago. They became very powerful. By A.D. 100, they had conquered the lands around them and ruled a huge empire. It was one of the mightiest empires in the ancient world.

● Different parts of the empire had very different climates. The Romans boiled in Egypt, where the summers were sweltering...

BRITAIN

Hadrian's Wall

London

FRANCE
(Gaul)

•Lyon

Alps

SPAIN

Pyrenees

ITALY

•Rome

Pompeii

Carthage •

AFRICA

● An old legend says that the city of Rome was first started by a man named Romulus. He and his twin brother Remus had been abandoned by their parents and were looked after by a wolf!

Did all the Romans live in Rome?

...but they shivered in the icy Swiss Alps and in northern Britain. These were the coldest places in the whole empire.

The city of Rome wasn't big enough for all the Romans! In total, there were about 50 million people in the empire, which stretched from Britain in the north to Africa in the south. Everyone in the empire was protected by Rome's armies and had to obey Rome's laws.

THE ROMAN EMPIRE A.D. 100

Caspian Sea

Black Sea

Constantinople

Athens · Ephesus

ASIA MINOR

Antioch

SYRIA

ARABIA

Mediterranean Sea

N

Alexandria

EGYPT

Red Sea

It would have taken nearly 100 days to travel on horseback across the whole of the empire. It was a journey of about 3,000 miles.

5

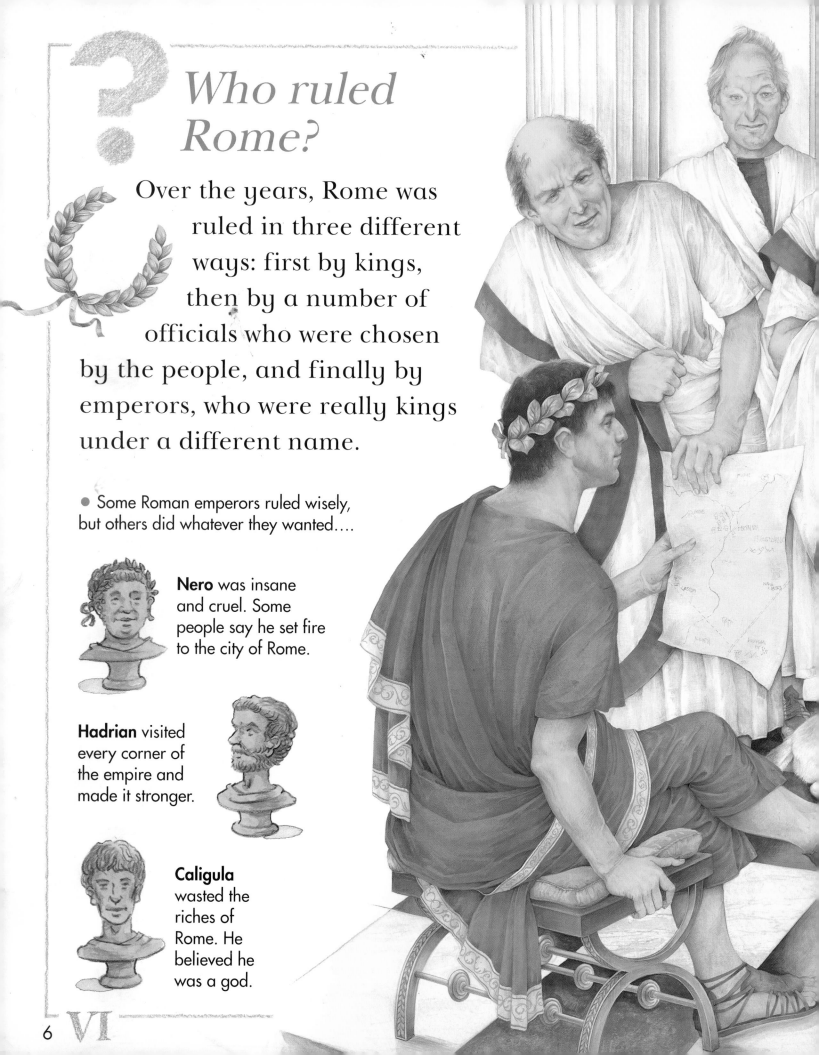

Who ruled Rome?

Over the years, Rome was ruled in three different ways: first by kings, then by a number of officials who were chosen by the people, and finally by emperors, who were really kings under a different name.

● Some Roman emperors ruled wisely, but others did whatever they wanted….

Nero was insane and cruel. Some people say he set fire to the city of Rome.

Hadrian visited every corner of the empire and made it stronger.

Caligula wasted the riches of Rome. He believed he was a god.

Who was born free?

Roman citizens were! Not only could they vote in elections, they also got free seats at the amphitheater and free use of the public baths. When times were hard, they even got free loaves of bread!

● Roman women did not have the same rights as men. They were not allowed to vote and had to obey their husbands or fathers. But that doesn't mean they always did!

Who slaved away for the Romans?

Most of the hard work in Rome was done by slaves. These men, women, and children were captured abroad and then sold in the marketplace in Rome. Each slave wore an identity tag with his or her master's name and address on it—just in case they got lost.

● The first Roman emperor was called Augustus. He was advised by a group of wealthy men, called senators, who were used to running the army and the government.

● Slaves were sometimes given their freedom after many years of good service, or if their master wanted to be kind.

When did the army use tortoises?

When Roman soldiers were advancing toward the enemy, they did a special trick called "the tortoise." They held their shields high above their heads to make a kind of shell. This protected them from enemy spears—but made it hard for them to see where they were going!

Dear Mom IV/VII/CIV
Having an awful time. The Barbarians are fierce and I think the Centurion hates me. Please send V sesterces for food.
Your loving son
Marcus XXX

● Soldiers were often hungry and cold. Many of them wrote letters home asking for extra food and clothing.

● Injured soldiers bandaged their wounds with cobwebs soaked in vinegar. This helped the soldiers, but wasn't so good for the spiders!

Which soldiers left home for 25 years?

Most soldiers had to stay in the army for 25 years. Those who were Roman citizens were luckier—they could leave after only 20 years. Soldiers had a hard life. They were far from home and had to put up with tough training and harsh punishments.

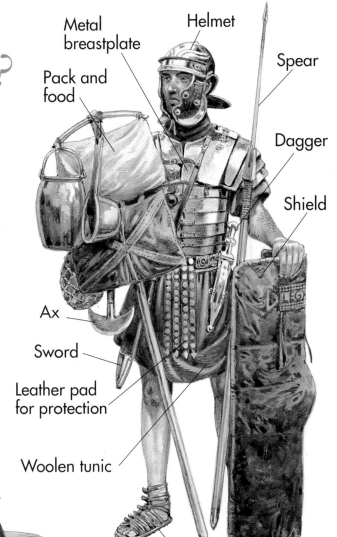

Metal breastplate

Helmet

Spear

Pack and food

Dagger

Shield

Ax

Sword

Leather pad for protection

Woolen tunic

Leather sandals

● In warmer parts of the empire, soldiers didn't wear much under their tunics. In chilly places they wore thick woolen underwear— just like the locals.

9

Who attacked the Romans with elephants?

In the 220s B.C. Hannibal was the leader of the Carthaginians in Spain. From there, he led a huge army and a herd of elephants across the Pyrenees and over the Alps to Italy, to fight the Romans for land. In battle, the elephants charged the Roman soldiers, who ran away in terror.

● Queen Cleopatra of Egypt used her beauty and charm against the Romans. She made two Roman commanders—Julius Caesar and Mark Anthony—fall in love with her.

● In Britain the Romans built Hadrian's Wall, which was 72 miles long. From this wall they could see if any Scots were attacking from the north.

• Forty thousand men and 37 elephants made the long, dangerous march from Spain over the Alps—the mountains in northern Italy. Sadly, many of them died along the way.

Which Roman guards went quack-quack-quack?

A flock of holy geese lived among the temples on Rome's Capitoline Hill. One dark night, a fierce tribe called the Gauls were planning an attack. They crept up the hill but were heard by the geese, who quacked a loud warning and saved the citizens of Rome.

Who was Queen Boudicca?

Queen Boudicca was a ruler in ancient Britain when the Romans invaded. Legend says she attached sharp knives to the wheels of her chariot, then drove straight into the lines of the approaching Roman army!

Who did the Romans worship?

Jupiter, king of the gods

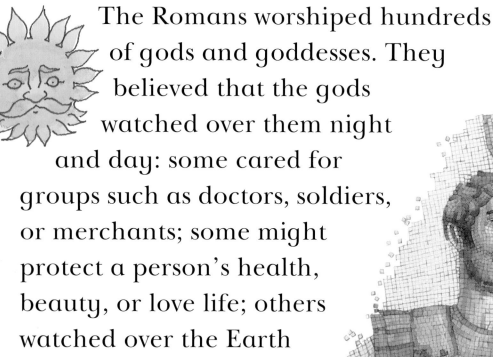

The Romans worshiped hundreds of gods and goddesses. They believed that the gods watched over them night and day: some cared for groups such as doctors, soldiers, or merchants; some might protect a person's health, beauty, or love life; others watched over the Earth and the sea.

● The Romans thought that snakes brought good luck, so they painted them on their walls.

Mars, god of war

● The Romans believed that spirits lived in the rivers, woods, and fields to protect the wild animals and plants that lived there.

Venus, goddess of love

Juno, queen of the gods

● Sick Romans prayed to the gods to cure them. If they got better, they left a thank-you present in the temple—a small model of the part of their body that had been cured.

Neptune, god of the sea

Diana, goddess of the Moon and of hunting

● The Romans built temples as homes for the gods. Each god or goddess had a temple of their own. It was built of the finest stone and decorated with statues and carvings.

Apollo, god of the Sun and of the arts

Why did Roman women look pale?

● Slaves mixed skin creams from all kinds of ingredients including flour, chalk, lead, and even donkey's milk.

Pale skin was a sure sign that a Roman woman came from a wealthy family. Poorer women had to work outside. Their faces burned in the hot summer sun, and became rough and red in the cold winter winds.

● Fashionable men wore perfume and makeup. They even had stick-on leather patches to hide any pimples or scars.

● The Romans used all sorts of beauty tools—combs and hairpins made of bone, heated curling irons, tweezers to pluck out stray hairs, and tiny spoons to scoop the wax from their ears.

How did Romans treat their hairdressers?

Most Roman noblewomen had slave girls to do their hair. Some of the women were cruel to their slaves. They jabbed them with hairpins if the girls pulled their hair, and might even whip them if the style came out wrong.

● Wigs were very fashionable. Blond hair came from German slaves. Dark glossy hair was bought from poor women in India.

Why did Romans wear togas?

Men wore togas to show that they were Roman citizens. Slaves could not wear them. An ordinary citizen's toga was plain white, a senator's had purple trim, and the emperor's was all purple. Women wore *pallas*—like togas, but in any color.

Where did Romans take baths?

In Roman times, many people went to the public baths, which were a little like today's health clubs. They went to the baths to exercise, play games, meet their friends, relax after a hard day's work— oh, and to get clean too.

● The Romans hardly ever used soap—but they weren't dirty. They rubbed oil all over their skin and then scraped the oil off with a blunt metal tool called a *strigil*. The dirt on their skin came off with the oil.

● Hot air from underground furnaces heated the water in the public baths. It also made the bottom of the baths very hot and some people wore sandals to avoid burning their feet!

- Some public baths had a library—very handy for people who liked reading in the tub.

Rise and Fall of Rome

Who went to the bathroom together?

The Romans often did. All cities had multi-seat public toilets, which were cheap to build and easy to clean. Sometimes as many as 16 people sat side by side, laughing and talking with each other.

OCCUPIED

- Most homes didn't have a toilet. Families used big pottery jars instead.

Who lived in high-rise apartments?

Space was short in Rome and most people lived in apartment blocks, about six stories high. The first floor had noisy stores and taverns. The top floor had stuffy attic rooms. The best apartments were in the middle.

● The Romans liked gardening. Rich people's gardens had pools and fountains. But even the poorest families kept flowerpots on the windowsill.

● Roman high-rises were so badly built that they often fell down. To stop accidents, the emperor Augustus passed a law forbidding any new building more than 65 feet high.

Which houses had holes in the roof?

Rich people's houses were built around an open-air courtyard. The open roof let in daylight and cool breezes during the summer, as well as chilly wind and rain in the winter.

Which guard dog was made of stone?

Next to the front door of many Roman homes was a mosaic—a picture made up of tiny pieces of colored stone—showing a fierce dog. Under it was the Latin phrase *Cave Canem*, meaning "Beware of the Dog," to discourage any burglars.

Who brought slaves, spices, and silk?

Merchants traveled to the ends of the empire and beyond to bring back goods for the citizens of Rome.

As well as ordinary things like corn and timber, they brought slaves from North Africa, spices from India, and beautiful silk from China.

● Ostia was the port of Rome. It lay on the coast, 15 miles from the city. Sacks of corn and jars of wine and olive oil were stored in warehouses at the port and sent up to the market by barge.

● Most merchants preferred to keep their ships in port all winter, safe from storms and shipwrecks.

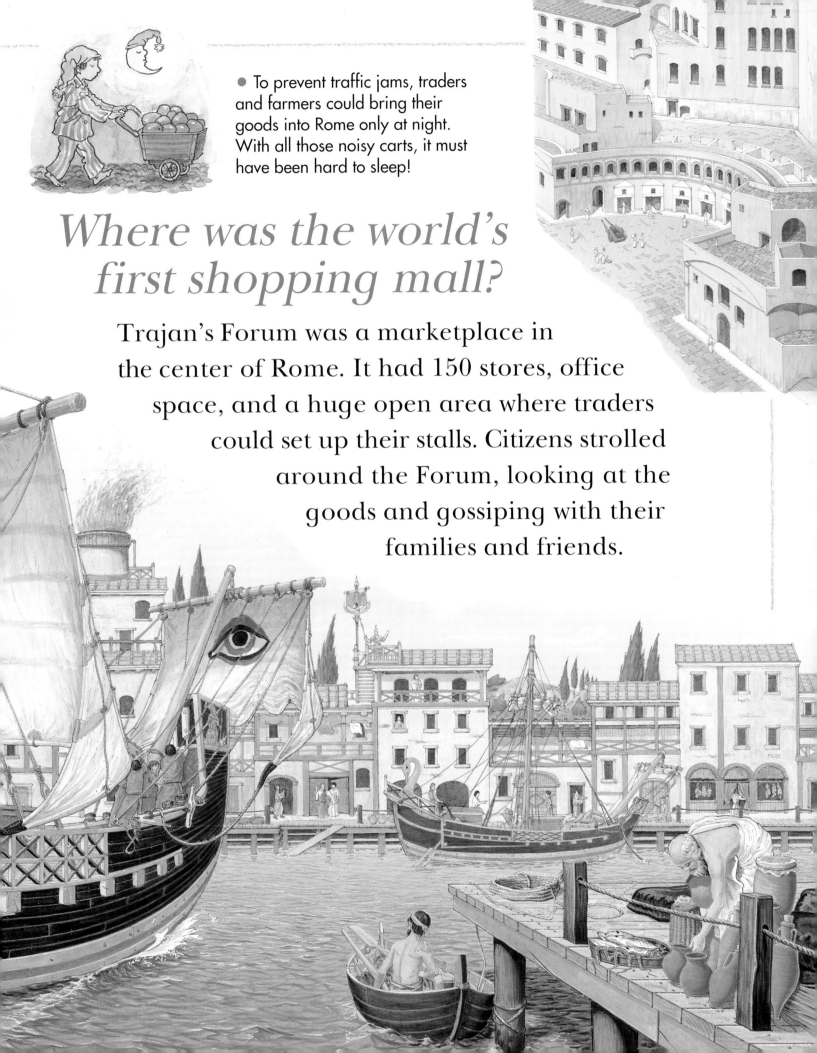

● To prevent traffic jams, traders and farmers could bring their goods into Rome only at night. With all those noisy carts, it must have been hard to sleep!

Where was the world's first shopping mall?

Trajan's Forum was a marketplace in the center of Rome. It had 150 stores, office space, and a huge open area where traders could set up their stalls. Citizens strolled around the Forum, looking at the goods and gossiping with their families and friends.

Did the Romans eat pizza?

Every day the Romans bought hot pies and tasty treats, a bit like modern pizzas, from the stores and taverns in the busy towns. The "pizzas" were topped with onions, fish, and olives—but not tomatoes, which were brought over from South America about 1,500 years later.

● The taverns did a roaring trade selling hot food and drink. Few families had a kitchen at home, and anyway, ovens were forbidden in high-rises, for fear of fire.

● In hot weather, rich people cooled their drinks with snow. It was carried down from the mountains by slaves.

Why did people throw up at banquets?

At the best banquets, many guests were too full for all the wonderful food and drink. To solve the problem, they'd sometimes go outside and make themselves vomit. Then they returned to the table to eat some more!

● Wealthy Romans ate all sorts of fancy foods, such as boiled ostrich, and dormice in honey. They also liked surprises. At one banquet, a roast pig was carved open and a flock of live birds flew out!

Who ate lying down?

Wealthy Romans didn't sit at the table. Instead, they lay propped up on their elbows on long wooden couches. This must have given them indigestion. Their children had more sense—they sat on stools close to their parents.

Who went to school in Roman times?

● Roman children only studied three subjects at school—reading, writing, and math.

Children from wealthy families went to school when they were seven years old. Poor children stayed at home. Some of them spent the day helping their parents in the house or out in the fields. Others were sent out to look for work or to play in the streets.

What language did Romans speak?

Everyone who lived in Italy spoke Latin. Everywhere else in the empire, people spoke their own local languages. But there were so many languages that people from all parts of the empire learned Latin, too, so that they could all understand one another!

● Girls left school at 11, but boys stayed on until they were 16 or 18 years old.

What did Roman children play with?

Many Roman toys and games were not unlike modern ones. Roman children used little round nuts as marbles and threw dice 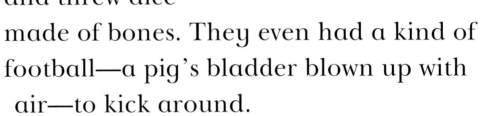 made of bones. They even had a kind of football—a pig's bladder blown up with air—to kick around.

CAESAR HORRIBILISSIMUS EST

● The Romans loved to scribble on walls. On many of their buildings you can still see the insulting things they wrote about their leaders and enemies— and even their friends!

● The Romans used letters for numbers: I was 1, V was 5, X was 10, L was 50, and so on. Have you noticed the Roman page numbers in this book?

I, II, III, IV, V, VI, VII, VIII, IX, X, XI, XII, XIII, XIV...

XXV

Why were Roman roads so straight?

The Romans were wonderful engineers. Before they built a road, they used measuring instruments to figure out where the road should go. They chose the shortest, straightest route between two camps, forts, or towns and they got rid of any bushes or buildings in the way. These roads linked the whole empire.

PLAN VIEW

SIDE ELEVATION

ARCHITECT
Marcu

● Road builders put milestones along the side of the road so that travelers knew how far they had gone. A Roman mile was 1,000 paces long.

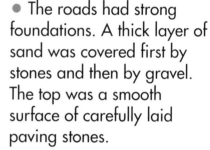

ROME
500
MILES

● The roads had strong foundations. A thick layer of sand was covered first by stones and then by gravel. The top was a smooth surface of carefully laid paving stones.

Which bridges were always full of water?

Aqueducts look like bridges, but instead of a roadway along the top they have a deep channel of water. The Romans built them to carry water from mountain streams to nearby cities. Without aqueducts, the people wouldn't have had baths, toilets, or fountains of fresh running water.

CLAUDIUS EMPEROR

●The Romans invented concrete by mixing lime, water, and the ash from volcanoes. This concrete was as strong as stone and it set hard, even under water.

●The Romans invented arches, too. Each arch rested on a wooden frame until the very last stone—the keystone—was in place.

Chapter 2

Will a New Logic of Management Emerge?

Michel Crozier

1

During the present period of accelerated change, organizational studies should focus again on the basic logic of management practices. This does not in any way mean that we should indulge in the normative orientations of business management teaching. But, that on the contrary, questions should be raised on the assumptions behind these orientations and their relationships with management models for that have become less and less appropriate with the problems organizations face in a postindustrial society.

When the focus on change becomes overwhelming the debate around the basic principles that were previously taken for granted once again becomes relevant. I believe that we are presently in the midst of such a period. And I also believe that sociological research could be and should be crucial to help experiment new methods and elaborate new principles and new reasoning. Normative theories should not be discarded lightly. When accepted as common knowledge, they have real consequences. At a time of rapid change when they become obsolete (to the necessary revolution in practices), positive research has a central role to play, in order to question outdated principles and also to help elaborate new ones. Such endeavours are not only fruitful for practice but will have an extremely favourable influence on research whose new relevance will help meet the challenge of an experimental situation.

From this point of view, ever since the time of Taylor the dominant logic of management has been the logic of rationalization. This logic was severely criticized from a humanistic and a political angle but also from a positivist sociological point of view. Nevertheless it has withstood all its critics from the only point of view that matters, i.e. *practice*. The attacks it withstood may have seemed devastating, at first, but they were gradually turned into new procedures for extending the domain of rationalization. This was especially true for the human relations challenge to rationalization which has given birth to new sophisticated techniques to include the rationalization of personnel management without changing the logic of economic rationality to which they were subordinated. This recurrent drift which has repeated itself since the 1930s has substantially weakened the impact of organizational research.

Organizational studies therefore have been pushed more and more towards abstract and deterministic models. Being part of "normal science" they have attracted less and less interest and in fact have lost touch with the crucial problems pertaining to practice.

2

The very long period of dominance of the logic of rationalization may now have come to an end. Rationalization is inescapable when the model cycle of economic activity is the mass production/mass consumption model. It becomes an impediment or a brake in development when the model is no more dominant. Indeed the acceleration of change in the economic and social fabric of our developed societies is such that it will force a major revolution in the logic of human activities of the magnitude of the Industrial Revolution of the nineteenth century as well as the Taylorian revolution of the early twentieth century.

There are at least three major trends that are upsetting our basic logic: the complexity of human interactions, the growing freedom of choice of individuals and the movement towards a service society.

The extraordinary complexity of technical, economic and social interactions in a world of explosive scientific development, global competition and global markets makes it increasingly difficult, if not impossible, to succeed with the traditional instruments of rationalization.

To quite an extent, managements's main task now appears to be the management of complexity. It becomes radically different, when the gradual increase in the degree of complexity is such that the nature of the phenomenon changes. The tools offered by the logic of scientific organization no longer work in such a context. This is already obvious for achieving effective cooperation between different sophisticated technical specialities in the elaboration of new products. The analytical breakdown of operations and their bureaucratic reconstruction stifles cooperation and prevents synergy. Moreover even conventional activities are threatened as soon as the complexity is such that human adjustment cannot help cope with the weight of the rigid impersonal theoretical model. Rationalization works well enough, when it can be counterbalanced by the ingenuity of the human actors. But when organizations become too big and too complex for actors to understand, when they become for most of the members a sort of Babel's Tower the erratic consequences of rational planning cannot be redressed.[1]

The second major trend, *the growing freedom of choice of individuals* and groups in a much more open society adds up considerably to the complexity of human interactions.

Statistics on patterns of human behaviour will not provide the answer. It has very narrow limits, since it cannot take into account learning practices that make it possible for operators to manipulate the system as well as cheat. Moreover the system is gradually disorganized. But freedom of choice has also an impact of its own. It weakens and ultimately destroys the patterns of obedience upon which hierarchical management must rely. Scientific management at its beginning believed it could eliminate hierarchy in as much as decisions would become scientifically rational. But experience proved that it could on the contrary survive only by reinforcing it.[2]

When people have the possibility to choose and end the relationships that are not satisfactory since they have other alternatives, the nature of the bargaining between supervisors and subordinates changes. Authority enforcement which used to be easy becomes difficult just at the time when the demand on it becomes much higher. So the tasks of management become much more difficult while the means at its disposal lose credibility.

The third major trend, *the development of a service society* exemplifies and reinforces these ongoing changes. The trend is even more profound than that of the Industrial Revolution which moved agricultural workers from the farm to the factory. Service activities, at the present moment, employ a great many more people than those employed in manufacturing. Industrial activities themselves are increasingly penetrated by service activities. The human and sociological basis of what we have called industrial society is in the process of disappearing and with it the kind of social and political conflict and consensus to which we were accustomed. Moreover the logic of economic activities is shifting. We are no longer dependent on the dominant cycle of mass production/mass consumption. We must also rely more and more on the new couple – high tech and services – which make the economy more dynamic than do the smokestack industries. The driving force of the mass production/mass consumption cycle was rationalization. The motor driving the new cycle of high tech/services is innovation. Rationalization is still indispensable but it is counter-productive if it stifles innovation.

If innovation becomes central for the logic of the new service society characterized by the complexity of human interaction and the freedom of the agents, the human resource becomes the rare resource. In order to succeed, management logic should be articulated around this rare resource and no longer revolve around the optimization of the use of technical and financial resources.[3]

Moreover the nature of human resources changes. It is not their number and availability which is relevant, but their quality from an individual and relational point of view. What makes the difference is neither the numbers nor the sum of individual competencies but the cooperative capabilities of a group of actors.[4]

Management and competence, therefore, will have to change from a technical and bureaucratic proficiency in mastering complexity to a capacity to create conditions for human groups to give the best of their resources to cooperate efficiently and to learn to innovate while taking upon themselves a greater share of the mastering of complexity.

In order to develop such skills management must understand rather than prescribe and command. It should have a much deeper knowledge of the relevant human games at all levels of the organization.

3

In this period of revolution in human activities the pressure for the emergence of a new logic of management does not stem from an idealistic normative movement as was the case previously. Management must change its logic because it has to face new problems which it cannot solve with the old logic. Its challenge becomes how to organize the enterprise or any kind of organization in such a way that human resources be tapped and more fully utilized. This is a rational challenge which has to be met with the help of positive knowledge and rational reasoning.

As it was the case in the Taylorian revolution, organization becomes again the crucial problem of management. Old principles have to be questioned not because they are wrong in absolute terms but because they do not fit into the new context.

The first revolutionary change that has to be achieved concerns structure and procedure. It is already on the way even if it is not yet really articulated as a full doctrine.

For 50 years there had been a concentration of efforts to develop more and more sophisticated structures and procedures in reaction to the growing complexity of a large-scale organization considered to be the embodiment of economic rationality. Organizational design was the supreme art. This type of response has already confronted the law of diminishing returns. More sophistication in staff and line or matricial structures end up in bureaucratic quagmire while they do prevent creativity.

The revolution of the 1980s is difficult to accept because it is paradoxical. The only practical answer to the main problem of complexity is simplicity. Rather than develop more and more sophisticated structures and procedures, one should simplify them, the operators should be professionalized. Intelligence should not be put in structures but in men and women. One cannot think about organizations in the way they were thought about in the 1900s – that is, to make great things with mediocre men. Now the issue is to make it possible for men and women to become less mediocre.

The principle of simplicity, as the new organizational principle, requires a complete reversal of business management logic. It runs counter to the teaching of business schools. It also requires the use of two other principles: the autonomy of operational units and major consideration to organizational culture.

The autonomy of organizational units has been recommended for a long time with the successive formula of management by objectives and profit centres. In the new logic it will develop under a new rationale. The only way to maintain large-scale organizations with simple structures is to give much more autonomy to their operational units. This is also the only way to professionalize line management, i.e. operational management at the expense of procedural management. The two principles will work together; it is not possible to have real autonomy within a complex structure with many echelons and large functional staffs.

If these new revolutionary principles were to be closely applied in practice, how could one maintain the necessary convergence of efforts, the coordination of policies and the implementation of a minimum of common strategy? The hierarchical system was not an end in itself or even a means for extracting as much as possible from a reluctant workforce, it was the instrument that seemed indispensable for maintaining an organization as a viable and if possible efficient entity. Even if one wants to not entirely get rid of it but at least to diminish its weight drastically one would have to look much more seriously into the ways cooperation is achieved in ongoing organizations.

Orders and preconceived rules have an importance to be sure but customary rules and the sheer results of the *de facto* games people have to commit themselves to may govern most of their day-to-day conduct.

This may not be enough. But one can argue if one raises the problem that one can accept a lesser degree of coherence than what is usually required in an organization. The policy to rely more on the initiative of the operational people releases a lot more initiative and energy. The trade-off between coherence and commitment may be solved in a more fruitful way by cutting through the bureaucratic maze. Finally there certainly is a certain minimum that one needs to rely upon but this may not require as much pressure as one thinks.

The pressure of the groups within the system, if well adjusted, can keep people in line without having to resort to rules and hierarchical orders. Within these limits customary rules of conduct sustained by a strong organizational culture constitute a very basic asset for an organization.

In the new societal context, reinforcing this culture and developing it may be one of the most important roles of management. This is where and when sociological research becomes crucial. Managers may understand too quickly the first elements of the problem and if convinced will act in a traditional voluntaristic way triggering strong reactions of rejection amongst their employees, especially middle-level executives: only research can demonstrate that one cannot shape an organizational culture according to one's own wishes even if these wishes are rational, generous and humanistic. The first investment to be made is an investment for knowledge in the patterns of relationships that do prevail and of the circumstantial constraints that have shaped them. Responsible action on the part of management will have to focus on the changing of these constraints and not on the direct shaping of the culture through motivational tools.[5]

In a series of studies of performing organizations in France in 1986 and 1987 we have been able to demonstrate the importance of these mechanisms very well. Motivational and communicational tools fail as well as direct structural constraints. What works are the organizational changes that make it easier and more rewarding for people to motivate themselves.

It is impossible and objectionable on moral grounds to try to motivate people by using psychological training to change their minds but one can create better relational conditions for them to actively motivate themselves.

For the last 15 years the more fashionable normative theories of management have revolved around the concept of strategy. The new logic of management does not discard strategy but makes it necessary to reconsider the meaning of strategy in a much more systemic and qualitative angle. Rational strategies of the firm as against the environment, the markets and the competitors can be valid only inasmuch as the internal system of the firm as an organization is capable of implementing them.

But knowledge of the internal system and its capabilities will not be enough. One will have to consider the functioning of the different systems that constitute the relevant environment of the organization. Markets for example, are not abstract constructs for quantitative calculus, they are human systems with qualitative regulations open to pressures and influence. Finally, the complex web of relationships between operators inside the organization and their partners in the different systems of the environment cannot be understood only in purely quantitative or even economic terms; it is a human relations system.[6]

There is no abstract rationality that could be imposed regardless of their constraints. Within the limits of a well-known and well-ordered American business game, these constraints could be ignored for a long time. But this is no more the case. We have moved not only theoretically but practically in a world that could be understood only within the paradigm of bounded rationality.

4

The emergence of a new logic of management will represent a major sea change for our ways of thinking as well as for our patterns of action and decision-making. It will have a major importance for organizational research. When fundamental principles are put into question, organizational problems become once again crucial. But this time when the deployment of human resources will determine the capabilities of an organization to be rational and therefore to succeed, the contribution of organizational research will become a major intellectual contribution.

At the same time organizational research will also have to transform itself drastically. To meet such a challenge it will have to change its course, its focus and its rationale. Instead of attempting to elaborate universal theories and principles and to examine the influence of variables in a deterministic conceptual framework it will have to revert to case-studies on which to build a better understanding of systemic models and to develop quasi-experimental research at the level of organizational units, organizations and systems.

i. Concrete Action Systems[7]

These should be the first focus of the new research orientation that we should encourage. The case-studies system which was the fashion of the 1950s make a comeback but in a significantly different way. In the 1950s, case-studies were basically ethnographic and the reasoning of their findings could easily be understood as the first hypotheses in order to elaborate rational organizations. Today we can focus on action systems as concrete identities in which the mechanisms have to be related to the functioning of the whole.

Very specific issues arise as soon as one accepts the use of the concept of the system in a serious, i.e. an empirical way: for example the issue of regulation, the issue of change, the issue of frontiers.

Regulation is the first and inescapable issue to be met. The mode of regulation of a concrete action system is its most significant characteristic. Experience has shown that it cannot be hypothesized in view of a few parameters. Only empirical analysis may help discover its basic mechanisms. The rationality of the actors' strategies and finally their modes of adjustment will be understood when one can obtain sufficient knowledge of the system in which they take place.

Normative management prescriptions on operational behaviour will lose relevance if they do not take into account the constraints of the system's mode of regulation. This problem becomes acute with the emergence of a new logic. Managers may have the best ideas about possible change necessary to implement the new logic, they will not be effective or they may even prove to be counter-productive if they don't understand the mode of regulation of the system of which they are in charge.

The new emergent logic requires – in order to be effective – a change in the mode of regulation. And one cannot change something one does not understand. However, systems have an extraordinary capacity to maintain themselves, i.e. their basic regulations against all pressures.

From such starting points there will gradually develop rich opportunities and mechanisms to go beyond simple case-studies and to compare modes of regulation; to discover which are the key elements, how they develop and may change. But, first of all we need a great many more case-studies across the board dealing with diverse situations. We need to develop more sophisticated methodologies to be able to make reliable diagnoses, hypotheses on which to build comparisons.

Change is, of course, the central problem but what appears to be crucial now is the change of the system and not the change of the persons or of groups of people. To focus on interpersonal relations, on groups and intergroup relations was a necessary step but certainly not enough. It is at the system level with its regulatory mechanisms that resistance and opening up to change can take place which does not mean that what happens at the concrete face-to-face level is irrelevant. On the contrary, the centre is most of the time more reactive than active.

Frontiers are not a menial issue since mechanisms of inclusion and exclusion have a direct impact on the regulation of a system and may be more open to clear choices. We could show, for example, that the decision that had the greatest impact on the regulation and, of course, on the functioning of some specific hospital units in our studies on this topic was not the choice made regarding the ways patients were admitted for dialysis machines. Decision-makers were unaware of its consequences. Neither the techniques, nor the administrative choices nor the rational culture made such a difference.[8]

ii. Loosely-coupled Systems

Among the most promising case-studies to be proposed to understand concrete action systems, the field of loosely-coupled systems may offer the best opportunities in view of the newly emergent logic of management.

The concept of loosely-coupled systems began as an abstract construct. But there is an empirical reality to support this intellectual approach. A great number of activities can be understood better with this concept than with the concept of organization. And these activities are rapidly growing in postindustrial societies where educational research and cultural problems have a decisive importance, when the frontiers of organizations are disintegrating, when delocalization is widespread, when the good management of networks of subcontractors may be more decisive than the bureaucratic control of productive units and wise parasitic symbiosis.

First results of our work have shown that these systems structure themselves around mechanisms of resource allocation. Public policy problems become a new field for these case-studies. The manner in which more rigorous evaluation procedures are conducted may help change systems empirically. Especially intriguing is the problem of the visibility of results and of the capacity to appreciate the contribution of each action for reaching them and finally the means for making actors conscious of it.[9]

The relationship between common knowledge[10] of the actors' interactions and their results may constitute one of the most important dimensions of the new kind of regulations necessary for the emergence of a new logic.

To understand the conditions of the emergence of a new logic of management the empirical analysis of some fast changing activities and areas in which new relationships are experimented will be especially rewarding. For example, the emergence and the restructuring of subcontracting networks, the externalization of most productive and functional activities in new entrepreneurial networks, the use of symbiotic relations and of parasitic activities as a new form of management. What can be understood in such cases is the relationship between consciousness and practice that will develop with new knowledge. Between hierarchies and markets innumerable new patterns can develop whose unstable regulations may evolve in new systemic forms.

Finally one should mention one new stimulating area that can be productive to the analysis of the problems that concern economists more and more: innovation, transaction costs, the economy of conventions. Even markets can be analysed as loosely-coupled systems. Their constitution, their development, their transformation should not be seen only as rational constructs. They take place within the constraints imposed on rationality by human games to be understood only through systems analysis.[11]

The most intractable problems raised in Eastern-European countries and the former Soviet Union with the attempts at reintroducing market relationships can be seriously analysed only with this new kind of reasoning. The near future will offer us the most extraordinary natural experiment to challenge our crude economic theories. It is quite clear already that economic calculus is helpless to predict not only outcomes but that it is not enough to supplement it with general psychological and political recipes built on our deterministic knowledge. New systems research is indispensable since the problem is the emergence of specific markets as really empirical human systems to be accepted by the participants with their inescapable hard regulations. Moreover there is not one market but innumerable specific markets which may be widely different since they are developing around widely specific material and informational constraints. Finally they are dependant on meta-markets which in the west have emerged through time in an empirical way whose rationality is *ex post*. How can new regulations emerge within the chaos brought about with the breakdown of the adjustment patterns built around the hierarchical order? We can hardly even raise this problem that brings us to the fundamentals of social science.

Human career patterns are one of the most crucial of these confusing issues. Nomenclature processes had been one of the major regulatory mechanisms that made it possible to manage the Eastern totalitarian systems. Their partial or total destruction forces upon these societies the problem of the alternate patterns that will develop in their place. When raising the problem conceptually as well as practically we may discover that our knowledge of such patterns that do exist in our much more open systems of the West remains still scanty, dispersed and poorly developed. Yet organizational capacities as well as market efficiency depends to quite an extent on the characteristics of our management systems to control careers and personnel deployment. These systems have evolved and they may be in crisis since they become a hindrance to innovation in the new logic of management. This is especially acute in the big bureaucratic public systems, in education, health and welfare.

iii. The Guidance of Change and the Management of Reform

Action will be another essential dimension of new developments in organizational sociology. The relationship of the sociologist to action will take a new turn with the emergence of the new logic of management. An empirical knowledge of systemic regulations of emerging new patterns and the possibility of change within formerly stable systems will become crucial for management. Research will make it possible to elaborate the methodology to develop such knowledge but it will have also to address the problem of how people can understand it, make use of it for their decisions within better-known systems and finally to implement change and begin reforms.

For making use of new knowledge information is not enough. Managers and people in general will have to internalize the new modes of reasoning of positive social science. Obstacles to change had been viewed too rapidly only in terms of lack of knowledge, vested interests and power relationships. It should be recognized that they may be due more and more to the constraints of specific mind-sets in tune with traditional logic.

The capacity to reason with a different logic appears to be a key skill for taking advantage of new opportunities. How it can emerge and develop through specific experiences, what are the conditions that are more conducive to that kind of learning – these are some of the problems that should and can be raised at the present moment.

Problems of training and educational methods can have a lot of relevance for understanding the development of such capacities. Older paradigms of double-loop learning are useful for raising these questions. So is the paradigm of common knowledge that helps understand the possibility of rapid change under specific circumstances and conditions. Experiments could be carefully monitored in specific cases of guided change.[12]

The processes of reforms conducted in organizational systems could provide numerous cases for research. Comparisons between such cases and those of training in educational frameworks made with the same intellectual paradigms will be extremely rewarding.

Generally social scientists can and should plead for massive investment in new research. It will be crucial to meet the challenges we are now facing not only with the rebuilding of Eastern societies but in the guiding of the accelerated patterns of change Western societies must undergo.

Notes

1 Perrow, Ch. (1984) *Normal Accidents*. New York: Basic Books.
2 Pavé, F. (1989) *L'Illusion informaticienne*. Paris: L'Harmattan.
3 Guyaz, J. (1981) *Innovateurs et Innovation: trente ans de création d'entreprises dans le domaine des services*, thèse de IIIème cycle, IEP de Paris.
4 Binst, M. (1989) *Le Mandarin Manager*. Paris: L'Harmattan.
5 Crozier, M. (1989) *L'Entreprise à l'ecoute: apprendre le management post-industriel*. Inter Editions.
6 Moullet, M. (1982) *La concurrence organisée*, Thesis, IEP, Paris, December 1982. Moullet, M. (1982) 'Modes d'échanges et coûts de transaction d'une approche comparative du marché et de la forme', *Sociologie du travail* 4.
7 Glaser, Barney / Strauss, Anselm (1967) *The Discovery of Grounded Theory*. Chicago: Aldine Publishing Company. Crozier, M. / Friedberg, E. (1978) *Actors and Systems*. University of Chicago Press.
8 Kuty, O. (1975) 'Orientation culturelle et profession médicale. La relation thérapeutique dans les unités de rein artificiel et son environnement', *Revue française de sociologie* 16 (2). Binst, M. op.cit. Gonnet, F. *Problèmes et perspectives de l'hôpital des années 80, analyse sociologique comparative de 3 modèles de fonctionnement*, Paris CSO to be published.
9 Friedberg, E. / Musselin, Ch. (1989) Enquête d'universités: *Etude comparée des universités en France et en RFA*. Paris: L'Harmattan.
10 Karl Weick is the first to have used this concept.
11 Favereau, O. (1989) 'Organisation et marché', *Cahiers du Crea* 13: 111-146. Boltanski, L. / Thévenot, L. (1987) *Les économies de la grandeur*. Cahiers du CEE, série Protée, Paris PUF.
12 Argyris, C. / Shon, D. (1974) *Theory in Practice: Increasing Professional Effectiveness*. San Francisco: Jossey Bass Publishers. Lewis, D. (1969) *Convention: A Philosophical Study*. Cambridge: Harvard University Press. Dupuy, J. P. (1988) 'Common Knowledge et Sens commun', *Cahiers du CREA* 11, avril.

PART II

CONCEPTS AND DISCOURSES IN ORGANIZATIONAL RESEARCH

CHAPTER 3

Metaphors of Time, Development and Decline in Organizational Discourses

Silvia Gherardi

1   Introduction

In organization studies, the temporal dimension is usually expressed by the image of a life cycle and in the concepts of change, growth, development and decline.

The aim of this article is to describe the mental images that the researcher or organizational actors possess of time and changes in an organization over time. I shall argue that the conception of time exerts a direct influence over both the way in which research into the organization is conducted (in the case of the researcher) and the way in which strategic decisions are taken or, more simply, the way in which organizational events are interpreted and explained (in the case of organizational actors).

Before beginning my analysis, I should first describe the context of the empirical research that has led to my present reflections on time, organizational development and decline, because I shall not be making any further direct reference to it. For a number of years I have studied the process whereby companies in crisis have been transformed into worker cooperatives: both in Italy and, from a comparative perspective, in Europe (Gherardi and Strati, 1988; Patton, 1989). When workers become managers, they find themselves faced by the problems of a company usually in decline; and should they be successful, they come up against problems arising from the growth and development of the company.

This is a relatively uncommon situation; and in studying it, I was struck by the metaphors used within companies to describe the process of recovery, treatment, sickness and health. I also began to interrogate myself concerning the images that I, as a researcher, had acquired from the literature: images which, for example, described a life cycle which begins with birth, not with the transformation of something old into something new. I thus began to write down and discuss the mental representations of the process of transformation held by the subjects concerned, because these representations affected their behaviour and their conception of time.

In order to give a rough idea to the reader of what I mean, the growth of the cooperative was, in some cases, conceived as a new branch growing out of the stump where the old tree had been cut down. The workers were thus gardeners who watched over a "natural" growth process which followed an "external" chronological time. This, together with the seasons, also carried the pattern of the company's growth encoded in its genetic heritage.

When the implications of the "gardener metaphor" were explored at meetings, it was usually strongly disliked by the workers: they felt that it was entirely unsuited to a situation where they had to manage a development process stemming from decline. By openly discussing which image of development was implicit in their discourse on the future of the cooperative, the actors were able to formulate their plans more coherently as a process of organizational development.

I shall not make overt reference to my research material in the following discussion. The literature of organization studies reports the same metaphors as I do – an endorsement which enables me to directly address the scientific community as I inquire into the metaphors we employ when deepening our knowledge on the processes of organizational change. In the course of our research, we use a variety of metaphors for change, and we encounter other subjects who likewise employ metaphors to build knowledge and to understand their/our reality.

In what follows, I shall briefly illustrate the role of metaphor in the interpretation and production of an organizational culture, thereby setting out the theoretical background to my analysis. I shall then illustrate the principal images that give social representation to the concept of organizational development by comparing it to the growth of a plant, to the psychological development of the individual or group, and to transpersonal archetypes. These images, which belong to an evolutionary paradigm, I shall counterpose with a dialectically-based image. I conclude by discussing the conceptions of time implicit in the various metaphors of organizational development here examined.

2   Metaphors and the Production of Meanings

We can gain a clearer idea of how a metaphor produces knowledge by examining an example of one (Rebulla, 1989: 57):

Memory, with its approximation and unreliability, with its tendency to alter original hues and contrasts, resembles the colour green: an unstable and mutable colour which, born brilliant and intense, reverts with time to its constituent yellow or fades to overoxidized black. In brief, it does not endure: it changes, it betrays its weakness and that of the painter. But in doing so, it behaves as the most human of colours, the one most susceptible to the onslaught of time, the one most ready to reveal the fragility of an artifact. Equidistant between blue and red, between the colour of the sky and the colour of hell, green is an aqueous and intermediate tint, the emblem of youth, of hope, and of things that do not add up. At least they do not add up for the painter, in his constant search for a permanent green, for a green that resists the passage of time, which does not immediately reveal his imperfection, the corruptibility of his tools, the vanity of his purpose.

Equally tepid and impermanent is memory: everything it recovers from the past is corroded or sublimated, too black or too yellow. Memory also suffers the attrition of time which alters its contours, fades its substance and changes its linearity.

Memory, colours, the transformation of colours over time, the colours of life, the alteration of time and of memory: colours and time speak of memory.

A metaphor comprises two concepts of different things, both active in the mind and expressed by a single word or phrase, the meaning of which results from their interaction (Richards, 1968: 89). The words in the above extract are conditioned by metaphor to yield a modified meaning (from literal to metaphorical). The outcome of the semantic shift is to show things in a certain manner; an effect produced by the semantic assimilation of words which refer to things alien to each other in our representation of the world.

The metaphor of memory sets up a powerful tension between two previously unrelated concepts. Black (1962) uses the term "generative" to describe metaphors that do more than merely suggest an analogy or a similarity, but themselves create the similarity we perceive between the terms of the metaphor. Metaphors therefore do not only serve to embellish discourse, to point out similarities, to describe unknown things by resorting to those that are familiar. They also serve to improve understanding, like the metaphors used in philosophical language.

Max Black was the first to argue that science employs metaphorical procedures. He claimed that the models of science fulfil the same function as metaphors in everyday language. More recent debate has also examined the use of metaphors in science (Black, 1962; Ricoeur, 1981; Boyd and Kuhn, 1979). In organization studies, in particular, Morgan (1980, 1982, 1986), Keeley (1980) and Manning (1979) have demonstrated the fruitfulness of an approach which makes explicit the epistemological presuppositions of the concept of "organization".

The use of metaphor performs an important role in the formation of language, the creation of new concepts and the construction of scientific theories. The researcher filters and structures his/her perceptions of the object of study through a metaphorical vision of the world based on the implicit or explicit analogies which frame his/her field of analysis. What Black called a generative metaphor is the invention of a similarity between things made separate by denomination. In this process, creative reassessment generates meaning by relating distant but never-theless connected things. Through the exploration of analogy (the "what is" and "what is not"), different meanings are fused together to constitute a new way of looking at things.

The concept of "organizational culture" itself, a concept which during the 1980s provided scholars with a fruitful approach to the study of organizations (Pondy and Frost, 1983; Turner, 1990; Gagliardi, 1990), was based on the juxtaposition of culture and organization; a procedure which drew on the potential of metaphorical expression (Smircich, 1983; Strati, 1992).

Metaphors are mental pictures which transmit information holistically, providing a coherent framework for the topic (Ortony, 1979) which is constitutive of the theory expressed, as well as being explanatory and pedagogic. In organizational discourses, metaphors diffuse social representations at the cognitive, emotional and behavioural levels, and influence perceptions and subsequent action.

The following section addresses two issues in particular: are development and decline totally separate phenomena? What conceptions of time are inherent in the metaphorical representation of organizational growth?

3   Growth and Decline

Since the 1970s, the phenomena of stagnation, the crisis of the welfare state and the process of deindustrialization that afflict society at large (Hirschman, 1970; Mensch, 1975; Olson, 1982) have been reflected in the greater attention paid by organizational studies to cases of organizational decline (Starbuck et al., 1978; Levine, 1978; Starbuck, 1965, 1982). The problems of how to define decline and how to distinguish between crisis and decline have been rarely addressed (Dyson and Wilks, 1983; Wetten, 1980); a methodological failure which suggests that further theoretical inquiry is necessary.

As March (1981, 1988) has pointed out, changes in organizations are not always "heroic" or dramatic events. Rather, they are frequently the outcome of a sequence of activities which shape organizational reality.

One should, however, distinguish (Watzlawich et al., 1974) between changes which come about within the structure of the system and those that alter the system itself. We may similarly distinguish between growth and development: growth continues within certain structures until it reaches a point beyond which the existing structure is no longer able to guarantee order. Consequently, either a process of decline is triggered or the structure moves to a higher level of development. When living organisms reach their inner limit of growth they enter a developmental crisis; artificial systems, however, do not.

In graphic terms, growth can be represented as a parabolic function and devel-opment as a series of steps. A classic example of a step function is the relationship between acceleration and gear-changing in a car, where a brusque shift between third and fourth gear does not usually provoke a crisis in the engine. Are organizations more akin to organic systems or to mechanical ones? And what are the implications of analogy with one or the other of them for research on organizations?

Let us assume that development and decline are not distinct phenomena, but rather two sides of the same coin.

For the time being, we can make use of a generally-accepted definition of decline (Pichierri, 1983, 1986) as a long-term process involving:
a) a deterioration in performance relative to institutional objectives;
b) a reduction in the dimensions/resources available.
And let us also accept for decline the most widely-acknowledged features of development, namely that:
• it is a discontinuous process;
• it is irreversible;
• it takes place in a series of stages;
• at each stage a specific structure appears;
• at each higher stage the structure becomes more differentiated.
We may therefore assert that the difference between growth and development is qualitative and not quantitative. An increase in certain variables (size, productivity, human and technological resources) represents a growth phenomenon as long as no change takes place in the framework of the system; an increase in these variables is indicative of development when the structural framework is altered. We may also assert that decline begins when the organization fails to respond to initiatives for change, or when it changes in an inappropriate manner (Gross, Giaquinta and Bernstein, 1971; Nelsen and Yates, 1978; Gamble, 1981).

Development and decline can be described from various and related perspectives which address the following:
a) the *direction* of development, a point of view which enables us to talk of evolution or involution;
b) *process*, a point of view which reveals the maturation and dissolution of structures and their arrangements;
c) the *situation*, a point of view which reveals the coexistence within the same organization of different structural forms during a particular phase of development;
d) development/decline as an *activity*, a point of view which reveals the components of corporate intentionality: planned change, innovative activity, or their counterparts that take the form of *laissez-faire*.
Each of these various perspectives, of course, entails different presuppositions and methodologies for research into organizational development/decline. In addition to the approaches listed above, this paper adds a further one: namely, the analysis of organizational culture and the social construction of time. In an earlier study

on the temporal dimension in decision-making (Gherardi and Strati, 1988), I developed the concept of "organizational times" in order to move beyond the commonplace notion of absolute, chronological and external time to one of time as a social factor, which I used to analyse of the plurality of times within an organization.

Organizational times are the various concepts of time expressed by organizational actors and arranged along various distinct dimensions of reality (Gherardi and Strati, 1988: 151):

- it is contained in the dialectic between internal and external time;
- it is involved in organizational planning activities, taking the form of the imaginative, predictive creation of the future context towards which an action is directed;
- it governs the sequence of the individual phases of a particular event;
- it provides the metaphor for the life of the organization and its stages of development (birth, maturity, decline);
- it symbolizes success through survival.

Accordingly, the next two sections explore metaphorical representations of development and decline using concepts of evolutionary, or alternatively non-evolutionary, time.

4   Analogies of Development and Decline in an Evolutionary Perspective

The theme of organizational development offers a series of analogies (a field pioneered by Penrose, 1952) which are of considerable interest for organizational theorists. I consider four main analogies here: the life of plants, the psychological maturation of the individual, the cycle of death and rebirth, and ontogenesis-phylogenesis.

The life of plants is perhaps one of the first and simplest analogies that come to mind, and it is one still extremely popular (Sackmann, 1989). Gardner (1965: 20) wrote:

> like people and plants, organizations have a life-cycle. They have a green and supple youth, a time of flourishing strength and a gnarled old age.

In this case, the passage of *chronological* time marks the movement from one stage to another. It illustrates the irreversibility and ineluctability of various life cycles, which all have a beginning and an end encoded in their genetic heritage. Decline is thus a physiological phenomenon.

Another common analogy is between the organization and the life of an individual; it fuses the passage of time with psychological maturation through a sequence of moments of existential crisis. Lippit and Schmidt (1967) have identified recurrent crises in each stage of development: birth (the creation of a new organization, survival as a viable system); youth (achieving stability, building a reputation and developing pride); maturity (becoming unique and adaptable, contributing to society). As the organization resolves each crisis (note that we are dealing here only with non-financial crises), it moves to a higher level of development. Thus development is not automatic but depends on how the organization responds to a crisis. Conversely, decline may be triggered by the organization's inadequate handling of a crisis or its outright failure to cope with it. Crises are most commonly triggered by unacceptably bad management, by drastic changes in demand or in the economic environment, by a high turnover in personnel which damages the organization's image among customers and suppliers, and – not least – by the fact that new managers only vicariously share the sense of sacrifice and dedication felt by the organization's founders (Lippitt and Schmidt, 1965: 107).

What marks the passage from one stage to the next is the *psychological* time of the maturation of the individual Ego as it undergoes crisis and the growth of moral awareness. On the subject of moral development, Piaget's stages of the growth of the individual, Culbert's stages of group development and Riesman's stages of social development have also been applied to organizations.

The cycle of death and rebirth is an image which replaces unidirectional evolution with a spiral or wave-like pattern in which the uppermost or lowermost points are not necessarily defined. This is a metaphor that is particularly common in studies of group development. However, characterizing the stages of organizational development according to the dynamics of only the dominant group, is an error of logical attribution (Bateson, 1979). Moreover, the groups studied are usually temporary (T-groups) or else created in artificial situations (in the laboratory or the classroom). Groups of people who work in organizations have rather different characteristics.

While acknowledging a certain "shift" in the subject of study, it may be of interest to cite the findings of organizational development research into the interaction between group and organization development (Lavoie and Culbert, 1978). Apart from the differing terminology used for stages, there is a general tendency in the literature to identify the structures and activities unique to each level (Tuckman, 1965). The first phase involves task orientation, dependence and boundary-testing. Typical of the second phase is intra-group conflict and an emotional response to task demands. The third phase is characterized by the open exchange of relevant interpretations. In the fourth phase, the group functions as a problem-solver and is distinguished by its functional relations and its constructive attempts at successful task completion. In previous phases, the typical features of organizational development are the definition of interpersonal boundaries and task-related behaviour: forming, storming, norming and performing.

Bennis and Shephard (1956) described these stages as dependence, counter-dependence, catharsis, enchantment, disenchantment and consensual validation. Slater (1966) identified them as unconscious shared fantasy, identification with the leader, revolt, common action, common experience, intimacy, consciousness.

Common to these authors is a *cyclical conception of time* where a given action is matched by a reaction, and where the end of one phase of the organization's life cycle does not signify its death but rather its rebirth as a new organization in the next phase. Greiner's classic pattern (1972) of evolution followed by a period of revolution, can also be fitted into this framework. Greiner describes, in fact, a linear form of development (creativity, direction, delegation, coordination, collaboration) in which the revolution phase is marked by the appearance of a specific crisis (of command, autonomy, control, bureaucracy and one left undefined because, Greiner argues, few enterprises reach this stage of development). Nevertheless, Greiner has sufficient evidence (which in any case can be readily provided by empirical research) to hypothesize a return to the initial phase of command crisis. In describing the development dangers due to collaboration, he cites the psychological saturation and the emotional and physical stress caused by group work. These symptoms obviously trigger demand for a centralized command which relieves subordinates from an excess of responsibility. The cycle may start up again, thus echoing the cyclical course of history described by Vico.

Ontogenesis as a repetition of phylogenesis is an image that construes cultural elements as a specifically social dynamic, innate to the development of human aggregates. The passage from one stage to another in group dynamics (Dunphy, 1968) is marked by the production of particular linguistic and imaginative forms organized into a group mythology: the myth of the "weak leader", the myth of the malicious and manipulative leader and, finally, the utopian myth. Attention is thus focused on the cultural elaboration of a solution to the crisis, on the premise that this is strongly influenced by the emergence of non-rational role specialists and by an underlying common meaning.

Mitroff and Kihlmann (1975; 1976) and Gustafsson (1983) pursue this line of inquiry by analysing organizations on the basis of their oral stories and myths. Also relevant here is the work of Miller and Friesen (1980), who single out nine archetypes of transition in development: fragmentation, entrepreneurial revitalization, consolidation, towards stagnation, towards centralization, boldness and abandon, maturation, trouble-shooting, initiation by fire and, finally, the formalization of stability. Berg (1979) also explores the emotional structures that frame organizational development and describes specific moments of revolution: dependency (structural revolution), neo-dependency (cultural revolution) and counter-dependency.

This kind of analysis brings out the relationship between the personal and the transpersonal in the development of specific cultural products. The background to these studies is provided by the work of Neumann (1949) on the levels of the development of consciousness: uroboric, creation, great mother and infant, great mother and adolescent, separation from world parent, dragon fight, captive and treasure. The passage from one stage to another is brought about by the *social time* inherent in history that transcends both the individual and the group.

5 From the Evolutionary Model to the Specialization-Differentiation Dialectic

The above outline of the principal analogies underlying various analyses of organizational development, has revealed the persistence of an evolutionary model based on higher-lower levels of development. This is not the place for a review of the extensive debate on the influence of evolutionary theory on the social sciences, nor of the criticisms brought against the "stage" models used in many disciplines. Nevertheless, given that these ideas have become an established component of the scientific tradition, one should also examine models that do not view the stages of development as necessarily hierarchical.

The premises of this second body of theory are the following:
a) change is inherent to the organization as a social system, in that problems arise for which no solutions of continuity exist (scarcity of resources, uncertainty in the processes of socialization, cultural transmission, orientation, aspiration, conflicting principles of organization, etc.);
b) the processes of change relate to the characteristics of the institutional structure and the problems that derive from it;
c) change is not rigidly determined by endogenous or accidental factors; instead, it is tied to the trend in the organization's dialectic with a changing environment.

In this model, specialization and differentiation induce some organizational functions (or institutional areas) to become dissociated (or loosely coupled in Weick's terminology, 1979) and closely dependent on roles or occupational communities which develop their own symbolically and organizationally significant images within the boundaries of the same system.

Development moves through various stages of specialization and differentiation. Specialization comes about when one of the areas of activity is developed independently by actors performing strategic roles. They strengthen their organizational unity and criteria of action, thereby enabling themselves to exploit the potential of technological innovation, cultural creativity, intra-organizational power and participation in decision-making. Differentiation is the phase when activities involving the exploitation of basic resources (economic, technical, human and motivational) and activities aimed at cultural hegemony are made relatively autonomous of the rest of the system. A surplus of resources is thus created which stimulates the institutionalization of these activities and presses for a new structural configuration and normative integration.

Movement from one stage to another comes about when the degree of differentiation in the organization can no longer be contained by the system. The actual form that change takes will depend on internal factors and pressures from the external environment. However, change does not take place independently of the existing institutionalized framework, nor of the premises for action within it, nor of the forms of conflict or orientation towards change inherent in its strategic behaviour. Nevertheless, although the growth of autonomy (the new potentialities for development and creativity) increases the organization's sensitivity towards specific sectors of the environment, this is not to imply that it acquires the ability to solve problems. Nor does it suggest that the outcome will be development rather than decline: the potentialities may be wasted, they may not cohere into new structural forms or, as Gardner writes (1965: 24), they may not be perceived:

> Most ailing organizations have developed a form of functional blindness to their own defects. They are not suffering because they cannot solve their problems, but because they cannot see their problems.

The response to problems of differentiation may take different forms. It may be a failure to find an adequate solution which leads to the death of the organization or to its partial disintegration. Or the organization may lead a parasitical existence on the margins of other organizations. Or it may regress to a less differentiated system in which numerous potentialities are allowed to lie dormant. Each new organizational set-up, once institutionalized, creates its own mechanisms for maintaining boundaries, for safeguarding change and for preserving its hegemony over other areas.

This dynamic is exemplified, albeit rather loosely, by Lievegoed's "four-leaf clover" model (1973), which comprises three phases: the pioneer phase, the differentiation phase and the integration phase. Decisive in the second phase, which is driven by the scientific organization of work, is the technical subsystem, while the third phase involves the rethinking of the entire organization in order to achieve the harmonious integration of the economic, technical and social subsystems. The reference here is to the system of organizations as a whole, not to the development of the individual organization: in this, Lievegoed's model is excessively deterministic.

By contrast, Eisenstadt (1964) proposes a more profound dialectically-based model based on social formations. Mintzberg (1978) pursues a similar line of analysis in his examination of the formation of a strategy (understood as a patterned sequence of decisions). A strategy follows a life cycle which moves through the stages of conception, elaboration, decline and death. Within this life cycle, periodic waves of continuity and change result from the interaction between the dynamic environment (which tends towards change) and the constraints of bureaucracy (which seek stabilization). The role of mediating between external dynamics (the environment) and internal ones (the bureaucratic tendency) is performed by the leadership, whose strategy expresses the totality of strategic decisions over time.

6   Conclusions

That which sustains the concept itself of development and decline is the passage of time. However, time is monolithic only to the extent that it is a measure of quantitative phenomena; otherwise it displays a multiplicity of dimensions (Ornstein, 1969; Zwart, 1975). My above analysis of the evolutionary analogies based on development and decline has evidenced:

a) chronological time;

b) psychological time;

c) social time.

A mental image of development grounded in chronological time (either linear or cyclical) views development and decline as phenomena induced by the passage of Newtonian time – as a factor external to the individual organization and to the actors within it. Time, in this case, is the all-encompassing container of all events.

In the case of psychological time, a dialectic is created between an external time (measured objectively) and a time internal to the processes of maturation and the resolution of specific crises. Organizational time is thus measured in contingent and variable durations.

The social time that determines the passage from one phase of development to the next, is still external to individuals and organizations. The unit of measurement for social time is also variable, and it is imprinted in the cultural heritage of a society.

Closer attention should be paid to the conception of time in the differentiation-integration model. One could, of course, interpret it "a-temporally", since the time of differentiation is followed by a time of integration, and so on, in an eternal alternation of the two times. But this would mean losing the dynamic character of the model. Movement from one phase to another is induced by the action itself of a temporal dimension internal to the process and unique to that particular organizational dynamic. There is, therefore, an organizational time which is specific to each organization and internal to it. Thus, the same organizational setting comprises a plurality of organizational times expressed in differentiated organizational choices and bound up with the specific dynamics of its development or decline.

The researcher must therefore not only analyse the plurality of organizational times that govern the ways in which actors structure their organization (Jaques, 1982); s/he must also examine the multidimensionality of the actors' conception of time. When organizational actors become aware that their organization is in decline and consequently develop an appropriate and coherent strategy, what time horizon do they apply to the origins of such decline? Does the passage of time that has provoked the symptoms of decline lie outside the organization in chronological or social time, or does it lie internally to it in psychological or organizational time?

Consideration of the analogies underlying the notion of development and decline reveals profoundly different meanings and problems. The analogy with the lives of plants depicts decline as a physiological feature of an organization approaching the end of its life cycle. The analogy with the psychological development of the individual preserves the concept of the life cycle. Here, however, the organization's inability to cope with crises triggers a specific pathology taking the form of either fixation at a particular stage or regression from "healthy" development. Decline, therefore, as well as being a psychological phenomenon, is also non-development as a pathological response which requires suitable therapy. It is at this point that the organizational consultant intervenes as the therapist.

Of prime importance in the analogy of death-rebirth is the concept of renewal – just as the image of the life cycle recalls the passage of the seasons and the alternation of day and night. Decline can therefore be conceived of as a temporary and physiological phenomenon, as a counter-reaction to development or even as a downturn prior to an upswing in the organization's fortunes. The renewal of people, structures and relations in an organization (which usually outlives the people who work within it) reinforces this image of recurrent regeneration.

The analogy of phylogenesis in the development of consciousness interprets decline as a cultural inability to handle change; that is, the organization's failure to develop interpretative schemata with which to process a reality that transforms itself dynamically into subject/object, inside/outside, I/non-I interactions. Adaptation to the environment therefore involves more than organic capacity; the organization must also evolve culturally so that it can cope with increasing degrees of complexity.

Although the specialization-differentiation model does not attempt to establish a hierarchy of stages of development, it nevertheless provides the researcher with a useful frame of reference: namely, the institutionalization of a new structural form which in itself gives no indication of the future direction of development, which is intrinsic within the differentiation process. This indication lies within the process of differentiation, particularly in the expression of internal and/or external hegemony. Attention thus shifts from the "naturalness" of development to power, leadership and the actors' world-view.

The hypothesis underlying my analysis is that researchers' mental images of their subject of study influence what they see of the world and how they interpret it. Also, the social representation of development expressed by organizational actors in their behaviour influences the "how" and "when" of their strategic response, when decline is perceived as such.

The analysis of analogies provides the researcher with fruitful access to the dynamics of development and decline by directing attention to:

- the response to crises and the capacity to "perceive" crisis indicators; that is, to perceive the reciprocal modelling of environment and organization;
- the elaboration of interpretative schemata of corporate culture;
- the systemic features of a structure in transition, organizational relations and processes of structural change;
- processes of intraorganizational and interorganizational conflict – whether this conflict takes the form of managerial group dynamics, or of the totality of long-term strategic decisions, or of the struggle for hegemony; and
- the temporal boundaries established by organizational actors to frame their life experiences.

Bibliography

Bateson, G. (1979) *Mind and Nature.* New York: Bantam Books.

Bennins, W.E./Shepard, H. (1956) 'A Theory of Group Development', *Human Relations* IX.

Berg, P. O. (1979) *Emotional Structures in Organizations: A Study of the Process of Change in a Swedish Company.* Lund: Dept. of Business Administration.

Black, M. (1962) *Models and Metaphors.* Ithaca: Cornell University Press.

Boyd, R./Kuhn, T. (1979) *Metaphor and Thought.* Cambridge University Press.

Culbert, S. A. (1975) 'Consciousness-Raising: A Five-Stage Model for Social and Organizational Change', in Cooper, C. L. *Theories of Group Processes.* New York: Wiley.

Dunphy, D. (1968) 'Phases, Roles and Myths in Self-Analytic Groups', *The Journal of Applied Behavioural Science* 4.

Dyson, K./Wilks, S. (eds.) (1983) *Industrial Crisis. A Comparative Study of the Study of State and Industry.* Oxford: Robertson.

Eisenstadt, S. N. (1964) 'Social Change, Differentiations and Evolution', *American Sociological Review* 26.

Gagliardi, P. (ed.) (1990) *Symbols and Artifacts.* Berlin: de Gruyter.

Gamble, A. (1981) *Britain in Decline. Economic Policy, Political Strategy and the British State.* London: Macmillan.

Gardner, J. W. (1965) 'How to Prevent Organizational Dry Rot', *Harper's Magazine,* October.

Gherardi, S./Strati, A. (1988) 'The Temporal Dimension in Organizational Studies', *Organization Studies* 9.

Gherardi, S./Strati, A. (1990) 'The Texture of Organizing an Italian Academic Department', *Journal of Management Studies* 27 (6).

Gherardi, S./Strati, F. (1988) 'Worker Takeovers: The Italian Experience', *Exeter European Studies* 1.

Greiner, L. E. (1972) 'Evolution and Revolution as Organizations Grow', *Harvard Business Review* 4.

Groos, N./Giaquinta, J./Bernstein, M. (1971) *Implementing Organizational Innovations. A Sociological Analysis of Planned Educational Change*. New York: Basic Books.

Gustafsson, C. (1983) 'Myths and Cultures: Their Relevance to the Theory of Management'. Paper presented to the VIth EGOS Conference, Florence, November 3-5.

Hirschman, A. O. (1970) *Exit, Voice and Loyalty. Responses to Decline in Firms, Organizations and States*. Cambridge, Mass.: Harvard University Press.

Jaques, E. (1982) *The Form of Time*. London: Heinemann.

Keeley, M. (1980) 'Organizational Analogy: A Comparison of Organismic and Social Contract Models', *Administrative Science Quarterly* 25.

Kohlberg, L. (1969) *Stages in the Development of Moral Thought and Action*. New York: Holt, Rinehart, Winston.

Lavoie, D./Culbert, S. (1978) 'Stages of Organizational and Development', *Human Relations* 31.

Levine, C. H. (1978) 'Organizational Development and Cut-Back Management', *Public Administration Review* 38.

Lievegoed, B. C. (1973) *The Developing Organization*. London: Tavistock Publications.

Lippit, G./Schmidt, W. (1967) 'Crises in a Developing Organization', *Harvard Business Review* 6.

Manning, P. K. (1981) 'Metaphors of the Field: Varieties of Organizational Discourse', *Administrative Science Quarterly* 26.

March, J. K. (1981) 'Footnotes to Organizational Change', *Administrative Science Quarterly* 26.

March, J. K. (1988) *Decisions and Organizations*. New York: Basil Blackwell.

Mensch, G. (1975) *Das Technologische Platt*. Frankfurt: Umschau Verlag.

Miller, D./Friesen, P. (1980) 'Archetypes of Organizational Transition', *Administrative Science Quarterly* 25.

Mintzberg, H. (1978) 'Patterns in Strategy Formation', *Management Science* 24 (9).

Mitroff, I./Kilmann, R. (1965) 'The Stories Managers Tell: A New Tool for Organizational Problem Solving', *Management Review* 64.

Mitroff, I./Kilmann, R. (1976) 'Analysis of Organizations Through Myths and Stories', in Kilmann, R./Pondy, L./Slevin, D. *The Management Organization Design*. New York: North Holland.

Morgan, G. (1980) 'Paradigms, Metaphors and Puzzle Solving', *Administrative Science Quarterly* 25.

Morgan, G. (1982) 'Cybernetics and Organization Theory: Epistemology or Technique?', *Human Relations* 7.

Morgan, G. (1986) *Images of Organizations*. Beverly Hills: Sage.

Nelsen, R./Yates, D. (1978) *Innovation and Implementations*. Lexington: Heath.

Neumann, E. (1954) *The Origins and History of Consciousness*. Princeton University Press.

Olson, M. (1982) *The Rise and Decline of Nations*. New Hartford, Conn.: Yale University Press.

Ornstein, R. E. (1969) *On the Experience of Time*. London: Penguin.

Ortony, A. (ed.) (1979) *Metaphor and Thought*. Cambridge: Cambridge University Press.

Patton, R. (ed.) (1989) Reluctant Entrepreneurs. Milton Keynes: Open University Press.

Penrose (1952) 'Biological Analogies in the Theory of the Firm', *American Economic Review* XLII.

Pichierri, A. (1985) 'Le déclin industriel', *Social Science Information* 2.

Pichierri, A. (ed.) (1986) *Il declino industriale*. Turin: Rosenberg and Sellier.

Pondy, L. et al. (1983) *Organizational Symbolism*. Greenwich: Jai Press.

Rebulla, E. (1989) *Carte Celesti*. Palermo: Selerio.

Richards, I. (1967) *La filosofia della retorica*. Milan: Feltrinelli.

Ricoeur, P. (1981) *Hermeneutics and the Human Sciences*. Cambridge: Cambridge University Press.

Sackmann, S. (1989) 'The Role of Metaphors in Organization Transformation', *Human Relations* 42 (6): 763-485.

Slater, P. *Microcosm: Structural, Psychological and Religious Evolution in Groups*. New York: Wiley.

Smircich, L. (1983) 'Concepts of Culture and Organizational Analaysis', *American Sociological Quarterly* 28.

Starbuck, W. (1965) 'Organizational Growth and Development', in March, J. *Handbook of Organizations*. Chicago: Rand-McNally.

Starbuck, W./Greve, A./Hedberg, B. (1978) 'Responding to Crises', *Journal of Business Administration* 9.

Starbuck, W. H. (1982) 'Congealing Oil: Inventing Ideologies to Justify Acting Ideologies Out', *Journal of Management Studies* 19.

Strati, A. (1992) 'Organizational Culture', in Széll, G. (ed.) *Concise Encyclopaedia of Participation and Co-Management*. Berlin: de Gruyter.

Torbert, W. R. (1974) 'Pre-Bureaucratic and Post-Bureaucratic Stages of Organization Development', *Interpersonal Development* 5.

Tuckman, B. W. (1965) 'Development Sequence in Small Groups', *Psychological Bulletin* 63.

Turner, B. A. (ed.) (1990) *Organizational Symbolism*. Berlin: de Gruyter.

Watzlawick, P./Weakland, J./Fish, R. (1974) *Change: Principles of Problem Formation and Problem Resolution*. New York: Norton.

Weick, K. E. (1976) 'Educational Organizations as Loosely Coupled Systems', *Administrative Science Quarterly* 21.

Whetten, D. A. (1980) 'Sources, Responses and Effects of Organizational', in Kimberly, J. R./Miles, R. H. (eds.) *The Organizational Life-Cycle*. San Francisco, Calif.: Jossey-Bass.

Zwart, P. J. (1975) *About Time*. Amsterdam: North Holland.

CHAPTER 4

The Enterprising Subjects of "Excellence"*

Paul du Gay

1 Introduction

In his 1938 lecture on "A Category of the Human Mind: the Notion of Person, the Notion of 'Self'", Marcel Mauss (1979) articulated what was to become one of the most scandalous axioms of the social sciences: the idea that the "person" or the "self" is a culturally and historically malleable creation. Since then, anthropological evidence and historical researches have indicated that the modern, western, "idea" of the person as a largely coherent, rational, conscious, and self-directed being is "a metaphysical fiction" (Beechey and Donald, 1986: x; Hirst and Woolley, 1982). As Mauss (1979: 90) argued "Who knows if this 'category', which all of us here today believe to be well founded, will always be recognized as such? It was formed only for us, among us".

This argument regarding the contextual nature of identities can be applied without hesitation to the arena of work and employment. As Claude Lefort (1986: 142) has suggested, for example, the category of "worker" does not connote some form of suprahistorical essence or "spirit" – as the notion of "alienation" appears to indicate – since it is, as Marx himself indicated, a "product of *history*". It only comes into being under certain historical and cultural conditions. Similarly, notions such as "job satisfaction" and "motivation" are not phenomena that exist in some timeless, universal realm waiting to be discovered by, and deployed within, managerial discourse. Both the basic concepts and the practices that bestow upon them a material reality are products of changes in the imagination and organization of work.

Given that any identity is basically relational in terms of its conditions of existence, any change in the latter is bound to affect the former. For example, if an employee's relations with his/her employing organization are discursively reconceptualized, then rather than having the same identity – the "employee" – in a new situation, a new identity is established.

However, for some marxists the "worker" is conceived as a transcendental *a priori* category representing the essence of every direct producer, "whose historically differentiated forms in relation to the conditions of production would merely constitute empirical variations" (Laclau, 1990: 25). Hyman (1987: 40), for example, argues that "shifting fashions in labour management" are purely and simply the outcome of an "originary" antagonism between "labour" and "capital". In this vision, the identity of both "labour" and "capital" is invariably represented as stable and unchanging, while lived history is reduced to a series of "empirical variations" on a constant theme. "Labour" and "capital" are conceived of as having an "essential", "real" identity that precedes or evades their dominant discursive articulation in any historical or cultural context. Needless to say, knowledge of this "real" identity is only available to those armed with the appropriate "gaze".

For proponents of this sort of position, at the heart of modern work organization there lies an "objectively" conflictual relationship. As Baldamus (1961: 105), for example, has put it

> as wages are costs to the firm, and the deprivation inherent in effort means costs to the employee, the interests of management and wage-earner are diametrically opposed.

At one pole there stand the "workers". With nothing to sell but their labour power, their "interests" can easily be delineated. Failing the complete transformation of already existing social relations, workers' "objective" interests lie in increasing wages, reducing working hours, minimizing "effort", and imposing various constraints upon "exploitation" by fighting for better conditions of employment and firmer legislative constraints upon the activities and ambitions of employers. At the opposite extreme are the employers and their "servants of power", management and the experts of symbolic mediation – occupational psychologists and the like – who service them. Their "objective" interests "are linked to the perpetual expansion of profit through increasing productivity, deskilling work, keeping wages low, weakening the collective power of workers, and reducing their capacity to disrupt the process of accumulation, while simultaneously casting a cloak of ideological legitimacy over the essentially exploitative nature of the employment relation" (Rose, 1990: 55-56).

From this perspective it is obvious that nothing short of a wholesale transformation of "society" will eradicate the "alienation" residing at the heart of modern work. In this model work entails the subordination of subjectivity. For Hyman and others, any programmes and practices that attempt to reorganize business enterprises and the subjective experience of work without tackling the fundamental "antagonism" between "capital" and "labour" must be little more than "shifting fashions", because they are obviously on a hiding to nothing. How subjects are positioned by, and use, these programmes and practices is of no concern because the latter are perceived to have no effect in overcoming the "objective" relations of alienation and exploitation.

However, for proponents of these "shifting fashions", the worker's subjective experience of work is of central importance. The advocates of various discourses and practices of work reform – Human Relations, The Quality of Working Life Movement, etc. – claim to be able to restructure the employment relation so as to make work more subjectively meaningful for those performing it, while simultaneously increasing profitability. These different discourses of work represent the subjectivity of the worker not only as an object to be developed rather than repressed, but also as a crucial determinant of organizational success. Through the medium of a variety of different programmes and human "technologies" – the use of human scientific knowledge to specify ways of doing things in a reproducible way – they have attempted to indicate that productive work can satisfy the worker, that the activity of working can provide empowering and fulfilling personal and social relations for those performing it, and that work is a route to self-fulfilment (Hollway, 1991; Rose, 1990).

As Rose (1990: 56) has argued

> Employers and managers equipped with these new visions of work have thus claimed that there is no conflict between the pursuits of productivity, efficiency, and competitiveness on the one hand and the humanization of work on the other. On the contrary, the path to business success lies in engaging the employee with the goals of the company at the level of his or her subjectivity, aligning the wishes, needs, and aspirations of each individual who works for the organization with the successful pursuit of its objectives. Through striving to fulfil their own needs and wishes at work, each employee will thus work for the advance of the enterprise; the more the individual fulfils him or herself, the greater the benefit to the company.

While it is undoubtedly true that these discourses and practices of work reform have played, and continue to play, an active part in reproducing hierarchies of power and reward at work, or that they have been consciously deployed at various times to attenuate the power of trade unions and their prerogatives for the representation of collective interests and the defence of collective "rights", it is equally important to note that they are not simply "ideological" distortions; in other words, that their claims to "knowledge" are not "false", nor do they serve a specific social function and answer to certain preformed economic needs. Certainly these discourses of work reform arise in specific political contexts, and have political consequences, but they are not merely functional responses to, or legitimations of, already existing economic interests or needs. Rather than simply reflecting a pre-given social world, they themselves actively "make up" a reality, and create new ways for people to be at work. As Miller and O'Leary (1986) have argued the "nature", or "essence" of the internal world of the business enterprise is a function of changes in practices of governing economic life, rather than the converse.

"Managerial thought" and other discourses of work reform play an active role in the formation of new images and mechanisms, which bring the government of the enterprise into alignment with political rationalities, cultural values and social expectations (Rose, 1989). In the process, people come to identify themselves and conceive of their interests in terms of these new words and images and formulate their objectives in relation to them. Changes in the ways of conceptualizing, documenting and acting upon the internal world of the business organization actively transform the meaning and reality of work. As Rose (1990: 60) has suggested these new ways of relating the attributes and feelings of individual employees to the objectives of the organization for which they work are central elements in the "fabrication of new languages and techniques to bind the worker into the productive life of society".

1.1   Governing the Work-based Subject

If management discourses play an active role in attempts to "govern" economic life through creating new ways for people to be at work, what exactly is the status of the term "government" in this context? Quite obviously "government" is not equivalent to "the Government" or "the State", and yet, as Rose's comments suggest, various discourses of work reform appear to be intimately linked to the political culture of the time. It is a shared "governmental rationality" (Foucault, 1991) which provides this link.

According to Foucault (1980: 221) "government" is a form of power referring to the "conduct of conduct": "to govern, in this sense, is to structure the possible field of actions of others"; that is to say, government is a form of activity aiming to shape, guide or affect the conduct of some person or persons. Government as an activity can concern the relation between self and self, private interpersonal relations involving some form of control or guidance, relations within social institutions and committees and, finally, relations concerned with the exercise of political sovereignty (Cousins and Hussain, 1984).

For Foucault, government is a "discursive" activity. All forms of government rely upon a particular mode of representation: the development of a language for delineating and depicting a certain domain that claims both to capture the nature of the "reality" represented, and, literally, to "re-present" it in a form suitable for deliberation, argumentation, scheming and intervention (Miller and Rose, 1990). Thus it is possible to see that the government of an economy, or of an organization, only becomes feasible through discursive practices that render the "Real" comprehensible as a particular "reality" with specific limits and distinct characteristics whose components are linked together in some relatively systematic fashion

(Hacking, 1983).[1] Particular programmes of intervention and rectification, and specific "technologies of government" follow on from this rendering of the "Real" into the domain of thought as a "reality".

However, "government" isn't simply about the ordering of activities and processes, it is intimately concerned with subjectification: government operates through subjects. As Foucault (1980; 1982) argued, forms of power "work" by constructing and maintaining the forms of subjectivity most appropriate to a given type of social practice/governmental rationality. Subjectivities are constituted by, and rendered instrumental to, a particular form of power through the medium of knowledges or technical *savoir faire* "immanent to that form of power" (Minson, 1985: 44-45). Thus power works in – and – through subjectivity. Different governmental rationalities are closely linked to conceptions and attributes of those to be governed. In other words, particular rationalities of government involve the construction of specific ways for people to be. In Ian Hacking's (1986: 234) phrase they actively "make up" people.

Because "government" is a "conduct of conduct", it presupposes rather than annuls the capacity of individuals as agents. As Foucault (1982: 221) suggests,

> when one defines the exercise of power as a mode of action upon the actions of others, when one characterizes these actions by the government of men by other men *(sic)* – in the broadest sense of the term – one includes an important element: freedom. Power is exercised only over free subjects, and only insofar as they are free. By this we mean individual or collective subjects who are faced with a field of possibilities in which several ways of behaving, several reactions and diverse comportements may be realized. Where the determining factors saturate the whole there is no relationship of power.

The relation between government and governed therefore depends upon an "unstable conjuncture" – it is "agonistic" – because this relation passes through the manner in which governed individuals are willing to exist as particular subjects. As Gordon (1991: 48) has suggested, "to the extent that the governed are engaged, in their individuality, by the propositions and provisions of government, government makes it's own rationality intimately their affair". In this sense, government is a very personal matter; it is bound up with "ethics". For Foucault (1984: 352) "ethics" has a very particular meaning: "the kind of relationship you ought to have with yourself, *rapport a soi* ... which determines how the individual is supposed to constitute himself *(sic)* as a moral subject of his own actions". Ethics are thus conceived as means by which individuals come to understand and act upon themselves in relation to the true and the false, the permitted and the forbidden, the desirable and the undesirable (Rose, 1990).

As I indicated earlier, the government of economic life across the twentieth century has entailed a range of attempts to shape and regulate the relations that individuals have with society's productive apparatus. From "Scientific Management" through "Human Relations" up to and including the contemporary programmes of "Excellence", the activities of individuals as "workers" have become "an object of knowledge and the target of expertise, and a complex web of relays has been formed through which the economic endeavours of politicians and businessmen have been translated into the personal capacities and aspirations of subjects"(Miller and Rose, 1990: 19). In other words, the identity of the "worker" has been differentially constituted in the changing practices of governing economic life. "Workers" and "managers" have been "made up" in different ways – discursively re-imagined and re-conceptualized – at different times through their positioning in a variety of discourses of work reform.

For the remainder of this chapter I will concentrate on the ways in which people are "made up" at work in the present by exploring the contemporary management discourse of "Excellence" and its relationship to the political rationality of "Enterprise". In particular, I will indicate how the expertise of Excellence provides the means whereby the politico-ethical objectives of neo-liberal government in the UK – or "Thatcherism" as it has popularly been known –, the economic objectives of contemporary business and the self-actualizing and self-regulating capacties of human subjects are linked together into a functioning network.

2   Enterprise Culture and the Discourse of Excellence

From the outset, the Thatcherite project not only involved an economic revival but also a moral crusade. As Margaret Thatcher herself argued, as early as 1975, "serious as the economic challenge is, the political and moral challenge is just as grave, and perhaps more so, because economic problems never start with economics" (quoted in Hall, 1988: 85). It was the difficult, often faltering, attempt to weave these economic and moral strands together that produced the Enterprise Culture as the symbol and goal of Thatcherism.

Although the concept of an Enteprise Culture was not at all well-defined in policy terms when the Conservatives first won power in 1979, it has since become extremely important in "justifying many of the policies the government has adopted, and in characterising the long term objectives of its programme and the kind of society it wants to see emerge" (Gamble, 1988: 137). Basically the government argued that the permissive and anti-enterprise culture that had been fostered by social-democratic institutions since 1945 had become one of the most serious obstacles to reversing decline. The economic and moral regeneration of Britain therefore necessitated exerting pressure on every institution to make it supportive of Enterprise.

In Britiain attempts to construct a culture of Enterprise have proceeded through the progressive enlargement of the territory of the market – the realm of private enterprise and economic rationality – by a series of redefinitions of its object. Thus the task of creating an "Enterprise Culture" has involved the reconstruction of a wide range of institutions and activities along the lines of the commercial business organization, with attention focused, in particular, on its orientation towards "the sovereign consumer". At the same time, however, the market has also come to define the sort of relation an individual should have with him/herself, and the "habits of action" he or she should acquire and exhibit. Enterprise refers here to the "kind of action or project" that exhibits "enterprising" qualities or characteristics on the part of individuals or groups. In this latter sense an "Enterprise Culture" is one in which certain enterprising qualities – such as self-reliance, personal responsibility, boldness, and a willingness to take risks in the pursuit of goals – are regarded as human virtues and promoted as such. As Keat (1990: 3-4) has indicated, in the contemporary discourse of Enterprise these two strands – the "institutional" and the "ethical" – are intricately interwoven.

> on the one hand, the conduct of commercial enterprises is presented as a (indeed the) primary field of activity in which enterprising qualities are displayed. And given that these qualities are themselves regarded as intrinsically desirable ... this serves to valorize engagement in such activities and hence, more generally, the workings of a free market economy. On the other hand, however, it is also claimed that in order to maximise the benefits of this economic system, commercial enterprises must themselves be encouraged to be enterprising, i.e. to act in ways that fully express these qualities. In other words, it seems to be acknowledged that "enterprises are not fully enterprising", and enterprising qualities are thus given an instrumental value in relation to the optimal performance of a market economy.

According to Colin Gordon (1991: 43), Enterprise has become an approach capable, in principle, "of addressing the totality of human behaviour, and thus, of envisaging a coherent, purely economic method of programming the totality of governmental action". In other words, Enterprise can be understood to constitute a particular form of "governmental rationality" (Foucault, 1991). As such it is not simply reducible to the politico-ethical project of Thatcherism. Rather than having an "originary" essence in, and unique "belongingness" to, the policies of successive Conservative administrations, the rationality of Enterprise permeates a plethora of discourses, programmes and technologies developed outside the field of formal or "official" Government. For example, one area in which the vocabulary of Enterprise has played a central structuring role is in management discourse.

According to Wood (1989: 387), one of the most distinctive features of "new wave management" is the shift it attempts to initiate from "reactive to proactive postures", from "bureaucratic" to "entrepreneurial styles of management" and, possibly most importantly, the new forms of work-based identity it tries to forge amongst all members of an organization. For Wood, the appeal of the new management discourse of "Excellence" has as much, if not more, to do with the *cultural* reconstruction of work-based identities as with the "values of the technologies or organizational forms they propose".

As Wood's comments indicate, one of the key elements in the contemporary discourse of work reform is the attention devoted to questions of "culture" and "identity". A cursory inspection of any number of recent management texts reveals the primacy accorded to "culture change programmes" as panaceas for all manner of organizational ills (Peters and Waterman, 1982; Ouchi, 1981; Kanter, 1990; Peters, 1987).[2] In this literature "culture" is paramount because it is seen to structure the way people think, make decisions and act in organizations. "Culture" is represented as an answer to the problems thrown up by the increasingly dislocated ground upon which globalized capitalism operates. As Laclau (1990: 56), for example, has argued, the less organizations are able to rely upon a framework of stable social and political relations, the more they are forced to engage in a project of "hegemonic construction". In other words, the effects of dislocation require constant "creativity", and the continuous construction of collective operational space that rests less on inherited objective forms (bureaucracy) and more on *cultural* reconstruction. Thus "new wave management" is concerned with changing people's values, norms, and attitudes so they make the "right" and necessary contribution to the success of the organization for which they work. To this end "Excellence" encourages managers to view the most "effective" and "excellent" organizations as those with "strong cultures" – patterns of meaning which enable all members of an organizaton to *identify* with the goals and objectives of the company for which they work.

According to Deleuze (1992: 3), amongst others, the corporation only becomes "cultural" – develops a "soul" – once "the market" has achieved a position of pre-eminence. The discourse of "Excellence" is therefore both symptom and effect of the increasing de-differentiation of Economy and Culture. As Jameson (1990: 29) has argued, the colonization of "Culture" by the market does not imply the disappearance or extinction of the cultural, rather it suggests a situation in which "the corporate is now at one with culture".

In effect, the "institutional" and "ethical" imperatives propounded by the advocates of Excellence are very similar to those proclaimed within the Thatcherite project: economic and moral revival through a programme of "cultural change". Like Thatcherism, the "Search for Excellence" requires a veritable "cultural revolution", one in which organizations and their members learn to "thrive on chaos" (in the decentred global free-market economy) and to renew continually their enterprising spirit. Thus, the vocabulary of Enterprise is a central structuring element in both of these projects. However, as I indicated above, "Excellence" is not reducible to "Thatcherism at Work". Although the discourse of Enterprise, and contemporary attempts to create an Enterprise Culture in the UK are virtually synonymous with the politico-ethical project of Thatcherism, they are not reducible to this phenomenon. Rather, Enterprise as a "governmental rationality" has entered people's daily lives in a number of ways not directly related to the policy initiatives of successive Conservative administrations (Robins, 1991; Held, 1991). At the same time, this also suggests that the removal of Margaret Thatcher from office in no way heralded the end of the project of Enterprise. Indeed, as Hall (1991: 10) has recently argued, the "entrepreneurial revolution" to which Thatcherism contributed with such passionate brutality "is still working its way through the system".

Although the *cultural reconstruction of identity* is central to the Excellence project, contemporary management discourse has been largely ignored within cultural analysis. Morris (1988: 22-23) has recently provided a convincing explanation for this neglect. According to her, there is a marked tendency within much cultural studies to assume that somehow the "economic" sphere has already been accounted for. Within this tradition a potentially de-alienated sphere of "consumption" is often counterposed to an alienated, deskilled and already determined world of paid employment. So while cultural analysis has paid considerable attention to the "pleasures" of and "play" of identities within contemporary cultures of consumption, it has tended to relegate the world of work and employment "to the realm of the *déjà vu*".

Meanwhile, within the sociology of work and employment, for example, where "economic life" is the central focus, the Excellence phenomenon has been accorded some considerable, though narrowly focused, attention. But while its theoretical underpinnings have been criticized, its empirical incidence debated, and its internal contradictions exposed (Storey, 1989), there has been little notice paid to the subjectivizing aspects of the Excellence project, and their relationship to the politico-ethical objectives of neo-liberal government in the UK. However, as I argued above, questions of discourse, subjectivity and identity have a key role to play in understanding the Excellence phenomenon and its linkage to the governmental rationality of Enterprise.

2.1 Work-based Identity and Management Discourse

A concern with the production of particular work-based identities is not unique to contemporary management discourse. As I argued earlier, throughout the present century multifarious schemes have been advocated by a plethora of "schools of thought" which attempt, both consciously and unconsciously, to eradicate conflict and contestability from organizational life through "integrating" the work-based human subject and the organization. This objective can be seen to underlie such seemingly diverse approaches as Mayoite Human Relations (Mayo, 1949; Roethlisberger and Dickson, 1939), the "Organizational Psycho-Technologists" (Herzberg, 1968; McGregor, 1960; Argyris, 1957), and the Quality of Working Life

Movement (Davis and Cherns, 1975), for example. Each of these projects assumed that it was possible (and indeed necessary) to reconcile the needs and desires of management and workers through the deployment of their own particular "expertise". In effect, whether articulated in terms of a "need" for "belongingness" (Mayo et al.), or as a desire for "self-actualization" (Herzberg et al.), what unites all of these projects is a concern with the production and regulation of particular work-based subjectivities.

According to Miller and Rose (1988: 172) these various schools of thought construct

> images of the enterprise, techniques of management, forms of authority, and conceptions of the social vocation of industry which can align the government of the enterprise with the prevailing cultural values, social expectations, political concerns and personal ambitions ... They have provided means for linking together changing political rationalities and objectives, the ceaseless quest of business for profitability and a basis for managerial authority, with interventions aimed at the subjectivity of the worker.

The Excellence project is firmly established on this trajectory. It follows in the footsteps of its predecessors in seeking to construct a vision of the enterprise as an "organic entity", but it does so through the articulation of a new vocabulary of the employment relationship in which the worker's relation to his/her work is re-imagined in line with prevailing ethical systems, political rationalities, and, of course, the profitability imperative. Within the discourse of Excellence the internal world of the enterprise is reconceptualized as one in which productivity is to be improved, production and service quality assured, "flexibility" enhanced, and innovation developed through the active engagement of the self-fulfilling impulses of all the organization's members" (Rose, 1989: 16).

Some critics of Excellence within the social sciences have emphasized the similarities between contemporary management discourse and previous programmes of work reform, and, in particular, its close resemblance to the Human Relations school (Turner, 1986; Silver, 1987). However, by concentrating almost exclusively on "continuity" and "homogeneity" within management discourse, these critics tend to downgrade the new ways for people to be at work present within the contemporary discursive formation. Within the Human Relations tradition, for example, the worker is considered, first and foremost, as a *social* creature seeking fulfilment of his/her needs for "belongingness" in the group relations of the workplace. With the contemporary "entrepreneurial order" (Miller and O'Leary, 1986), however, the worker is represented as an *individual* in search of *meaning* in work, and wanting to achieve fulfilment through work. Excellent organizations are those that "make meaning for people" by encouraging them to believe that they have control over their own destinies; that no matter what position they may hold in an organization their contribution is vital, not only to the success of the company for which they work, *but also to the enterprise of their own lives*. Peters and Waterman (1982: 81, 56), for example, approvingly quote Nietzsche's axiom that "he (*sic*) who has a *why* to live for can bear most any *how*". They argue that "the fact ... that we think we have a bit more discretion leads to much greater commitment" and that "we desperately need meaning in our lives, and will sacrifice a great deal to institutions that will provide meaning for us. We simultaneously need independence, to feel as though we are in charge of our destinies, and to have the ability to stick out". In this vision, work is a sphere within which the individual constructs and confirms their identity. "Excellent" organizations get the most out of their employees, not by manipulating group human relations to secure a sense of "belonging", but by harnessing "the psychological striving of individuals for autonomy and creativity and channelling them into the search of the firm for excellence and success" (Miller and Rose, 1990: 26).

In other words, "Excellent" companies seek to cultivate "Enterprising subjects" – autonomous, self-regulating, productive individuals (Gordon, 1987; Rose, 1989; 1990). Here, Enterprise refers to those plethora of "rules of conduct" for everyday life mentioned earlier: energy, initiative, self-reliance and personal responsibility, etc. This "Enterprising self" is a calculating self; a self that "calculates *about* itself, and that works *upon* itself in order to better itself" (Rose, 1989: 7-8). Thus Enterprise designates a form of rule that is intrinsically "ethical" in Foucault's sense of the term: good government is to be grounded in the ways individuals govern themselves; as well as inherently "economic", enterprising self-regulation accords well with Jeremy Bentham's rallying cry of "Cheap Government!".

For Peters and Waterman (1982: 238-239) Excellent organizations are those which create a "powerful focus of identification" by activating the individual's capacities for "self-motivation" and "enterprise"

> there was hardly a more pervasive theme in the excellent companies than *respect for the individual*. That basic belief and assumption were omnipresent ... what makes it live at these companies is a plethora of structural devices, systems, styles and values all re-inforcing one another so that the companies are truly unusual in their ability to achieve extraordinary results through ordinary people ... These companies give people control over their destinies; they make meaning for people. They turn the average Joe or Jane into winners. They let, even insist that, people stick out. They accentuate the positive.

For the advocates of Excellence, governing the organization in an "Enterprising" manner requires a judicious mixture of centralized control and individual autonomy. According to Peters and Waterman (1982: 318), Excellent companies must be "simultaneously loose and tight": "organizations that live by the loose/tight principle are on the one hand rigidly controlled, yet at the same time allow (indeed, insist on) autonomy, entrepreneurship, and innovaton from the rank and file". Thus the Excellent firm is one that engages in a *controlled de-control*, or, to deploy Foucault's (1988b) terminology, one that "totalizes" and "individualizes" at one and the same time.

According to its proponents, the key to "loose/tight" is "culture": the effective management of symbols, meanings, beliefs and values is held to transform an apparent contradiction – between increasing central control while extending individual accountability and responsibility – into "no contradiction at all" (Peters and Waterman, 1982: 321). If an organization has an appropriate "culture" of Excellence, if all its members adopt an "Enterprising" relationship to self, then efficiency, economy, autonomy, quality and innovation all "become words that belong on the same side of the coin" (Peters and Waterman, 1982: 321).

Although the recourse to "culture" by advocates of "Excellence" is often criticised within the social sciences for its "remarkable vagueness" (Howard, 1985), Peters (1988: 404), for example, is adamant that the "corporate culture" only finds life "in details, not broad strokes". In other words, the "culture" of the business enterprise is only operationalized through particular practices and technologies – through "specific measures" (Hunter, 1987).

Rather than being some vague, incalculable "spirit", the culture of Enterprise is inscribed into a variety of mechanisms – application forms, recruitment "auditions", communication groups and the like – through which senior management in "Excellent" companies seek to delineate, normalize and instrumentalize the conduct of persons in order to achieve the ends they postulate as desirable. Thus, governing the business organization in an Excellent manner involves cultivating enterprising subjects through the development of an (simultaneous loose/tight) "enabling and empowering vision" (Peters, 1987) articulated in the everyday practices of the organization.

2.2   The "Enterprising" Subjects of "Excellence"

According to the doyenne of contemporary management discourse, Rosabeth Moss Kanter (1990: 9-10), "by 1983" the figure of the entrepreneur had become "the new culture hero" of the Western world. According to Kanter the term "entrepreneur" no longer simply implied the formation of an independent business venture, rather it had traversed its traditional limits and now referred to the application of "entrepreneurial principles to the traditional corporation, creating a marriage between entrepreneurial creativity and corporate discipline, cooperation and teamwork".[3] This "intrapreneurial" or "post-entrepreneurial" ("because it takes entrepreneurship a stage further") "revolution" therefore provides the possibility for every member of an organization to express "individual initiative" and to fully develop their "potential" in the service of the corporation. In effect, enterprising Excellence offers the individual the opportunity to feel "in business for oneself inside the modern corporation", and therefore the all important experience of "ownership" (Pinchot, 1985; Kanter, 1990; Sabel, 1990).

Hence, while "Enterprise" still designates an economic form, it also indicates a category of activity to be encouraged by specific programmes of intervention and rectification in economic life, and a certain way in which aspects of economic, social and cultural life should be "problematized and programmed" (Rose, 1989: 3-4). Problems are conceptualized in terms of a "lack of Enterprise"; the solutions to which are to be found by actively fostering and utilizing the "enterprising ca-pacities" of individuals, "encouraging them to conduct themselves with boldness and vigour, and to drive themselves hard to accept risks in the pursuit of goals" (Rose, 1989: 3-4). Individuals are deemed capable of identifying themselves with the goals and objectives of their employing organization to the extent that they interpret them as both dependent upon and enhancing their own skills of self-development, self-presentation, self-direction, and self-management.

The enterprising vision of "Excellence" provides a novel image of the worker, the organization, and their relationship one with the other. It posits a "post-hierarchical", entrepreneurial future where the "old bureaucratic" emphasis on or-der, uniformity and repetition is gradually replaced by an entrepreneurial emphasis on "can do" creativity (Kanter, 1990; Boyne, 1990).[4] The choice presented is stark: to survive in the dislocated, decentred, increasingly competitive and chaotic global economy "companies must either move away from bureaucratic guarantees to post-entrepreneurial flexibility or ... stagnate" (Kanter, 1990: 356). The message clear: organizations must shift from "formality" to "flexibility" in all their activities and relations. "Formal rules" as to how work should be done must be replaced by "implicit expectations" as to how work should be done. This requires that every employee make the goals and objectives of his/her employing organization their own personal goals and objectives, thus ensuring that s/he will deploy their "autonomy" and "creativity" correctly from the organization's point of view. Hence, again, there is the insistence on the construction and promulgation of a "strong corporate culture" which reconciles the autonomous aspirations of the self-steer-ing individual employee with the collective entrepreneurialism of the flexible cor-poration. According to Peters and Waterman (1982: 72)

> virtually all the excellent companies are driven by just a few key values, and then give lots of space to employees to take initiatives in support of these values – finding their own paths, and so making the task their own.

Thus the "expertise" of Excellence provides techniques for mapping the cultural world of the business organization in terms of its success in engaging with and building upon the motivations and aspirations of its inhabitants. Through the medium of various technologies and practices inscribed with the presuppositions of the Enterprising self – techniques for reducing dependency by reorganizing management structures ("de-layering"); for cutting across internal organizational boundaries (the creation of "special project teams", for example); for encouraging internal competitiveness through small-group working; and for eliciting individual accountability and personal responsibility through peer-review and performance appraisal schemes, etc. – the internal world of the business organization is re-conceptualized as one in which customers' demands are satisfied, productivity enhanced, quality assured, innovation fostered, and flexibility guaranteed through the active engagement of the self-fulfilling impulses of all the organization's members. In this way, the autonomous subjectivity of the productive individual has become a central economic resource; that is the "strategic human resource" (Storey, 1989).

Within the discourse of Excellence, work is characterized not as a painful obligation imposed upon individuals, nor as an activity only undertaken by people for the fulfilment of instrumental needs and satisfactions. Work is itself a means for self-fulfilment, and the road to company profit is also the path to individual self-development and growth.

In this way, the worker is made "subject", in that s/he is both "subject to someone else by control and dependence, and tied to his (*sic*) own identity by a conscience or self-knowledge. Both meanings suggest a form of power which subjugates and make subject to" (Foucault, 1982: 212). In other words, a person's sense of who and what they are is constituted and confirmed through their positioning within particular relations of power. These relations are both "technological" and "economical": "technological", in that they are exercised in and through specific "knowledges"; "economical" in that their effect is to create and sustain a "self-governing" subject. According to Gordon (1991: 44), Enterprise is the contemporary "care of the self" which government commends as the corrective to collective greed.

As Foucault (1988c: 92) has argued, the exercise of power "depends on an unstable conjuncture". Power is always productive, not merely repressive of culture. And it is precisely the positive aspects of power/knowledge relations which makes them so plausible, so effective/seductive. Thus, the "expertise" of Excellence can be seen to play the role of "cypher" between people's evaluations of themselves and the "programmatic" aspirations of economic authorities (Rose, 1990). The "power" of this "expertise" lies in its promise of an effectiveness lodged in objectivity, and its manifest commitment to people's sense of who and what they are. As Rose (1989; 1990), for example, has argued, expertise is constitutive of subjectivity. Its languages permeate people's ways of thinking, its judgements enter into people's evaluations, and its norms into their calculations. At the very moment when they aspire to freedom and try to realize autonomy, people are bound not only to expert knowledge but to the project of their own identities.

Thus the establishment of "connections" and "symmetries" between the self-development of the worker and the increased competitiveness and flexibility of the corporation

> enables an alignment to take place between the technologies of work and the technologies of subjectivity. For the entrepreneurial self, work is no longer necessarily a constraint upon the freedom of the individual to fulfil his or her potential through strivings for autonomy, creativity and responsibility. Work is an essential element in the path to self-realization ... The government of work now passes through the psychological strivings of each and every individual for self-fulfilment (Miller and Rose, 1990: 27).

3 Enterprise, Excellence, Thatcherism

It is now possible to see how the language of Enterprise does not simply attempt to fashion the way owners and managers of capital calculate and activate business strategies in the marketplace, it is also inscribed within contemporary management discourse where it has been formulated into a series of technologies of regulation for governing the internal life of the modern corporation in order to secure business success. This success is premised upon an engagement by the organization of the "self-fulfilling impulses" of all its individual employees, no matter their role within the enterprise. Excellence plays the role of "relay" between objectives that are economically desirable and those that are personally seductive, "teaching the arts of self-realization that will enhance employees as individuals as well as workers" (Rose, 1989: 16). The discourse of Excellence brooks no opposition between the mode of self-presentation required of managers and employees, and the ethics of the personal self. Becoming a better worker is represented as the same thing as becoming a more virtuous person, a better self. In other words, within the discourse of Excellence, *technologies of power* – "which determine the conduct of individuals and submit them to certain ends or domination, an objectivizing of the subject" – and *technologies of the self* – "which permit individuals to effect by their own means or with the help of others, a certain number of operations on their own bodies and souls, thoughts, conduct and way of being, so as to transform themselves in order to attain a certain state of happiness, purity, wisdom, perfection or immortality" – are imperceptibly merged (Foucault, 1988a: 18). The values of self-realization, of personal responsibility, of "ownership", accountability and self-management are both personally attractive and economically desirable.

This "autonomization" and "responsibilization" of the self, the instilling of a reflexive self-monitoring which will afford self-knowledge and therefore, self-mastery, makes paid work (no matter how "objectively" alienated, deskilled, or degraded it may appear to social scientists) an essential element in the path to self-fulfilment and provides the *a priori* that links together work and non-work life.

The "employee", just as much as the "sovereign consumer", is represented as an individual in search of meaning and fulfilment, one looking to "add value" in every sphere of existence. Paid work and consumption are just different playing grounds for the same activity; that is, different terrains upon which the enterprising self seeks to master, better and fulfil itself. In the discourse of Excellence the relations between "production", "consumption", between the "inside" and "outside" of the corporation, and, crucially, between work and non-work based identities, are progressively blurred (Sabel, 1990).

However, the "expertise" of Excellence doesn't just act as a "relay" between the self-steering capacities of subjects and the goals of industry, it also plays a vital "translating role" between the government of the enterprise and the politico-ethical objectives of neo-liberal government in the UK. Through deployment of the vocabulary of Enterprise, contemporary management discourse establishes "connections and symmetries" between the concerns of owners and managers of capital to maximize the performance and productivity of their organizations, political concerns about the government of the productive, moral and cultural life of the "Nation", and techniques for the government of the subject. Excellence helps link these together into a "functioning network" (Miller and Rose, 1990: 26-27).

Thus the Thatcherite belief that Britian's moral and economic regeneration can only come about through the destruction of the "dependency culture" and its replacement by a culture of Enterprise is mirrored almost exactly in the logic of Excellence. What is seen as an increasingly competitive and chaotic global free market "that can't be bucked" demands that the corporation – like the State – shed its "dependency mentality" and cultivate some "entrepreneurial spirit". "The traditional corporation is in such turmoil that it can no longer carry the weight of ... society's expectations of permanence, to which a variety of welfare benefits are tied"(Kanter, 1990: 357).

According to the Confederation of British Industry (1988: 59-60), for example, the "productivity imperative" calls for a restructured corporation with "lower manning levels and more flexible and wider job specification". In turn, this is deemed to require "a necessary parallel change ... towards greater individual responsibility on the part of all employees and, in consequence, the development of self-management at all levels". Again the message is clear: "the free ride is over, you're on your own". From now on it is up to individuals to secure their own future through their own efforts. In "post-entrepreneurial" times people's careers

> are more dependent on their own resources ... This means that some people who know only bureaucratic ropes are cut adrift. It means that incomes are likely to fluctuate rather than increase in an orderly fashion every year ... It means more risk and uncertainty ... No longer counting on the corporation requires people to build resources in themselves, which ultimately could result in more resourceful people (Kanter, 1990: 357-358).

The assumption is that "post-entrepreneurial strategies are more motivating for people" because they allow everyone the opportunity to be in business for themselves "inside ... the large corporation". The promise is that the corporation itself "should reap benefits too, in increased productivity" (Kanter, 1990: 357-358).

This vision of the corporation again echoes familiar ("organic") theories of society. According to critical management theorists such as Legge, Storey, and Sisson (1989), "new wave" management discourse is really "no more or less than a reflection of the rise of the new right – whether in the U.K. or the U.S.A.". For Legge (1989: 40), Excellence provides that "different language" which "our new enterprise culture demands ... one that asserts management's right to manipulate *and* ability to generate and develop resources". Indeed, as Storey and Sisson (1989: 168-172) have indicated, "the powerful advocacy of the 'excellence literature' has been supported massively by the government and its agencies" – for example through the Department of Trade and Industry's (the Department of Enterprise as Lord Young referred to it) "Enterprise Initiative". Nonetheless, despite this committed promulgation, they continue, the facts suggest that the "Excellence vision is not being adopted in most organizations". So, whilst they acknowledge the importance of contemporary management discourse in articulating "a coherent and convincing *Weltanschauung*", they still posit an enormous gap between representation and reality.

Interestingly, it is a self-styled "post-marxist", Andre Gorz, who takes this view of contemporary developments to its logical conclusion. Gorz (1989: 66) argues that contemporary images of the enterprise

> as a place where employees can achieve personal fulfilment is ... an essentially ideological invention. It conceals the real transformations that have taken place, namely that enterprises are replacing labour by machines, producing more and better with a decreasing percentage of the workforce previously employed, and offering privileges to a chosen elite of workers, which are accompanied by unemployment, precarious employment, deskilling and lack of job security for the majority.

While the "transformations" Gorz refers to are "real" enough, they are never just given, as he seems to imply, but are always discursively constituted. Unlike many other post-marxists (Hall, 1988; Laclau and Mouffe, 1985; Zizek, 1989), Gorz views ideology as simply a negative force, hiding or distorting a more "truthful" reality. Thus the desire to establish a clear and transparent relationship between the socially active signifier and the real relations to which it might refer is expressed in a vocabulary of truth and falsity: ideology is a simulacrum, it disguises, travesties and blurs reality and "real" relations.

In a very orthodox (and extremely non-post-marxist) fashion, any acknowledgement of the ideological status of Excellence can also be seen to be, at one and the same time, a condemnation. As a counterweight to the "essentially ideological" (whatever that is), Gorz appears to invite the reader to view instead what is actually (i.e. non-ideologically) happening on the ground by taking a close look at "real" material circumstances. Nonetheless, while it is undoubtedly true that "material circumstances" matter profoundly, these circumstances are always "ideologically" (ie. discursively) defined. The subjects of ideology are never unified and integral selves, however; they are "fractured, always in process and strangely composite" (Hall, 1988: 9-10). People make identifications symbolically, through social imagery, in their imaginations. To maintain a totally perjorative attitude towards ideology, to refer to it as a con-trick, distortion, or simply as a marginal or secondary concern, leads to a certain neglect of, Reich's words, "what goes on in people's heads" (Smith,1988).

3.1   Enterprise and Excellence: Ideology/Antagonism/Fantasy

As I have indicated, questions of ideology/discourse are absolutely central to the Excellence project, and cannot be regarded as secondary or dependent factors. Ideology has "real", "material" effects which cannot be reduced to, or simply read as, the "reflexive" accounts of some "original" or determining factor. As Hall (1988: 9-10) has indicated, "all economic and political processes have ideological 'conditions of existence'".

Like the Thatcherite project of an Enterprise Culture, Excellence is an attempt to redefine and reconstruct the economic/cultural terrain, and to "win" social subjects to a new conception of themselves – to turn them into "winnners", "champions" and "everyday heroes". As Wood (1989) has argued, Excellence is about the politics of identity; contemporary management discourse attempts to enable all sorts of people, from highest executive to lowliest shop-floor employee, to see themselves reflected in the emerging conception of the "enterprising organization", and thus to come increasingly to identify with it. In this sense, Excellence can be conceptualized not only as "cultural technology" (Hunter, 1987), but also as "organic ideology"; as attempting to articulate into a configuration different subjects, different identities and different aspirations.

To appeal to the "logical contradictions" of contemporary management discourse, and to the even more basic underlying "contradictions of capitalism" (Legge, 1989: 43; Hyman, 1987), in order to show that this project can never "really work" is to misunderstand the ways in which ideology operates. For ideology doesn't "work" in a logical intellectual fashion. It doesn't collapse as the result of a logical contradiction because it does not obey the logic of rational discourse (Hall, 1988; Zizek, 1991). Rather it is closer in discursive structure to the logic of the "dream-work" than to that of analytic rationalism (Hall, 1988: 86). As Wright (1987: 8) has commented, "management thinking is superior to merely rational science in that it brings the lifeworld along with it. It entails no break with everyday experience; there is no question of having to 'save the appearances' after meaning and scientific truth have taken off into a realm of their own".

The discourse/ideology of Excellence connects across different positions and divergent terrains, between seemingly disparate, and often contradictory ideas. Just like "Thatcherism", Excellence is "multifaceted" – operating on several fronts at one and the same time, linking together diverse strands into a "functioning network" (Hall, 1988: 166; Miller and Rose, 1990). Arm in arm with the New Right, Excellence has unfolded a positive conception of the Enterprise Culture which it would be dangerous to dismiss simply as "hype" or a "fad". Through deployment of the vocabulary of "Enterprise", Excellence appears to have established a "translatability" between the economic objectives of employers and managers of capital, changing political rationalities, and the desires of the self.

Exactly whose identities are being discussed here? At one level it is quite clearly the "character" of the "Manager" (MacIntyre, 1985) at whom these "technologies of the self" are aimed. After all, its managerial staff, rather than more lower-level employees who have sustained the remarkable sales figures of the Excellence literature and attended the screenings of Tom Peter's *A Passion for Excellence* video (a very common event throughout a wide range of British companies in recent years). For the manager there is tangible sense in which economic success, career progress, and personal development intersect in this new expertise of autonomous subjectivity: the closer to the centre of the "organizational network" you are located, the more likely it still is that the interests of organizational development and "personal" development coincide. In turn, this suggests that not all employees will be subjects in the new regime of the self. Those on the "margins", or, in this case, the "periphery", continue to be governed in more visible, and less subtle ways; subject to "coercion" rather than "seduction" (Bauman, 1988; Rose, 1989). Nevertheless, Excellence *is* explicitly aimed at everyone. No matter what role they perform within an organization, it is argued, everybody can and will benefit from cultivating some "enterprising spirit" and aspiring to Excellence. That is how they can become virtuous, resourceful, and "empowered" human beings, so the argument goes.

Excellence is very much a crusade, promulgating the faith that everyone can be "won over". Almost all the "new cultural intermediaries", or "experts", of Excellence firmly reject the idea that "culture change" at work is only enabling for a minority of the workforce. Instead they appear to believe that the interventions they propose in the internal world of the economic enterprise will transform what was previously a minority experience into the life of the majority. This is particularly true in relation to the notion of "self" they encourage all workers to adopt. "Self-management" is the key here: "how to handle yourself to your own best advantage" (Kanter, 1990). The cultural intermediaries of Excellence advise all workers to "make a project of themselves" (Bourdieu, 1984; Featherstone, 1987; Bonner and du Gay, 1992). In other words to work on their relations with employment, and all other areas of their lives, in order to develop a "lifestyle" which will maximize the worth of their existence to themselves.[5]

According to some commentators (Townley, 1989), technologies of regulation based on this faith in Excellence are being deployed more extensively by employers to cover a much wider range of employees. More systematic selection and appraisal technologies – personality profiling and psychometric testing, biodata, and per-formance-related reviews – are being targeted at sections of the workforce they had not previously covered. As Townley (1989: 93-98) has noted, "no longer confined to managerial levels, careful selection screening, and regular formal monitoring of performance are increasingly becoming the experience of those at lower levels of the organizational hierarchy, especially blue-collar employees". These developments are interpreted as expressing an increasing concern amongst employers with the behavioural and attitudinal characteristics of the employee as an *individual*. The more extensive deployment of technologies of regulation can be seen therefore as a "strategic" response by employers to the problems of gov-ernment involved in the "move away from the direct and technical supervision of work, to the greater degree of 'discretion', or 'flexibility', being devolved to the individual ..." (Townley, 1989: 93-98).

Although enormous gaps remain between the programmatic aspirations of employers and managers, and the actual "usage" (or "consumption") of these technologies in the practice of everyday working life by those at whom they are aimed, this does not mean that the whole entrepreneurial edifice of Excellence can be dismissed with disdain as yet another failure. Government is an inherently Sisyphean endeavour. The impossibility of government is the very motor of the "will to govern". What is important here is the establishing of those "connections and symmetries" described by Miller and Rose (1990) between changing political rationalities and objectives, the profitability imperatives of contemporary business, and interventions aimed at the subjectivity of the employee.

Since work-based identity can no longer be guaranteed in any foundational sense by "class position", or by the "mode of production" of themselves (Hall, 1988; Laclau, 1990), the "subjective" moment becomes central politically, culturally, and ideologically. The project of reconstruction advocated by the experts of "Excel-lence" is not some side-show to the main event of global economic restructuring, rather it is an essential element in the very process of restructuring itself. As Laclau (1990: 56), for example, has argued, "the more dislocated is the ground on which capitalism operates, the less it can rely on a stable framework of stable social and political relations" and the more central becomes the cultural moment of "hegemonic construction". Excellence attempts to redefine the terms in which the social rela-tions of work and employment are imagined. For unless people identify with and become subjects of a new conception of "work", "business", or "society", it is un-likely it will emerge.

According to Hall (1988: 167), "Thatcherism" as an ideology works by address-ing "the fears, anxieties, the lost identities of a people. It invites us to think about politics in images. It is addressed to our collective fantasies, to Britian as an imagined community, to the social imaginary". Excellence appears to operate in a similar vein, offering people the fantasy of "Entrepreneurship". It promotes an image of "self-determination" at work, inviting people to feel as if they are their own bosses – to experience "ownership" – and to become "entrepreneurs of themselves".

In the US context, as Guest (1990: 390) has indicated, Excellence has enjoyed enormous success because, like "Reaganism", it managed to capture "the essence of the American Dream". He argues that it is precisely because Excellence plays on fantasies of "the opportunity for progress, or growth, based on individual achievement" that it has gained "a stubborn hold on the American mind" (Guest, 1990: 391).[6] By drawing attention to the importance of "dreams", "images" and "fantasy" in the operation of Excellence, Guest has performed a great service. However, it is one he quickly undermines by giving way to the desire to reintroduce a reality/representation dichotomy. While he argues that Excellence addresses and connects with ordinary people's aspirations and displays "the good intention" of turning them into "reality", he concludes that "the evidence suggests this is no more than a fantasy, a dream" (Guest, 1990: 391). What is this evidence? Once more it is "objective material circumstances".

Rather than exploring the level of "ideological fantasy" at which Excellence "structures social reality", Guest tries to establish a clear and transparent relationship between the socially active signifier and the real relations to which it might refer. Not surprisingly, it proves impossible to break out of the ideological dream by "opening our eyes and trying to see reality as it is", by throwing away the ideological spectacles: as the subjects of such a post-ideological, objective, sober look, free of so-called ideological prejudices, as the subjects of a look which views the facts as they are, we remain throughout "the consciousness of our ideological dream" (Zizek, 1989: 48).

What, then, does it mean to suggest that "ideological fantasy structures reality" itself? Well, firstly, it suggests that a certain "misrecognition" characterizes the human condition. In Lacanian terms, this "misrecognition" occurs because all attempts to capture the "Real" symbolically ultimately fail. There is always a "leftover", a "surplus" separating the "Real" from its symbolization. However, for this very reason "misrecognition" is not synonymous with the traditional concept of "false consciousness". Rather than viewing ideology as a "false" or "illusory" representation of reality, it is reality itself which should already be conceived of as "ideological". As Zizek (1989: 21) argues "'*ideological*' *is a social reality whose very existence implies the non-knowledge of its participants as to its essence*". Ideology is a fantasy-construct that serves as a support for "reality" itself. The function of ideology "is not to offer us a point of escape from our reality but to offer us the social reality itself as an escape from some traumatic real kernel" (Zizek, 1989: 45).

This "traumatic real kernel" is the "surplus", the left-over separating the Real from its symbolization. To attempt to come to terms with this "excess" requires an acknowledgement of a certain fundamental deadlock (what Laclau and Mouffe have termed "antagonism"), "a hard kernel resisting symbolic integration-dissolution" (Laclau and Mouffe, 1985, 1987; Zizek, 1989). In this way it is possible to see what Laclau and Mouffe (1985) are suggesting when they say that "Society doesn't exist". They are certainly not lending support to the Thatcherite dictum that "there is no such thing as Society, just individuals and their families". Rather they are attempting to indicate that "the social" is "always an inconsistent field structured around a constitutive impossibility", a fundamental antagonism. "Society never fully manages to be society because everything in it is penetrated by its limits, which prevents it constituting itself as an objective reality" (Laclau and Mouffe, 1985: 127). However, because society is always traversed by an antagonistic split which cannot be integrated into the symbolic order "the stake of ideological fantasy is to construct a vision of society which does exist, a society which is not split by an antagonistic division, a society in which the relation between its parts is organic, complementary" (Zizek, 1989: 126).

The discourse/ideology of "Excellence" operates with such a "unitary frame of reference" (Fox, 1974). The vision it projects is of a cohesive but inherently "flexible" organization where an "organic" complementarity is established between "the greatest possible realization of the intrinsic abilities of individuals at work" and the "optimum productivity and profitability of the corporation" (Kanter, 1990; Pascale, 1991). In this vision, the "No Win scenario" associated with a "mechanistic", "bureaucratic" lack of Enterprise is transformed into a permanent "Win/ Win situation" through the active development of a "flexible", "creative", and "organic" entrepreneurialism (Pinchot, 1985: 38). For Excellence, as for Thatcherism, economic and moral revival involves the construction of an appropriate culture of Enterprise: Enterprise is their "ideological fantasy". Both of these evangelical projects are engaged in struggle against lack of Enterprise, which they conceptualize as a fundamental cause of social antagonism, a disease spreading through the social body destroying "initiative", "innovation", "creativity" and the like. This debilitating "lack" can only be overcome, and social harmony restored, it is suggested, through the promotion and development of Enterprise in both its distinct senses. In other words, the symbolic enemy – "bureaucracy" and its associated evils – may only be defeated by summoning up and unleashing the forces of Enterprise and, in particular, the remarkable powers of its "everyday hero" – the private, possessive, competitive, enterprising individual (man).

In their respective visions, lack of Enterprise appears to be a foreign body introducing corruption into the pure, sound social fabric. However, in effect, "lack of Enterprise" is akin to a "symptom", the point at which the immanent social antagonism erupts on to the surface of the social, the point at which, to recall Laclau and Mouffe, it becomes apparent that the organization/society "doesn't work". Thus, "lack of Enterprise" is basically the means, for both Excellence, and Thatcherism, of taking into account, of representing their own impossibility. It is the expression of the ultimate impossibility of their respective projects – of their "immanent limits". Rather than being a positive cause of social antagonism, "lack of Enterprise" is just the expression of a "certain blockage" – of the impossibility which prevents the organization/society from achieving its full identity as a closed, homogeneous totality.

4 Some Concluding Remarks

As Wright (1987) has indicated, the rise of both Excellence and Thatcherism has prompted frequent derision and disdain from various figures who view themselves as representatives of a deep and authentic humanism (the "artist", the "scholar", etc.). While there may be a certain (simple) consolation in equating the contemporary discourse of Enterprise with the merely "philistine", Wright suggests, such a response misplaces its critical energies – indicating a powerful cultural elitism, while missing the point completely. The projects of both Excellence and Thatcherism deserve altogether more serious attention. As Gordon (1987: 300) has argued, rather than being a travesty of genuine value, the triumph of the entrepreneur is directly related to "a profound mutation" in governmental rationality: "Here a certain idea of the enterprise of government promotes and capitalizes on a widely disseminated conception of individuality as an enterprise, of the person as an entrepreneur of the self".

The key features of contemporary political rationalities and technologies of government has been the connections they have tried to establish between the self-fulfilling desires of individuals and the achievement of social and economic objectives. As Rose (1989: 24) has indicated, the success of neo-liberalism in Britain (as elsewhere in the West), with its flagship image of an "Enterprise Culture", "operates within a much more general transformation in 'mentalities of government' in which the autonomous, responsible, free, choosing self ... has become central to the moral bases of political arguments from all parts of the political spectrum". It is the vocabulary of Enterprise which establishes an affinity between "Excellence" and the neo-liberal government in the UK. The expertise of Excellence provides the means whereby the politico-ethical objectives of neo-liberalism in the UK, the economic objectives of contemporary business, and the self-actualizing and self-regulating capacities of human subjects are linked together into a "functioning network". By so doing Excellence establishes "connections and symmetries" between "the way we are governed by others and the way we should govern ourselves" (Rose, 1989: 3).

However, as even Miller and Rose (1990: 10) admit, "government is a congenitally failing operation". The "Real" always escapes attempts to govern it because there is always a "surplus" separating the Real from its symbolization. Whether expressed in terms of "ideology" or "cultural technology", therefore, the most that government can hope for is to manage this "lack of fit" without ever resolving it. Nonetheless, at one and the same time, this very "impossibility" of government justifies and reproduces the attempt to govern.

Notes

*   A different version of this article appeared under the title 'Enterprise Culture and the Ideology of Excellence' in *New Formations* 13, Spring 1991: 45-61.
1   Ian Hacking (1983) delineates the triptych Real – Representation – Reality. Reality is "a lower order concept" formed through the practice of representation.
    The "Real" – in the Lacanian sense – is an impossible entity to fully represent, but its effects cannot be avoided. The "Real" is a "hard kernel" (Zizek, 1989) resisting symbolic integration/dissolution and yet only through trying to represent it can its effects be grasped. In other words, the "Real" is an entity which must be constructed retroactively so that the distortions of the symbolic structure can be accounted for. As Lacan (1987:7) puts it, "I always speak the truth, not the whole truth because there's no way to say it all. Saying the whole truth is materially impossible: words miss it. Yet it is only through this impossibility that the truth holds onto the real".
2   There can be little doubt that the Excellence literature has touched a nerve. The acknowledged leader of the field, Peters and Waterman's *In Search of Excellence*, remains the best-selling business book of all time, with worldwide sales of over five million by 1985.
3   According to the cultural critic Judith Williamson (1991: 28), the language of Enterprise has surpassed the boundaries imposed by even this looser definition. "What intrigued me", she writes, "is not only that enterprise now means business, but the fact that ... it can be seen as ... a personal attribute in its own right. The language has colonized our interiors; if you can't speak it, you haven't got it!".
4   As William Connolly (1987: 138) has indicated "equality" and "excellence" tend to be mutually exclusive categories:
    "To honor equality (an admirable thing) is also to demean excellence in certain ways; to institutionalize individualism is to sacrifice the solace and benefits of community; to exercise freedom is to experience the closure which accompanies choice among incompatible and often irreconcilable projects; to secure stable identities through gender demarcation is to exclude the hermaphrodite from such an identity and to suppress that in others which does not fit neatly into its frame; to prize the rule of law is to invite the extension of litigiousness into new corners of social life; to institutionalize respect for the responsible agent is to sow institutional disrespect for those unqualified or unwilling to exercise such responsibility; to give primacy to mathematicization in the social construction of knowledge is to denigrate individuals whose thought escapes that mold and to depreciate ways of knowing which do not fit into its frame. And lest the point be misread, to reverse these priorities would be to install another set of losses and impositions."

5   As Wright (1987: 8-9) has observed, "Excellence works in the everyday world, diversifying consumer lifestyles as it goes". It is a defining feature of members of the new expanding "service"/middle class, to which the "cultural intemediaries of Excellence" belong, to seek their "occupational and personal salvation in the imposition of new doctrines of ethical salvation" (Bourdieu, 1984: 365). In other words, by encouraging as many people as possible to share its "investment orientation to life" at work, as well as in all other spheres of existence, this social grouping is engaged in a symbolic action which not only produces the need for its own goods and services, but also, in the long run, legitimates itself and the lifestyle(s) it puts forward as a model.

6   Silver (1987: 124-125), another commentator on the links between "Excellence" and "neo-conservatism" in the USA, argues that the appeal of Excellence is located in its cry to American employees to "stand tall" again, rather than feeling inferior to their international competitors (particularly the Japanese) , and that this rallying call "fell on the same receptive ground as Reagan's exhortations to the American people to 'feel proud to be American', and one might argue, the same receptive ground as such popular cultural phenomena as Rambo and Rocky, which are also celebrations of extraordinary effort from ordinary people".

References

Baldamus, W. (1961) *Efficiency and Effort*. London: Tavistock.

Beechey, V./Donald, J. (eds.) (1986) *Subjectivity and Social Relations*. Milton Keynes: Open University Press.

Bonner, F./du Gay, P. (1992) 'Representing the Enterprising Self: Thirtysomething and Contemporary Consumer Culture', *Theory, Culture and Society*, 9 (2): 67-92.

Bourdieu, P. (1984) *Distinction* (trans. R. Nice). London: Routledge.

Burchell, G./Gordon, C./Miller, P. (eds.) (1991) *The Foucault Effect: studies in governmentality*. Brighton: Harvester Wheatsheaf.

Confederation of British Industry (1988) *People – The Cutting Edge*. London: Confederation of British Industry.

Connolly, W. (1987) *Politics and Ambiguity*. London: University of Wisconsin Press.

Cousins, M./Hussain, A. (1984) *Michel Foucault*. London: Macmillan.

Davies, L./Cherns, A. (eds.) *The Quality of Working Life* (2 Vols.). New York: The Free Press.

Deleuze, G. (1992) 'Postscript on the Societies of Control', *October* 59: 3-7.

Foucault, M. (1982) 'The Subject and Power', pp. 208-226 in Dreyfus, H. L. /Rabinow, P./Foucault, M. *Beyond Structuralism and Hermeneutics*. Brighton: Harvester Wheatsheaf.

Foucault, M. (1984) 'On the Genealogy of Ethics: An Overview of Work in Progress', pp. 340-372 in Rabinow, P. (ed.), *The Foucault Reader*. Harmondsworth: Penguin.

Foucault, M. (1987) *The Use of Pleasure: the History of Sexuality* volume two. Harmondsworth: Penguin.

Foucault, M. (1988a) 'Technologies of the Self', in Martin, L.H. et al. (eds.) *Technologies of the Self*. London: Tavistock.

Foucault, M. (1988b) *The Care of the Self: the History of Sexuality,* Volume 3. Harmondsworth: Penguin.

Foucault, M. (1991) 'Governmentality', pp. 87-104 in Burchell, G. et al. (eds.) *The Foucault Effect: Studies in Governmentality.* Brighton: Harvester Wheatsheaf.

Fox, A. (1974) *Beyond Contract.* London: Faber and Faber.

Gamble, A. (1988) *The Free Economy and the Strong State.* London: Macmillan.

Gordon, C. (1987) 'The Soul of the Citizen: Max Weber and Michel Foucault on Rationality and Government', pp. 293-316 in Whimster, S./Lash, S. (eds.) *Max Weber: Rationality and Modernity.* London: Allen and Unwin.

Gordon, C. (1991) 'Governmental Rationality: an Introduction', pp. 1-51 in Burchell, G. et al. (eds.) *The Foucault Effect: Studies in Governmentality.* Brighton: Harvester Wheatsheaf.

Gorz, A. (1989) *Critique of Economic Reason.* London: Verso.

Guest, D. (1990) 'Human Resource Management and the American Dream', *Journal of Management Studies* 27, September: 377-397.

Hacking, I. (1983) *Representing and Intervening.* Cambridge: Cambridge University Press.

Hacking, I. (1986) 'Making up People', pp. 222-236 in Heller, T.C. et al. (eds.) *Reconstructing Individualism.* Stanford: Stanford University Press.

Hall, S. (1988) *The Hard Road to Renewal.* London: Verso.

Hall, S. (1991) 'And not a shot fired', *Marxism Today* December: 10-15.

Held, D. (1991) 'Democracy, the Nation-state and the Global System', *Economy and Society* 20 (2): 138-172.

Herzberg, F. (1968) *Work and the Nature of Man.* St. Albans: Staples Press.

Hirst, P./Woolley, P. (1982) *Social Relations and Human Attributes.* London: Tavistock.

Hollway, W. (1991) *Work Psychology and Organizational Behaviour.* London: Sage.

Howard, R. (1985) *Brave New Workplace.* New York: Viking Press.

Hunter, I. (1987) 'Setting Limits to Culture', *New Formations* 4: 103-123.

Hyman, R. (1987) 'Strategy or Structure? Capital, Labour, and Control', *Work, Employment and Society* 1 (1): 25-55.

Jameson, F. (1984) 'Postmodernism, or the Cultural Logic of Late Capitalism', *New Left Review* July/August: 53-92.

Jameson, F. (1990) 'Clinging to the Wreckage – a Conversation with Stuart Hall', *Marxism Today* September: 28-30.

Kanter, R. (1990) *When Giants Learn to Dance.* London: Unwin Hyman.

Keat, R. (1990) 'Introduction', pp. 3-10 in Keat,R./Abercrombie, N. (eds.) *Enterprise Culture.* London: Routledge.

Lacan, J. (1987) 'Television', *October* 40: 1-50.

Laclau, E. (1990) *New Reflections on the Revolution of Our Time.* London: Verso.

Laclau, E./Mouffe, C. (1985) *Hegemony and Socialist Strategy.* London: Verso.

Lash, S. (1988) 'Discourse or Figure ? Postmodernism as a 'Regime of Signification''', *Theory, Culture and Society* 5 (2-3): 311-336.

Lash, S. (1990) *Sociology of Postmodernism.* London: Routledge.

Lefort, C. (1986) *The Political Forms of Modern Society.* Cambridge: Polity Press.

Legge, K. (1989) 'Human Resource Management: a Critical Anaylsis' in Storey, J. (ed.) *New Perspectives in Human Resource Management.* London: Routledge (19-40).

MacIntyre, A. (1985) *After Virtue.* London: Ducksworth.

Mauss, M. (1979) *Sociology and Psychology*. London: Routledge and Kegan Paul.

Mayo, E. (1933) *The Human Problems of an Industrial Civilisation*. New York: Macmillan.

McGregor, D. (1960) *The Human Side Of Enterprise*. New York: McGraw-Hill.

Miller, P./O'Leary, T. (1989) 'The Entrepreneurial Order', Paper presented to the 5th Annual UMIST/Aston Conference on the Organization and Control of the Labour Process.

Miller, P./Rose, N. (1988) 'The Tavistock Programme: the Government of Subjectivity and Social Life', *Sociology* 22 (2): 171-192.

Miller, P./Rose, N. (1990) 'Governing Economic Life', *Economy and Society* 19 (1): 1-31.

Minson, J. (1985) *Genealogies of Morals*. London: Macmillan.

Morris, M. (1988) 'Banality in Cultural Studies', *Discourse* 10: 2-29.

Ouchi, W. (1981) *Theory Z*. Reading, Mass: Addison-Wesley.

Pascale, R. (1990) *Managing on the Edge*. Harmondsworth: Penguin.

Peters, T./Waterman, R.H. (1982) *In Search of Excellence*. New York: Harper and Row.

Peters, T. (1988) *Thriving on Chaos*. Basingstoke: Macmillan.

Pinchot, G. (1985) *Intrapreneuring: why you don't have to leave the corporation to become an entrepreneur*. New York : Harper and Row.

Robins, K. (1991) 'Tradition or Translation: National Culture in its Global Context', pp. 21-44 in Corner, J./Harvey, S. (eds.) *Enterprise and Heritage*. London: Routledge.

Roethlisberger , F.J./Dickson, W.J. (1939) Management and the Worker. Cambridge, Mass: Harvard University Press.

Rose, N. (1989) 'Governing the Enterprising Self', Paper presented to a Conference on the Values of the Enterprise Culture, University of Lancaster, September.

Rose, N. (1990) *Governing the Soul*. London: Routledge.

Sabel, C. (1990) 'Skills Without a Place: The Reorganization of the Corporation and the Experience of Work', Paper presented to the British Sociological Association Annual Conference, University of Surrey, Guildford, April.

Silver, P. (1987) 'The Ideology of Excellence: Management and Neo-conservatism', *Studies in Political Economy* 24: 105-129.

Smith, P. (1988) *Discerning the Subject*. Minneapolis: University of Minnesota Press.

Storey, J. (ed.) (1989) *New Perspectives in Human Resource Management*. London: Routledge.

Storey, J./Sisson, K. (1989) 'Looking to the Future', pp. 167-183 in Storey, J. (ed.) *New Perspectives in Human Resource Management*. London: Routledge.

Townley, B. (1989) 'Selection and Appraisal: Reconstituting Social Relations ?', pp. 92-108 in Storey, J. (ed.) *New Perspectives in Human Resource Management*. London: Routledge.

Turner, B. (1986) 'Sociological Aspects of Organizational Symbolism', *Organization Studies* 7: 101-115.

Williamson, J. (1991) Column in *The Guardian* newspaper (04/07/1991) (p. 28).

Wood, S. (1989) 'New Wave Management ?', *Work, Employment and Society* 3 (3): 379-402.

Wright, P. (1987) 'Excellence', *London Review of Books* May: 8-11.

Zizek, S. (1989) *The Sublime Object of Ideology*. London: Verso.

CHAPTER 5

Understanding the Subcontracting Relationship: The Limitations of Transaction Cost Economics

Hans Berger, Niels Noorderhaven,
Bart Nooteboom and Bartjan Pennink[1]

1   Subcontracting and Transaction Cost Reasoning

Frequently, firms enter into long-term relationships with other – formally-independent – firms to which they contract out certain production-related tasks. This kind of long-term relationship ("the subcontracting relation") fits into a strategy of balancing flexibility with predictability. The firm putting out the job can concentrate on its core business and technology; and because of its more limited commitments in terms of, for instance, specialized assets, it can enjoy an enlarged capability to adapt to changes in market circumstances and technological developments. At the same time, it creates a high level of predictability in its interaction with part of its environment. Thus long-term subcontracting relations can intuitively be understood as a viable answer to the environmental uncertainty and complexity with which many firms have to cope.

At the same time, this kind of long-term relationships between formally independent firms pose some interesting theoretical problems. The perspective assumed in this paper is that of transaction cost economics (TCE), a theory that has repeatedly been invoked in the description and explanation of make-or-buy decisions and the concomitant economic structures, of which the subcontracting relation is an example (Heide and John, 1990; Masten, 1984; Monteverde and Teece, 1982; Walker and Poppo, 1991; Walker and Weber, 1984).

From a TCE point of view, the subcontracting relation is the outcome of a trade-off between different production technologies with differential production costs and different governance structures with differential transaction cost features (Williamson, 1975, 1985). In a nutshell, TCE makes us expect subcontracting relations if non-trivial economies can be realized by applying a special-purpose technology (as opposed to a general-purpose technology) but if this special-purpose technology is not fully specific to one individual trading partner. Thus, an independent firm, aggregating demand from various client firms, can presumably achieve economies of scale or scope inaccessible to an entity integrated into the client firm.[2] However, a pure market relationship would pose unacceptable hazards to the trading partners because of the transaction-specific nature of investments. Consequently a governance structure somewhere between the extremes of market and hierarchy will be implemented, leading to a mutual long-term commitment between otherwise independent parties.

In this paper, we will not take issue with the main contention of TCE, namely that the occurrence of subcontracting relations has to do with transaction-specific investments. However, we find altogether unsatisfactory the way in which the governance structures associated with subcontracting relations are conceptualized in TCE. Williamson (1985: 71-72), with apparent assent, refers to Macneil's concept of "relational contract" to describe the governance structure ruling long-term bilateral trading relations. A relational contract as described by Macneil "grows" over time, rather than being fixed once and forever at the moment of agreement; it forms a "mini-society" in its own, in which norms that foster compliance – partly internalized by the parties, and partly enforced by the community – increasingly come to influence the behaviour of the parties more and more (Macneil, 1978: 901; 1980: 71ff.).

However, after having hailed Macneil's "thoughtful and provocative" contribution, Williamson hardly uses the concept, elaborating instead on examples of "private ordering", i.e. arrangements between parties that are of a self-enforcing nature because of the carefully established balance in dependencies (Williamson, 1985: Chapters 7 and 8). The two characteristics of relational contracts pointed at above, the development of the relationship over time and the arising of norms governing the behaviour of the parties, are pushed into the background in these chapters. In fact, Williamson explicitly dismisses the importance of socially-mediated rules or norms;[3] and his phrasing clearly suggests that the "private orders" discussed, are the result of rational and conscious *ex ante* choices made by the parties rather than of an autonomous process of development.[4]

The tension between the concepts of "relational contract" and "private ordering" is unsatisfactory from a theoretical point of view. In the context of this paper, however, it is more important that the premature dismissal of development over time and social norms seems to be counter-productive in the study of subcontracting relations. For one thing, in some accounts of subcontracting, social norms are pointed at as an explanatory factor of prime importance. Thus, Dore (1983: 470) places a social norm at the centre of his explanation of Japanese subcontracting: "[the Japanese] most commonly say: benevolence is a duty. Full stop. It is that sense of duty – a duty over and above the terms of written contract – which gives assurance of the pay-off which makes relational contracting viable".

As far as the development of exchange relations over time is concerned, there is a strong theoretical basis for the assumption that repetition of patterns of interaction (e.g. in the context of a transaction) can lead to cooperative behaviour (Axelrod, 1984) and to the alignment of expectations, the formation of habits, and the institutionalization of behaviour (Berger and Luckmann, 1966). Moreover, even casual conversations with practitioners make clear that "unwritten laws of the trade" and good personal relationships between buyer and seller are immensely important in industrial markets, a conclusion endorsed by Macaulay's (1963) and Beale and Dugdale's (1975) empirical observations.

Accordingly, we propose that a TCE-based analysis of subcontracting relations is best served by a hark back to the concept of "relational contract" emasculated by Williamson, and by an elaboration of the idea that exchange relations develop gradually over time and are supported by an amalgam of legal and social enforcement mechanisms – as well as by benign intentions of the parties. We will do this by taking much more seriously than Williamson the bounds to the rationality of the parties to a transaction as well as by reasoning out how these boundedly rational parties go about in their dealings with the environment. More specifically, the following sections of this paper will focus on three dimensions of exchange relations: the temporal, the cognitive, and the social dimension. In Section Two, we will first discuss the temporal dimension, because the assumption of a more "dynamic" perspective has important ramifications for the other two dimensions. Next, Section Three will turn to the cognitive dimension of exchange relations and challenge the assumptions with regard to knowledge, preferences and opportunism that are routinely made in received TCE. Building on the ideas pertaining to the cognitive dimension, in Section Four we will subsequently discuss the social dimension. On the basis of these two sections, we will elaborate in Section Five on the concept of "trust" – one alien to TCE in its present form, but in our view indispensable for an understanding of subcontracting relations. In Section Six, we will work out the implications for empirical research into subcontracting relations as well as report on a research project in which we are currently engaged.

2   The Temporal Dimension: Transaction and Relation

Before turning to a discussion of the temporal dimension, we will have to settle a preliminary question, namely the shift from transaction to relation in the analysis.

The transaction purportedly is the basic unit of analysis in TCE. But in this paper, we will focus on the exchange relation rather than on the transactions taking place between the parties. This shift could be justified by pointing out that Williamson himself also tends to slide to a discussion of relations rather than of transactions. More relevant, however, is the fact that strict concentration on a focal transaction would blind us to an important feature of subcontracting relations, namely that an exchange relationship developed in the context of transactions with regard to a specific good can subsequently form a channel for future streams of transactions with regard to other goods. For this reason, we will in the remainder of this paper focus on the relationship between a firm putting out jobs and its subcontractors, rather than on the jobs themselves.

In making a start with the incorporation of the time dimension into a TCE-like theoretical framework, a closer look at Macneil's (1974) landmark study of "relational contract" is apposite.

Macneil juxtaposes two views on exchange and contract: the "discrete" and the "relational" view. According to the discrete view, transactions – even if taking place within established relationships – can usefully be treated as independent events. In this perspective, a focal transaction is seen as isolated from all other relations and obligations between the parties in question and with third parties, i.e. the transaction is assumed to take place within a social vacuum. Furthermore, the temporal dimension is assumed away by the fiction of "presentiation": the future is treated "as if it were already there", and the original exchange agreement is assumed to reflect perfectly all relevant aspects of this future. The corresponding legal standpoint is that of "classical" contract doctrine: the original exchange of promises ("the meeting of the minds") is the sole source of all rights and obligations in the context of the exchange.

On the other hand, according to the "relational" view a focal transaction can never be completely isolated from other interactions between the parties and society at large. As far as the time dimension is concerned, the relational view rejects presentiation, and emphasizes that the uncertainty with regard to the future should be taken seriously. Thus, in the relational view, agreements will pertain to the continuous process of decision-making necessary to adapt to ever-changing circumstances, rather than trying to distribute rights and duties once and for all.

The corresponding view on contract law is that of "relational contract theory". According to this view, the relationship between exchanging parties, far from being fixed at the moment of agreement, in many cases gradually changes and develops over time; and contract law should recognize this rather than cling to the life-buoy of the largely-fictitious "original agreement".

Integrating the concept of "relational contract" in a theory of subcontracting relations, means acknowledgement of the fact that business relations are initiated, developed, and strengthened through interaction. Interaction per se refers to the temporal dimension: it is a series of successive mutually-related individual actions. If the importance of the temporal dimension is conceded, it means that a given transaction relationship can never be explained completely on the basis of cross-sectional analysis or transversal in time alone. The form of a relationship that can be observed at a given moment, has grown through a process of cumulative causation during the time the parties interact. As will be expounded in the following sections of this paper, rules and expectations with regard to transactions may be institu-tionalized to such an extent that they are no longer questioned by the parties. Institutionalization may take place within the dyad, i.e. be idiosyncratic to the relationship, but may also arise outside of the transaction relation, e.g. in the form of the traditions of an industry (Ford, 1978).

In the context of a TCE-like analysis two consequences of a process of interaction should be emphasized. Firstly, interaction tends to entail the investment of resources in the relationship – resources that subsequently cannot be put to use elsewhere. If nothing else, at least attention is "invested" in a relationship. But frequently, other non-redeployable resources will be invested as well (cf. Håkansson 1982, 1989). Secondly, interaction also spontaneously tends to generate safeguards for the risks associated with such transaction-specific (or rather: relation-specific) investments, through the alteration of preferences and the emergence of norms.

Below that, we will first discuss in Section Three the cognitive dimension (pertaining among other things to the preferences of transaction partners) – and subsequently, in Section Four, go into the social dimension (pertaining to the generation of norms influencing transaction behaviour).

3   The Cognitive Dimension: Learning and Bonding

Williamson (1985: 143-144) grants that "the study of economic organization in a regime of rapid innovation poses much more difficult issues than those addressed here" and that "[n]ew hybrid forms of organization may appear in response to such a condition ... [m]uch more study of the relations between organization and inno-vation is needed". Since business is at present striving under such a "regime of rapid innovation", further insight is of some importance. For this focus, we can no longer take knowledge and preferences as givens; they must be made endog-enous. In our study of transactions, we need to both include the role of relations between transaction partners in the formation of knowledge and preferences and deal with the implications for uncertainty and opportunism – as well as the result-ing effects on transaction costs, the choice of governance structures and the design of governance schemes.[5]

In TCE, bounded rationality is taken to arise from the scarcity or cost of infor-mation and limited capacity for information processing. If rationality were un-bounded, all possible contingencies could be foreseen – even those arising from opportunism – and could be incorporated in a contract prior to commitment. But there is more to the boundedness of rationality that is relevant to TCE. As pointed out above, we propose that the temporal dimension of transacting should be incorporated in the analysis. A consistent addition of the time dimension should proceed from the comparative statics of standard TCE to dynamics. True dynamics requires that one breaks through the traditional assumption in mainstream (neoclassical) economics of given preferences, given technology and knowledge that are in principle available to all. In time, the bounds of knowledge, preferences and perceived risk of opportunism may shift. To incorporate this, one needs a theory of knowledge (epistemology), and – in particular – a theory of acquisition and change of knowledge (genetic epistemology).[6]

Implicitly, neoclassical theory and TCE assume that while information may be costly to obtain and capacity to process it may be costly or limited, all information is in principle available to all "from the shelf" in a given form, containing or generating objective truth. The underlying empiricist epistemology, however, is defunct and has been since the philosopher Kant. In terms of Kantian "critical" philosophy, mainstream economics is uncritical of perception and knowledge.[7]

Perception and thought are conditioned by categories of understanding, in the double sense of being made possible *and* being limited by them. Apart from giving form or coherence to otherwise incomprehensible sense impressions, categories perform the heuristic function of shutting out impressions that do not fit the present purpose. To be receptive to and explicitly aware of all available bits of information all the time, regardless of context or purpose, would eliminate all purpose. The problem increasingly is not how we can obtain all available information, but how we can ignore irrelevant information. We set agendas for rational evaluation according to the context, and do not consider what is not on them. As discussed by Simon (1983), it is the role of our emotions to set or shift the agenda, triggered by a shift of context. Emotions have survival value in calling attention to priorities.

To be effective, organizations also have to define the relevant in order to shut out noise, and this requires some coordination of the perceptions and perspectives of individuals within the firm. This function is performed by administrative and social routines, as well as being supported by the use of symbols and rituals. As a result, different organizations not only have different preferences but entertain different perceptions, and interpret the same phenomena differently. What is perceived, known and communicated in a firm depends on its past – embodied in its culture and routines – and on its context. As discussed by Pfeffer and Salancik (1987), there will be some variance of perception and preference within a firm according to the function, i.e. the resource that is represented. Different functions will interpret the interest of the firm from different perspectives but on the basis of a common experience, position and orientation of the firm. To be effective, one needs a focus; but having a focus means not to see everything.

In decision-making, economics focuses on the choice between given alternatives, but the prior issue concerns the identification of alternatives and the objective of choice.[8] The point now is that the value of transaction relations lies not only – and perhaps not primarily – in satisfying wants according to present preferences and knowledge, but also – and perhaps primarily – in developing new perceptions, understanding and preferences. This may be called the "transcendental" role of transactions or transaction relations (in a Kantian sense). This transcendence has two effects relevant to TCE: learning and bonding.

In learning, interaction with the transaction partner creates the awareness of new options or new outcomes of previously recognized options, and creates the capacity to utilize them. In other words: it enhances one's potential. A partner may be chosen for his/her expected capacity for such enhancement, rather than only for the capacity to satisfy demands presently perceived. But the point then is that a commitment to continuity of the relation has to be made, since the enhancement of potential takes time. Categories of knowledge are often acquired and developed in practice (in learning by doing), whereby they may be "tacit" (cf. Michael Polanyi)[9] and cumulative. It is difficult to be critical of one's own knowledge or skill if they are tacit.

As taught by Rogers (1983), the first stage in the adoption of something new is awareness of a need and the availability of the novelty to satisfy it. With tacit knowledge this may be problematic; and in order to achieve awareness, one may need a transaction partner who takes a different perspective and has different but complementary experience. Next, when awareness has been created and one wants to adopt a novel way of doing things, tacit knowledge is hard to adopt from someone else, particularly through more explanation and specification of rules. If at all, tacit knowledge can be transferred only by ostension (showing how one does it), or after it has been made more explicit. When knowledge is cumulative, it is difficult to transfer because it requires underlying capabilities to be effective. When knowledge is tacit or cumulative or both (the two tend to go together), transfer is more easily performed by the transfer of the person (or the firm) in which the knowledge is embodied, or by working together.

The difficulties that arise in the acquisition of knowledge, due to categories of perception and understanding and their variance between firms – as well as the tacit and cumulative nature of much knowledge – have several implications for TCE. Firstly, as discussed, they yield what we called a transcendental value of transaction partners. Secondly, they point out that in order to benefit from this, a relation must be to some extent lasting. Thirdly, they raise obstacles for the make-or-buy decision: due to problems of technology transfer, one may not be able to produce an input, no matter how specific it is to one's own needs; on the other hand, one may not be able to contract production out to an independent producer, no matter how few transaction-specific investments are required. Thus, we may well observe transaction relations in spite of highly transaction-specific investments, either because the relation is chosen for its (unique or indispensable) potential for learning, or because the user would simply not be able to produce the item himself. Conversely, one may see several firms in an industry producing an input that does not require investments specific to the input for any one firm, because there simply is no independent supplier capable of producing and delivering it.

Concerning the third implication (but not the first two), we grant that these situations do not represent equilibria: in due course users may take care to develop the technology to produce inputs requiring highly transaction-specific investments; and where there is demand for some more or less standard input for an industry, some supplier will rise to the occasion. But disequilibria may last for a while, and may show up in observations.

If we allow for learning, which constitutes a shift of knowledge, we should also allow for shifts in preferences, which constitute a change of objectives or values. This brings us to the effect that a transaction relation may have on the commitment to that relation. Commitments may grow stronger, which we call "bonding", or they may grow weaker. A bond is something that constitutes a "glue" or "cement" for relations and which is related to the concept of trust (Section Five). In the process of bonding, the commitment to the relation increases, and the exercise of op-portunism is thereby reduced. This relieves the problem of bounded rationality: with less threat of opportunism, there is less one needs to foresee and take into account. One feels confident to look less at safeguards against opportunism and more at opportunities for further learning or improvement of quality.

There is bonding in a weak and in a strong sense. In "weak bonding", potential opportunism (the scope of it, or the inclination towards it) is unmodified. In that sense, preferences or values have not shifted; but, out of self-interest, opportunism is not exercised. The reason may be that one has already invested so much in the relation that the switching cost or loss of reputation involved in its breaking up due to the exercise of opportunism is too great. Weak bonding corresponds to the "lock-in" of standard TCE. In "strong bonding" preferences have shifted to narrow the boundaries or scope of opportunism: one *wants* to be less opportunistic, apart from direct self-interest. Strong bonding may be individualized, relating only to a specific partner in a specific transaction relation. Or it may be generalized, relating to similar relations in general, because experience has led to the adoption of a new behavioural norm or a new organizational procedure. Of course, experience may also work the other way around: the generation of antipathy or hatred, or the breakdown of some previously held norm. We will return to the question of the emergence of norms in the following section.

The shifting of preference or values also has possible empirical implications for TCE. If relations "go well", in the sense that bonding takes place, attention to safeguards against opportunism may rapidly subside. Firms which have experienced no failed relations may become naive: few safeguards may be made in spite of highly transaction-specific investments. While this may be warranted within a given market and region where the experience was obtained, a step outside may be punishing. Conversely, one may observe sudden breakdowns of relations with inducements that seem only slight: betrayal of confidence on some minor point may cause a shift in perception, preference or behavioural norm. Cultural differences that may be determined by region, industry or membership of associations, may play an important role in this. Thus, safeguards may differ according to region, club membership, industry or other cultural traits of the transaction partner. This brings us to the subject of the next section.

4   The Social Dimension: Norms and Solidarity

A peculiar ambivalence with respect to the social dimension of transaction relations can be noticed in TCE. Williamson (1985) rejects the "legal centralism" that lies at the basis of classical legal doctrines of contract and of mainstream economic theory; and insists that "the limits of contract and of the courts (should be) recognized from the outset" (p. 166) and that attention should be focused on the mechanisms of private ordering. At first glance, this stance seems to coincide with that of legal scholars devoted to the development of an "empirical view of contract" and the study of the working of legal contract rules in their interaction with other-than-legal social mechanisms.[10]

However, at the end of the day Williamson does not fill up the "social vacuum" of classical legal contract doctrine. Rather, in the two chapters on private ordering of his (1985) study, he ventures into an explanation of exchange relations in the absence of *any* kind of external enforcement mechanism, relying on the binding force of mutual dependency only. Compared with the meticulous basically asocial reasoning in these two chapters on private ordering, the various allusions to social factors[11] acquire a merely ornamental aspect. Thus, in its 1985 codification, TCE displays the same insensitivity to the social embeddedness of exchange observed by Granovetter (1985) in Williamson (1975).

The escape from legal centralism into self-enforcement leads to serious analytical problems. In Noorderhaven (1992), these problems are demonstrated for an extreme case – namely Telser's (1980) analysis of self-enforcing agreements between opportunistic parties with, as its only safeguard, the threat of discontinuing the series of exchanges. However, as reliability is explicitly assumed *not* to be a personality trait in Telser's analysis, such a threat is incredible. Exploitation in a previous transaction is a sunk cost to a rational party; in Telser's analysis, it should not influence expectations with regard to the probability of future exploitation.

More in general, an extreme methodological/individualist approach cannot explain the social institutions that are a *conditio sine qua non* for any kind of exchange to take place (Lowry, 1976; Macneil, 1974). In fact, complete methodological individualism becomes impossible if knowledge, as in the present paper, is assumed to be imperfect (Levy, 1985). Let us therefore venture to look beyond the exchanging dyad and consider possible influences of the social environment.

Analogously to the distinction between "weak" and "strong" bonding in Section Three, a distinction between social influences mediated by considerations of self-interest and by considerations of solidarity can be made. With regard to the first category, reputation effects are of central importance. If the probability of exploitation depends not only on the objective characteristics of the exchange situation but also on the individual propensity to act opportunistically, a bad reputation will lead to high transaction costs. In this situation, it will frequently pay to forego opportunities for immediate gains in order not to risk future transactions (Klein, 1985).

But reputation effects by no means form a panacea for all transaction problems caused by opportunism (Williamson, 1985: 396). The efficacy of reputation effects depends among other things on the speed and reliability of information dissemination. In view of the assumptions with regard to human cognition formulated in Section Three serious impediments to the working of reputation effects should be expected. This forecloses the adoption of reputation as *the* safeguard in exchange entailing transaction-specific investments. But reputation effects positively need to be taken into account in the analysis of subcontracting relations.

"Solidarity" has to be differentiated from self-interest as a motive for human action. If one acts on the basis of solidarity, the interests of others are given more weight than narrow self-interest. As the "others" will most of the time belong to a group of which the focal individual is also a member, solidarity does not necessarily conflict with self-interest, although this will most of the time be the case if only short-term effects are considered. In the long run, preservation of the group may very well be the best way to promote self-interest.

However, action on the basis of solidarity is presumed not to be guided by such "enlightened" considerations of self-interest, but rather by social norms. Social norms are motives for human actions that cannot be reduced to rational calculation of self-interest and that form imperatives of the type of "Do X" or "If others do Y then do X", or "Do X if it would be good if everyone did X" (Elster, 1989). To be rightly called "social", norms should be shared by a group of people, and at least partly sustained by their approval and disapproval. "A norm, in this perspective, is *the propensity to feel shame and to anticipate sanctions by others at the thought of behaving in a certain way*" (Elster, 1989: 105; emphasis in the original).

Here again, self-interest tends to get back in by the back door: social norms may be obeyed not only because they are internalized and form part of decision-makers' preferences, but also because of fear of sanctions. The operation of this second category of norm-following behaviour is analogous to the reputation effects discussed above. Although the two motivational bases can never be completely separated, we are primarily interested in the first category of norm-following behaviour here, the case in which one obeys a social norm "just" because one thinks it is the right thing to do. Doubtlessly, social norms play an important role in business behaviour as well; the findings of Macaulay (1963) and Beale and Dugdale (1975) are positive in this respect. After all, a business firm deals with its environment through individual employees who are members of various partly-overlapping communities: branch organizations, professional societies, regional networks and so on. The individual and the organizational levels interact through "mechanisms (that) are easy to intuit, if ponderous to spell out" (Dore, 1983: 466). We will not pursue this question here but merely state that norms governing individual behaviour have an indirect bearing on interorganizational dealings.

The question of self-interest or solidarity is a matter of degree. As pointed out above, exchange is possible only within a social matrix, and even hard bargaining between strangers is restricted by rules (otherwise bargaining would quickly degenerate into physical violence). Thus, transactions in which a relatively unfettered pursuit of self-interest is accepted, can be said to be reigned by "weak solidarity"; and transactions in which self-interest is relegated to the background, by "strong solidarity" (Lindenberg, 1988). The question of whether a transaction is governed by a regime of "weak", "strong" or "moderate" solidarity, is closely related to the cognitive dimension discussed in Section Three. The attenuation of the propensity to opportunism as a result of the interaction within an exchanging dyad, amounts to a shift from the "weak solidarity" pole to the "strong solidarity" pole. But, as will be put forth below, interaction within the dyad is not the only source of solidarity. The wider context of the relationship may also generate norms that lead to solidarity in exchange relations.

Two questions pertaining to social norms arise: the content of the norms that may be expected to lead to stronger solidarity in exchange relations, and the mechanisms producing these norms. As far as the former is concerned, we will not go into any detail: as will be explained in Section Six, we do not intend to measure specific norms directly in our empirical analysis of subcontracting relations. Suffice it to refer to Macneil's (1980: 64ff.) distinction between four categories of "relational norms": role integrity, preservation of the relation, harmonization of relational conflict and supra-contractual norms. All these norms have the effect of making behaviour in the context of exchange relations more predictable.

With regard to the emergence of norms, however, we will be somewhat more specific. This is necessary because the relational contract theory that provided the impetus for our incorporation of temporal and social aspects in a TCE-like analysis, is not very clear on this point.

According to Macneil (1987: 274) patterns of behaviour in exchange relations give rise to norms, "a case of an 'is' creating an 'ought'". Macneil refers to Lewis

(1969) and Ullmann-Margalit (1977) for a description of the process of the generation of norms; but with this, he seems to be begging the question, for the game-theoretical analyses in these two studies fall short of describing the process of norm generation. A rational reconstruction in terms of game theory can identify social contexts "which are prone to generate norms" (Ullmann-Margalit, 1977: 197), but this does not amount to an account of the actual generation of norms. Ullmann-Margalit admits that "the non-formal, contextual features of the situations represented by the game matrices, play a decisive role in explaining the generation of social norms. These connotations, however, remain outside the game-theoretical treatment" (p. 14-15).[12]

In our view, Ullmann-Margalit's ultimate failure to account for the emergence of norms is due to the fact that the time dimension tends to evaporate with her use of game theory and pay-off tables. And the temporal dimension is crucial in an explanation of norms or – more in general – cooperative behaviour (Axelrod, 1984: 182). Berger and Luckmann's (1966: 50ff.) reconstruction of the process of institutionalization provides an example of the kind of "dynamic" reasoning that could lead to an explanation of the emergence of norms. According to Berger and Luckmann, any human activity that is repeated frequently is subject to habitualization. Habitualization frees the individual from a plethora of decisions, and thus provides "a psychological relief". Habitualization subsequently forms the basis of institutionalization, when habitualized actions are reciprocally typified by interacting parties (Berger and Luckmann, 1966: 53-54):

> A watches B perform. He attributes motives to B's actions and, seeing the actions recur, typifies the motives as recurrent. As B goes on performing, A is soon able to say to himself, "Aha, there he goes again". At the same time, A may assume that B is doing the same thing with regard to him. From the beginning, both A and B assume this reciprocity of typification. ... The most important gain is that each will be able to predict the other's actions. Concomitantly, the interaction of both becomes predictable.

Much in the same way, the interaction within the dyad of two exchanging parties – say, a firm putting out a job and its subcontractor – could be reasoned to lead to regularities in behaviour that give rise to norms. The established way of doing things becomes the prescribed way of doing things, because unwarranted disruptions endanger a valued relationship.

The account of the origin of institutionalization can also be used to suggest how norms from the social environment can come to have a bearing on a transaction relationship. Berger and Luckmann continue their analysis by assuming that other parties join A and B's social universe (Berger and Luckmann, 1966: 55):

The institutional world, which existed *in statu nascendi* in the original situation of A and B, is now passed on to others. This means that the institutions that have now been crystallized (for instance, the institution of paternity as it is encountered by the children), are experienced as existing over and beyond the individuals who "happen to" embody them at the moment. In other words, the institutions are now experienced as possessing a reality of their own, a reality that confronts the individuals as an external and coercive fact.

Likewise, norms that have been validated in other social settings – e.g. the business community at large – may influence behaviour in exchange relations.

To be sure, with the above we have not by a long shot provided a dynamic account of the emergence of social norms. According to Elster (1988: 365), many stories can be told about how norms may emerge, "[b]ut to tell a story is not to provide an explanation". Norms, in Elster's view, "result from psychological propensities about which we know little" (ibidem). Let us then refrain from telling one more story about the genesis of norms but conclude that the assumption that norms – as arising in the context of the focal relationship itself as well as carried over from other social settings – influence transaction behaviour and may lead to an attenuation of self-interest and opportunism consistent with intuition and with the limited empirical evidence available (Macaulay, 1963; Beale and Dugdale, 1975). On top of that, it is in line with the view on human cognition expounded in Section Three.

5   Under the Blanket of Trust

The line of thought followed in this paper up to this point can be summarized as follows:
1) The characterization of the subcontracting relationship in received TCE as one of "private ordering" is unconvincing because it puts too high a strain on the purportedly bounded rationality of economic agents, assuming a social vacuum and neglecting the temporal dimension by proposing that the "private order" is designed *ex ante*.
2) A hark back to the concept of "relational contract" leads to the acknowledgement of the need of integrating the temporal dimension into the analysis. In time, processes of interaction may be expected to induce relation-specific investments, but safeguards for these investments are also generated spontaneously.
3) These expectations correspond with the conclusions from an exploration of the cognitive dimension of exchange. Transaction relations play an important role in the production of knowledge and the constitution of preferences. Thus interaction in the context of a valued exchange relation may lead to "strong bonding": the emergence of shared norms inducing an alignment of preferences, thus endorsing the preservation of the relationship.

4) Apart from the changes in preferences caused by the interaction within the exchanging dyad, a transaction relation may also be protected against opportunism by social norms generated outside the dyad, e.g. within regional or professional business communities. This is the case if the relation is governed by a "strong solidarity" regime. "Strong solidarity" is very much like "strong bonding", but basically exogenous to the relation.

The view on exchange relations expounded here is represented schematically in Diagram 5.1.

In this section, we will follow up on these ideas and make a first step in the direction of their operationalization. In doing that, we will use the blanket concept of "trust". "Trust", in our analysis, refers to preferences benign to the preservation of the relationship, as well as to the social norms that enable parties in an exchange relationship to renounce enforcement mechanisms such as "private ordering", legal contracts, etc. It corresponds to the area enclosed by a dotted line in Diagram 5.1, where it is purposely used as a "blanket" concept covering the benign preferences and relational norms that we do not intend to measure directly.

Diagram 5.1: Strong and Weak Bonding and Solidarity

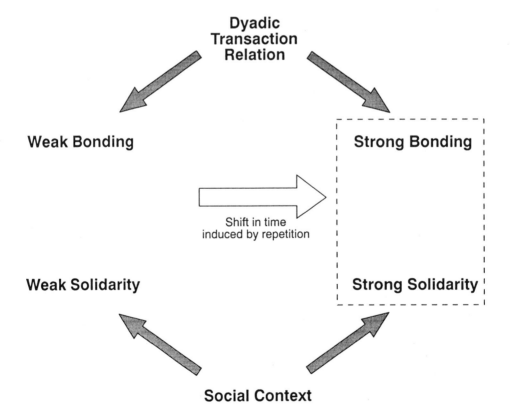

But before we can make use of the term, we should determine what properly goes under the name of trust. At first glance, trust seems to be fundamentally arational if looked upon from an economic perspective. Consider, for instance, the definition used by Baier (1986: 49):

> "Trust ... is letting other persons (natural or artificial, such as firms, nations, etc.) take care of something the truster cares about, where such 'caring for' involves some exercise of discretionary powers."

This is an accurate description of what in the economic literature is called a principal-agent relationship.[13] But, whereas in the principal-agent literature all attention is geared to the specification of (presumably externally enforceable) contracts in order to mitigate the risks associated with this class of relations, the point of trust is precisely the *absence* of such safeguards. It seems as if economic theory and the concept of trust are completely incompatible.

Yet trust is by no means necessarily a-rational. That this may seem to be the fact from the perspective of economics is caused by the extremely stylized version of the concept of "uncertainty" employed by mainstream economics and, to a lesser degree, by branches like agency theory and TCE. If, on the other hand, uncertainty is taken seriously, trust can very well be seen as a rational strategy. Luhmann (1979: 15) sees trust as a necessary mechanism "for the reduction of a future characterized by more or less indeterminate complexity". But trust is not only a general condition without which the complexity and uncertainty of the world would be "beyond human endurance", it is also an expedient that can be available to a greater or a lesser degree in a specific exchange relationship.

Trust, according to Luhmann's account, can be of two kinds: personal trust and institutional trust.[14] We will use Luhmann's concepts somewhat liberally here, and regard as "personal" the trust between specific individuals (natural persons) as well as between specific organizations. This kind of trust is generated in the interaction between the parties concerned (cf. Luhmann, 1979: 42ff.). Institutional trust, on the other hand, is trust in the functioning of a system. This kind of trust tends to be independent of the identity of the agents that happen to assume specific positions at a certain point in time (Luhmann, 1979: 57). Trust in the way business deals are performed in a particular industry or region, would be examples of the kind of institutional trust to which we allude. Institutional trust does not emerge within a specific dyad but is generated more diffusely in a wider social setting, carrying over into many individual relationships.

To the distinction between personal and institutional trust a second distinction can be added: trust as the expectation of technical competence, and trust as the expectation that the other party will demonstrate a special concern for one's interests (Barber, 1983: 14). In some cases, the goodwill of the other party is the only thing that counts; but in other cases, the good intentions of the other are not sufficient. One also has to be assured that the other person has the technical capability to look after one's interest in a competent way. This second differentiation is pertinent because both kinds of trust, "competence" trust and "goodwill" trust, are important in the context of subcontracting. Distinguishing several possible manifestations of trust adds to the measurability of the concept in empirical research.

In other words, this is the ratio for introducing the concept of "trust": we intend to use it as a blanket covering the changes in preferences endogenous to the transaction relation and the exogenous social norms that lead to an inextricable amalgam of strong bonding and strong solidarity. We assume that strong bonding and strong solidarity will tend to go together anyway, so that putting them under one blanket implies no indecency. However, strong bonding in a generally weak solidarity regime is also imaginable, as well as the reverse. Arguably, interaction within transaction relations will be more protracted under a regime of strong solidarity and thus more likely to lead to strong bonding than under a regime of weak solidarity. But exceptions may occur.

In the next section, we will explain how we intend to use, in an TCE-like analysis of subcontracting relations, a concept of trust acknowledging the importance of the temporal, cognitive, and social dimension of transactions.

6   Implications for Empirical Research

The theoretical considerations expounded in the foregoing sections form the basis of an empirical research project carried out by the authors of this paper. This project comprises a small number of case-studies of subcontracting relations between a firm putting out jobs (the "focal firm") and a number of its subcontractors.

The design of these case-studies is two-tiered. First, in-depth interviews with key functionaries from the focal firm and from 10-15 of its subcontractors are conducted. At this stage, information is gathered with respect to specific characteristics of the firms concerned, market conditions, technologies used, etc. These interviews are also used to draw up a written questionnaire to be used in the second tier. Subsequently, in the second tier, these questionnaires are sent to representatives of a large number of subcontractors and to all relevant functionaries at the focal firm.

This type of case-study will be repeated several times with different focal firms. Inter-case comparison is important because idiosyncratic, firm-specific effects can have an important bearing on make-or-buy decisions – and consequently, on the subcontracting relations of a focal firm (cf. Monteverde and Teece, 1982). Furthermore, as will be argued below, inter-case comparison can be useful to investigate the influence of the particular social setting of the subcontracting relations of a focal firm. The results of the case-studies will be used to test two sets of hypotheses: one set based on received TCE, and one set based on our restatement of the theory.

Diagram 5.2: Hypotheses Based on Received TCE

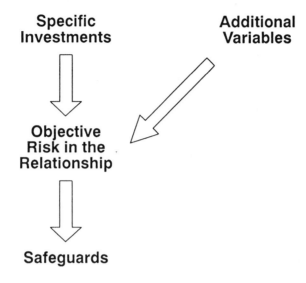

According to received TCE, the specificity of investments in durable physical assets, human capital, location, and dedicated assets (together with some additional variables like market risk and dependency of the other party) determine the risk in the transaction relation. This risk in turn determines the degree in which legal and other-than-legal safeguards are employed. Specificity of investment is measured directly in the research, as are the additional variables. "Risk" is a construct based on these various variables. The safeguards are measured directly and have to do with such elements of legal contracts as duration and termination clauses – as well as with elements of private ordering such as participation in the ownership of transaction-specific tools and machinery, risk-sharing devices, etc. Schematically, the system of hypotheses based on received TCE looks like Diagram 5.2.

According to TCE (as restated by us), specificity of investments etc. influences the *perceived risk* in the transaction relationship; and it is this perceived risk rather than some objectively measurable risk that is the determinant of the degree in which safeguards are used. The concept of perceived risk does better justice to the cognitive dimension discussed in Section Three of this paper. Moreover, in this view, there is a second important source of influence on perceived risk: trust. Trust in turn is assumed to be determined by the history of the relation.

Perceived risk will be measured directly, using Likert-type scales. Trust is a construct on the basis of measurements of the history of the relation. Trust will also be measured directly, but the function of these measurements is to distinguish between different types of trust (personal/institutional; competence/goodwill) rather than to establish the degree of trust available. Interpersonal comparison of trust is

likely to be just as problematic as interpersonal comparison of utility. The history
of the relation will finally be measured by looking at the number of years that the
relationship has already existed, as well as at the development in the relationship
in terms of volume of trade and involvement of the subcontractor in product design.
The system of hypotheses based on our restatement of TCE is pictured schematically
in Diagram 5.3.

In the research design described above, the social dimension is largely omitted
within case studies. However, questions with regard to the influence of branch-
specific or regional norms are included in the questionnaire. These can be used for
comparison between cases if the focal firms are from different branches and/or
regions. Differences between the relative importance of different sorts of trust may
be expected to correspond with branch-specific and regional differences. Thus, we
would expect that relatively more importance is attached to personal trust in a social
setting characterized by "weak solidarity" than in a setting with "strong solidarity".
In the latter case, a strong influence of branch-specific or regional norms attenuating
the need for personal trust will be reported. Although measurement problems
abound, exploration of inter-branch, interregional and even international cultural
differences in principle also seem to be possible in this way.

Diagram 5.3: Hypotheses Based on Restated TCE

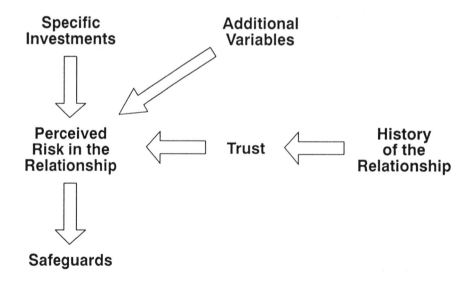

Notes

1   Berger, Nooteboom and Pennink work at the University of Groningen; Noorderhaven
    works at Tilburg University. This paper is a first product of a joint research project,
    sponsored by the Economics Research Foundation which is part of the Netherlands'
    Organization for Scientific Research (NWO).

2   Cf. Williamson (1975: 16-19; 1985: 92n; id.: 116). The main argument is that an
    integrated firm, in order to produce the component in question at an optimal level, would
    have to sell part of its output to its competitors reluctant to deal with it because of
    strategic hazards. The argument appears to be somewhat of an ad hoc nature.

3   In response to a suggestion that private ordering is feasible only if supported by
    communitarian values, Williamson states rather categorically that "such baggage is
    both unneeded and unhelpful. The study of economic organization is better served, I
    submit, by focusing on the purposes served" (1985: 166). Some 40 pages further,
    Williamson states that "the feasibility of crafting superior *ex ante* incentive structures
    warrants more attention (than exogenous norms of cooperative behaviour)" (1985: 204-
    205).

4   Vide phrases like "bilateral (private ordering) safeguards are carefully crafted" (1985:
    106), and "suppliers are assumed to be farsighted" (id.: 164). There is a notable tension
    between this creeping presumption of all but perfect rationality and Williamson's general
    assumption of bounded rationality; see also Noorderhaven and Stassen (1992).

5   As in the work of Williamson, "governance structure" refers to market governance,
    hierarchy or some mixed form such as bilateral or trilateral governance. The term
    "governance scheme" refers to a specific scheme worked out in a mixed structure to
    contain risks.

6   For a more detailed discussion, see Nooteboom (1991), which draws from the work
    of Michael Polanyi and Jean Piaget.

7   Similar criticism of the epistemological foundations of neoclassical economics and
    TCE was given earlier by Etzioni (1988) and Hodgson (1988), among others.

8   The difference between choice and the prior identification of alternatives is related to
    the well-known difference between risk and more radical uncertainty (as discussed by
    Frank Knight and Keynes). Under risk, the class of alternatives and their outcomes is
    known, and uncertainty is limited to the question of which outcome will be realized
    with what probability. Under uncertainty, one does not know all alternatives or
    outcomes.

9   Williamson is one of the rare economists to have recognized the relevance of Michael
    Polanyi's work for economics, but has not fully carried through the implications of
    tacit knowledge for TCE.

10 E.g. Blegvad (1990), Galanter (1981), Macaulay (1963, 1966, 1984, 1985), Macneil
    (1974, 1978, 1980), and Vincent-Jones (1989).

11 E.g. (1985: 22): "customs, mores, habits, and so on ... have a bearing"; (id.: 122):
    "cultural and institutional checks on opportunism"; (id.: 406n): "(a)ttention to behavioral
    and governance features that transcend bargaining frameworks ... may be needed".

12 As Lewis (1969) addresses coordination problems, characterized by the absence of
    divergence of interests, the omission (at least in the more formal analysis: in the
    accompanying text Lewis does occasionally address process aspects) of the temporal

dimension is less serious in his study than in Ullmann-Margalit's. It is not very difficult to imagine how a convention solving a coordination problem arises and becomes established. In the case of the Prisoner's Dilemma dealt with by Ullmann-Margalit, however, incentives for breaching established or nascent norms may exist at any point in time, making the genesis much more problematic.

13 In her discussion of trust, Shapiro (1987) explicitly uses principal-agent terminology.

14 Luhmann (1979) uses the term "system trust" for what is here called institutional trust. We prefer the term "institutional trust" because it fits in with Berger and Luckmann's (1966) terminology.

References

Axelrod, R. (1984) *The Evolution of Co-operation.* New York NY: Basic Books.

Baier, A. (1986) 'Trust and Anti-trust', *Ethics* 96: 231-260.

Barber, B. (1983) *The Logic and Limits of Trust.* New Brunswick NJ: Rutgers University Press.

Beale, H./Dugdale, T. (1975) 'Contracts Between Businessmen: Planning and the Use of Contractual Remedies', *British Journal of Law and Society* 2: 45-60.

Berger, P.L./Luckmann, T. (1966) *The Social Construction of Reality.* Garden City NY: Doubleday.

Blegvad, B.M. (1990) 'Commercial Relations, Contract, and Litigation in Denmark: A Discussion of Macaulay's Theories', *Law & Society Review* 24: 397-411.

Dore, R. (1983) 'Goodwill and the Spirit of Market Capitalism', *The British Journal of Sociology* 34: 459-482.

Elster, J. (1988) 'Economic Order and Social Norms', *Journal of Institutional and Theoretical Economics* 144: 357-366.

Elster, J. (1989) *The Cement of Society; A Study of Social Order.* Cambridge etc: Cambridge University Press.

Etzioni, A. (1988) *The Moral Dimension; Towards a New Economics.* New York NY: Free Press.

Ford, I.D. (1978) 'Stability Factors in Industrial Marketing Channels', *Industrial Marketing Management* 7: 410-422.

Galanter, M. (1981) 'Justice in Many Rooms: Courts, Private Ordering, and Indigenous Law', *Journal of Legal Pluralism and Unofficial Law* 19: 1-47.

Granovetter, M. (1985) 'Economic Action and Social Structure: A Theory of Embeddedness', *American Journal of Sociology* 91: 481-510.

Håkansson, H. (ed.) (1982) *International Marketing and Purchasing of Industrial Goods – An Interaction Approach.* Chichester: Wiley.

Håkansson, H. (1989) *Corporate Technological Behaviour: Co-operation and Networks.* London: Routledge.

Heide, J.B./John, G. (1990) 'Alliances in Industrial Purchasing: The Determinants of Joint Venture Action in Buyer-supplier Relationships', *Journal of Marketing Research* 27: 24-36.

Hodgson, G.M. (1988) *Economics and Institutions.* Oxford: Polity Press.

Klein, B. (1985) 'Self-enforcing Contracts', *Journal of Institutional and Theoretical Economics* 141: 594-600.

Levy, D.M. (1985) 'The Impossibility of a Complete Methodological Individualist', *Economics and Philosophy* 1: 101-108.

Lewis, D.K. (1969) *Convention; A Philosophical Study.* Cambridge MA: Harvard University Press.

Lindenberg, S. (1988) 'Contractual Relations and Weak Solidarity: The Behavioral Basis of Restraints on Gain-maximization', *Journal of Institutional and Theoretical Economics* 144: 39-58.

Lowry, S.T. (1976) 'Bargain and Contract Theory in Law and Economics', *Journal of Economic Issues* 10: 1-22.

Luhmann, N. (1979) *Trust and Power* (H. Davis, J. Raffan and K. Rooney, trans.). Chichester etc.: John Wiley (Original work published in 1973/1975).

Macaulay, S. (1963) 'Non-contractual Relations in Business; A Preliminary Study', *American Sociological Review* 28: 55-70.

Macaulay, S. (1966) *Law and the Balance of Power.* New York NY: Russell Sage Foundation.

Macaulay, S. (1984) 'Law and the Behavioral Sciences; Is There Any There There?', *Law & Policy* 6: 149-187.

Macaulay, S. (1985) 'An Empirical View of Contract', *Wisconsin Law Review* 1985: 465-482.

Macneil, I.R. (1974) 'The Many Futures of Contracts', *Southern California Law Review* 47: 691-816.

Macneil, I.R. (1978) 'Contracts; Adjustment of Long-term Economic Relations Under Classical, Neoclassical, and Relational Contract Law', *Northwestern University Law Review* 72: 854-906.

Macneil, I.R. (1980) *The New Social Contract.* New Haven CT: Yale University Press.

Macneil, I.R. (1987) 'Relational Contract Theory as Sociology: A Reply to Professors Lindenberg and de Vos', *Journal of Institutional and Theoretical Economics* 143: 272-290.

Masten, S.E. (1984) 'The Organization of Production: Evidence from the Aerospace Industry', *Journal of Law and Economics* 27: 403-417.

Monteverde, K./Teece, D.J. (1982) 'Supplier Switching Costs and Vertical Integration in the Automobile Industry', *Bell Journal of Economics* 13: 206-213.

Noorderhaven, N.G. (1992) 'The Problem of Contract Enforcement in Economic Organization Theory', *Organization Studies* 13: 229-243.

Noorderhaven, N.G./Stassen, Y.E.D.M. (1992) 'Hybride verticale relaties en de transactiekosteneconomie: Overzicht en kritiek', forthcoming in *Tijdschrift voor Economie en Management.*

Nooteboom, B. (1991) *Cognition, Evolution and Dynamics in Transaction Cost Theory.* Research Report School of Management and Organization, University of Groningen.

Pfeffer, J., and G.R. Salancik (1978) *The External Control of Organizations: A Resource Dependence Perspective.* New York NY: Harper & Row.

Rogers, E.M. (1983) *Diffusion of Innovations.* New York NY: MacMillan.

Shapiro, S.P. (1987) 'The Social Control of Impersonal Trust', *American Journal of Sociology* 93: 623-658.

Simon, H.A. (1983) *Reason in Human Affairs.* Oxford: Basil Blackwell.

Telser, L.G. (1980) 'A Theory of Self-enforcing Agreements', *Journal of Business* 53: 27-44.

Ullmann-Margalit, E. (1977) *The Emergence of Norms*. Oxford: Clarendon.

Vincent-Jones, P. (1989) 'Contract and Business Transactions: A Socio-legal Analysis', *Journal of Law and Society* 16: 166-186.

Walker, G./Poppo, L. (1991) 'Profit Centers, Single-source Suppliers, and Transaction Costs', *Administrative Science Quarterly* 36: 66-87.

Walker, G./Weber, D. (1984) 'A Transaction Cost Approach to Make-or-buy Decisions', *Administrative Science Quarterly* 29: 373-391.

Williamson, O.E. (1975) *Markets and Hierarchies: Analysis and Antitrust Implications.* New York NY: Free Press.

Williamson, O.E. (1985) *The Economic Institutions of Capitalism; Firms Markets, Relational Contracting.* New York NY: Free Press.

PART III

NON-PROFIT ORGANIZATIONS AND VOLUNTARY ASSOCIATIONS

CHAPTER 6

The Challenges to Creating and Maintaining Non-profits in Newly Emerging Market Economies

Howard P. Tuckman
Cyril F. Chang

1   Introduction

A major challenge facing newly emerging market economies (hereafter called NEMEs) in Eastern Europe is how to provide social services such as health care, education, and the arts. The enchantment with free markets in these countries is likely to be tempered as citizens realize that market economies will not provide some of the key social services previously delivered by their governments. In viewing how countries in the West provide such services, it is important to understand that non-profit organizations in Western Europe and North America have played a major role in filling the gaps left by market economies.[1] Non-profits offer benevolent and fraternal services, provide charity and education, and offer training and other manpower services that help market economies to function efficiently and equitably.[2]

Those overseeing the transition to market-based economies in Eastern Europe must determine the role that non-profits play in their countries. This paper is designed to explain the reasons why non-profits are valuable in a market economy and to explore the challenges involved in creating an environment favourable to their existence. It begins with a discussion of why market economies fail to provide certain public services at the levels desired by society. It then considers the reasons for favouring non-profits over for-profits as providers of social services. The problems associated with establishing a fertile setting for non-profits are introduced and five environments within which non-profits operate are discussed; legal, financial, market, internal, and regulatory. The paper ends with a summary of the advantages of the non-profit form in social service delivery.

2   The Market Economy and The Role of Non-profit Organizations

2.1 Economic Rationale

Economists have examined the question of why a market economy is unable to provide certain types of services (Bator, 1958; Buchanan, 1968). Their analysis indicates that when producers cannot receive sufficient revenues to cover production costs and allow an adequate return to investment, these services will not be produced. One situation in which this occurs is where the characteristics of a service are such that non-paying individuals cannot be excluded from its use. The problem is compounded when one person's consumption of the service does not prevent another from using it, as in the case of defence or police protection. Economists refer to goods and services exhibiting the above two characteristics as "public goods" (Musgrave and Musgrave, 1984, Ch. 3). It is recognized in the economics literature that insufficient amounts of public goods will be produced by free markets because producers cannot earn sufficient revenues to finance production.

A second case of market failure arises when the market is dominated by a few large producers. In such a market, the quantity of output is lower and the price paid by consumers is higher than they would be if the market were competitive with a large number of producers. This makes it desirable for the government to regulate the industry or to subsidize production to the desired level (Scitovosky, 1971). Subsidies may also be warranted if the production cost of a particular service is sufficiently high that the price charged by its producers excludes persons deemed by society to be in need of the service, or if additional consumption of a service yields to society benefits not captured in the transaction between producer and consumer. This "merit goods" case arises when society believes that subsidy of a particular good is warranted by the externalities it generates (Musgrave and Musgrave, 1984, Ch. 4).[3]

Social service delivery is subject to one or more of sources of market failure. For example, public health programmes are a type of public good. These programmes fit the first characteristic for a public good because they yield an indivisible gain to the members of society. They also fit the second because non-contributors cannot be excluded from the benefits that these programmes create. A similar situation applies to research to cure AIDS, research organizations that study socio-economic issues, and/or activities that foster peace or the preservation of the environment. Societies subsidize education in part to insure that it is produced in greater amounts than would prevail in free markets, usually on the premise that it provides benefits beyond those who receive it. Education subsidies may also be motivated by a desire to insure higher quality than prevails in the market-place.

Subsidies may also be justified when a service is considered to be so important that society chooses not to exclude individuals from its use. In the area of medical services, for example, debate rages as to whether it is moral and ethical to deny life-saving technologies to patients simply because they cannot pay for them (Tuckman and Chang, 1991: 115).[4]

2.2 Political Rationale

A political explanation has also been advanced for why market economies produce less than ideal levels of social services based on the assumption that, in a democratic political system governed by majority vote, government offers sufficient social services to satisfy its median voter (Weisbrod, 1988). This political system can leave an unsatisfied minority, especially if voters differ in the amount of social services they desire. Dissatisfaction arises because voters are not asked to pay a price equal to what they believe a service is worth. Those who pay more for a service than they think it is worth want less produced; those paying less want more of it. Only in the rare case where the tax levied on voters is equal to the value they place on the available service will discontent be avoided. A tax system that assigns the right amount of tax to each voter is difficult to design. This is why a democratic country is likely to have minorities willing to pay for more social services. In a market economy, these minorities and other interested parties can form organizations to provide higher levels of the desired services and the non-profit form provides a vehicle for them to do so.

2.3 Government / Non-profit Collaboration

Government plays an important role collecting taxes and insuring provision of social services. Its coercive powers enable it to raise funds from individuals who oppose provision of public goods. Because it can potentially collect taxes from everyone, it has fund-raising powers far in excess of those of non-profits and it has a legal justification for taxing individuals, as well as control over the amounts it takes in. Hence, it is not surprising that government is the primary source for financing social services in most Western countries.

   While government is a major funding source, whether it should also produce and deliver social services is debatable. Government production and ownership have been a principal tenant of socialism. However, alternative possibilities for social service provision exist and these have been adopted in varying degrees in the West. Among the most interesting is government / non-profit partnership (Salamon, 1987: 113). This approach assumes that each party has something to offer the other. Government can generate reliable resource streams, set priorities for social service provision based on a democratic process, offset the paternalism of the non-profit sector, and regulate non-profit behaviour. Non-profits can "personalize" social service delivery, operate on a small scale, adjust the care they provide to meet client needs, and compete in market settings. For Salamon, collaboration between government and the non-profit sector with the former providing services and the latter insuring financing is "... the preferred method for responding to the human needs of an advanced industrial society".

2.4   The Role of the Non-profit Sector

What distinguishes non-profit organizations from other private enterprises is that they are barred from distributing profits to the individuals who exercise control over them (Hansmann, 1981). Non-profits can make profits from their operations but cannot distribute them to their owners or managers. In contrast, for-profits are allowed to distribute profits to their stockholders. Government can and does delegate provision of some social services to for-profit firms. However, strong arguments exist favouring the use of non-profit providers to deliver social services. Consider the informational asymmetry and other arguments that favour non-profit providers.

2.4.1 Informational Asymmetry

One of the strongest arguments for why non-profits should be the preferred vehicle for delivery of social service type public goods is that some services are of such a nature that ordinary contractual arrangements do not provide the purchaser with sufficient assurance that the contracted services will be performed in the intended manner. For example, Hansmann (1981) notes that the financiers of CARE, an international relief organization, have limited contact with the recipients of their largesse.[5] Consequently, donors know very little about whether the service they financed was performed. They could spend time and money to investigate but most do not because the cost of policing is too great for this to be feasible. Hence, they must trust the entity providing the service. For Hansmann (1981), the source of trust in non-profits is the prohibition against distributing surpluses to owners and managers. This interdiction provides a disincentive for managers to use funds for purposes other than those intended by the financiers because non-profit managers cannot personally gain by doing so.

A number of cases exist where a financier has limited knowledge of how the services financed are performed. Government purchases of nursing home services for the elderly, of day care services for the young, clinical services for the sick, and care and feeding of international refugees are examples. Because an asymmetry of information exists between providers who know what services they produce and financiers who do not, a strong element of trust must exist in providing services financed by a third party. Particularly where critical services are involved, as in the provision of medical care, non-profits have an advantage as the vehicle to receive third party funds because they have less of an incentive to misuse funds than for-profits.

Table 6.1:   **Expenditures and Assets of the Several Types of Non-profit Organizations in the US**

Organizational Mission/Industry	Annual Expenditure		Total Assets	
	Dollars	Per cent	Dollars	Per cent
A. Arts/Culture	$6,671	2.37%	$14,552	2.42%
B. Education	56,551	20.08	157,490	26.14
C. Environment	713	0.25	2,598	0.43
D. Animal Related	871	0.31	1,876	0.31
E. Health - General	149,511	53.09	181,866	30.18
F. Mental Health	2,568	0.91	1,584	0.26
G. Disease Related	3,664	1.30	5,357	0.89
H. Consumer/Legal	1,061	0.38	493	0.08
I. Crime/Deliquency	242	0.09	210	0.03
J. Employment/Jobs	1,667	0.59	1,578	0.26
K. Food/Agriculture	822	0.29	1,009	0.17
L. Housing/Shelter	1,727	0.61	6,225	1.03
M. Public Safety	247	0.09	411	0.07
N. Recreation/Sports	920	0.33	1,347	0.22
O. Youth Development	1,922	0.68	3,376	0.56
P. Human Services	15,077	5.35	22,121	3.67
Q. International	886	0.31	818	0.14
R. Civil Rights	192	0.07	154	0.03
S. Community	6,604	2.34	8,236	1.37
T. Philanthropy	515	0.18	122,837	20.39[a]
U. Science/Soc Sci	2,416	0.86	3,108	0.52
V. Public/Society	1,424	0.51	4,315	0.72
W. Religion Related	7,581	2.69	12,131	2.01
Y. Unclassified	17,788	6.32	48,821	8.10[b]
Total Charity (A-Y)	$281,640	100.00%	$602,817	100.00%[c]
Philanthropy Organizations	9,653[d]			
Mutual Benefit Organizations	16,616[d]		66,817[d]	
Grand Total	$307,909		$609,330	

Notes: a) Expenditures for those organizations that file Form 990-PF are listed separately to avoid double-counting in the charity subtotal. b) Unclassified entities are the 501(c)(3) organizations for which a National Tax Exempt Entities (NTEE) Major Group Code has not been assigned. c) These totals are a compilation including tax returns from 1987, 1988, and 1989. d) Excluded from the percentages. e) The Y category includes the Teachers Insurance and Annuity Association and College Retirement Equities Fund. Other similar organizations are organized under 501(c)(1).

Source: National Center For Charitable Statistics at Independent Sector, NTEE Master File of Non-profit Organizations as of November 1990. These totals change as new organizations are added to the NTEE master data base, closed organizations are deleted, and unclassified organizations are assigned initial NTEE codes. Data are from the latest tax returns for 501(c)(3) organizations that (1) existed in 1987 and (2) filed a return during 1987, 1988, or 1989.

2.4.2 Diversity of Functions

Non-profits perform many diverse functions in the United States, as demonstrated by the National Taxonomy of Exempt Entities (NTEE) prepared by the Independent Sector, a Washington-based non-profit organization for the promotion of voluntary activities. Table 6.1 shows the annual expenditures and assets of charitable non-profits as of November 1990. Note that the non-profit expenditures reported to the Internal Revenue Service (IRS) are over $281 billion. (The GNP in the US was $5,400 billion in 1990.) Note too the great diversity in the functions that non-profits perform in the American economy. In part, this diversity reflects prevailing attitudes concerning what constitutes activity appropriate to the non-profit sector. In part, it reflects the American preference for a limited role for central government. Americans have a strong preference for using the non-profit sector to provide health and education services. As measured by the Independent Sector, these two activities represent almost three quarters of the total non-profit expenditures reported to IRS.[6] Finally, note that reported asset holdings of American non-profits were twice the size of aggregate expenditures.[7]

2.4.3 Pros And Cons of Non-profit Delivery

Douglas (1987) emphasizes several advantages that non-profits offer. Relative to governments, non-profits provide greater diversity of service provision, reflect a fuller range of views on social issues because many small organizations can be created to reflect constituent views, are better able to experiment with new approaches, less bureaucratic, less politically constrained, and more quick in responding to changes in the needs of their service populations than government. They may also be less costly to operate to the extent that they can use volunteer labour. Moreover, because they are not governmental entities they are free of the restrictions placed on public organizations (Tuckman, 1984; 1985).

Non-profit organizations also have several disadvantages. They can be insulated from competition in the marketplace, causing them to deliver services inefficiently. Because they are run by non-elected officials, they can be clubby, elite, and removed from the society that finances them and the people they serve. In the absence of public scrutiny of their finances, a potential also exists for abuse of the public trust.

3   Challenges to Establishing an Effective Non-profit Sector

This part of the paper examines the challenges that face newly emerging market economies (NEMEs) that wish to establish non-profit organizations. To simplify the analysis, the challenges are presented in the context of the environments in which they occur. Five environments are considered; legal, financial, market, internal, and regulatory. The important social and political environments are complex and lie beyond the ken of the present paper.

3.1 The Legal Environment

A major challenge exists in creating a legal environment in which non-profits can thrive. Among the issues that arise in the establishment of this environment are the right of non-profits to exist, their permissible purposes, their corporate rights, and what constitutes acceptable fiduciary behaviour on their part.

3.1.1 The Right to Exist

At the core of the legal environment is an entitling statute or statutes that recognize the right of non-profit organizations to exist. Non-profits in both England and the United States trace this right to England's Elizabethan Poor Law (An Act For the Relief of the Poor, 43 Eliz, 1601). This law, as demonstrated by the attorneys in the US *Girard Will Case*, was simply a formalization of a long series of other statutes existing in English law. Hall (1987: 4-6) indicates that during the period following the American Revolution of 1776, "lawyers and legislators began – in a fashion dictated largely by local and regional concerns – to draw on the English legal and organizational precedents of the previous two centuries". However, it was not until the massive wave of immigration in the mid and late 1800s that attitudes towards non-profits changed and massive numbers of new welfare organizations took hold.

Legal statutes give legitimacy to the non-profit sector by providing government sanction for the existence of the sector. Government statutes grant legal recognition to the non-profit form and set forth the rights and responsibilities of non-profit organizations. They also determine when non-profits can form and when they should be terminated.[8] Thus, the first challenge facing a NEME is to frame a legal statute that provides for the non-profit form, if this does not presently exist.

3.1.2 Permissible Purposes

It is not easy to define permissible purposes for non-profit organizations. Such purposes include but need not be limited to, the delivery of charitable, social, cultural, religious, educational, intellectual, and quasi-political services. No simple way exists to draw a line delineating the activities that non-profits should be permitted to perform. The American experience is helpful in illustrating this point. Because non-profit organizations in the US are created under the laws of individual states rather than under a single federal law, differences exist in the permissible purposes defined by the states. At the heart of the issue is whether to allow non-profits to perform specific functions or whether they should be free to engage in any activity as long as it is not unlawful.[9] Some states in the US limit non-profits only to the performance of charitable, educational, scientific, and fraternal purposes.

Others define the term charity broadly and do not spell out specific activities that are acceptable. In still other states, the set of activities allowable under Section 501(c)(3) of the Federal Internal Revenue Code is used as a standard for permissible activities, despite the fact that no specific criteria are spelled out to select the purposes allowed in this code.[10]

At present, no uniform set of criteria exist for defining what is an acceptable purpose for a non-profit organization. In the research community, experts differ in their opinions on what is an acceptable purpose. Some experts, like Hansmann (1981: 521), argue that restriction of the purposes for which non-profits can be formed is less important to society than the restriction of right to distribute profits to owners and managers. They take the position that economic factors will limit the activities that non-profits seek to perform. Others, like Swain (1983), believe that the purposes for which a non-profit can be formed should be carefully circumscribed.[11]

3.1.3 Corporate Rights

In many Western countries, the corporate form enjoys advantages not available to other business entities. Among other things, these involve the right to own property, to pay taxes, and to incur debt as an entity separate from its owners. Since ownership resides in the corporation rather than its managers or owners, it has the right to perpetual existence. Its ability to own properties, to perpetual life, and to offer limited liability to its owners for the debts it incurs make this organizational form more attractive to both for-profit and non-profit firms than other forms such as single proprietorship and partnership. The experience of the US is again useful in understanding the value of the corporate form. Although the US became a country in 1776, it was 108 years before the corporate form received full legal acceptance. While it is unclear to what extent this slowed the growth of the non-profit sector, most of the development of this sector occurred only after the corporate form was fully sanctioned in the late 1800s (Hall, 1987: 6).

NEMEs face several issues in deciding whether to grant corporate status to non-profits. The first relates to whether to allow a non-profit perpetual rights to its property. If this is allowed, ownership will reside in the organization itself rather than in its founders or current managers. Once a non-profit corporation's purpose is judged to be permissible, it will have the right to perpetual existence, as long as its behaviour does not violate regulatory standards. The decision to grant perpetual life assumes that an organization will carry out its purpose and that its activities will benefit society. As long as it exists, it will retain title to its property. Governments in NEMEs must make a decision as to whether this is an acceptable arrangement and how, if at all, they plan to limit the lifespan of non-profit organizations.

A related question involves whether non-profits should have the right to accumulate unlimited assets. Asset accumulation is critical to the financial health of an organization. However, there may come a point where excess asset accumulation occurs. For example, a non-profit may accumulate assets for 30 years while expending little of available resources in support of its purpose or it may take in assets at a rate substantially greater than it expends them. At some point, society has an interest in insuring that its productive wealth is not tied up in support of one activity or in unproductive uses. At present, the literature does not contain any guides as to when asset accumulation becomes excessive (Tuckman and Chang, 1991). The US imposes no limits on the asset accumulation of operating non-profits while Canada limits the amount of new assets that non-profits can amass. Policy makers in NEMEs will have to decide among alternative ways of dealing with this question.

A third issue concerns what should be done with the property of a non-profit upon its dissolution. Hansmann (1981: 574) argues that the distribution of assets to non-profit's members creates a loophole in the prohibition against the distribution of profits because it presents opportunities for self-dealing when a non-profit terminates operation. A danger exists that non-profits will accumulate assets and, at a future date, dispense them to the individuals who control them. This problem, together with the fact that some donors provide assets to a non-profit with the clear intent of devoting them to particular uses into perpetuity, suggest that a need exists for limits on how the assets of a defunct non-profit should be disposed of. One solution is to require that the assets of an expiring non-profit be passed to other non-profits or presented to the government for disposition. Another is to allow sale with the proceeds to revert to another non-profit with similar purpose.

3.1.4 Fiduciary Behaviour

Non-profits operate with the understanding that they have a fiduciary responsibility towards both the people who finance them and the populations they serve. An issue arises as to whether and how to regulate the behaviours of non-profit managers. Hansmann (1981) argues that regulation is largely not necessary since the constraint on asset distribution assures trustworthy behaviour on the part of non-profit managers. Other scholars of non-profits see a need for a detailed definition of acceptable behaviour. Among the issues to be resolved are whether to establish limits on the size of the salaries paid to administrators, on "self-dealing", on the extent to which salaries are based on performance, and on potential conflict of interest situations (Young, 1989).[12]

A particularly difficult problem can arise in the case of private foundations. Under US law, non-profit private foundations exist for the purpose of channelling money to other organizations engaged in charitable causes. Non-profits in this category differ from other non-profits in that they are open-ended in purpose (but the causes that they give to must be charitable), give money to others to perform services rather than dispensing them directly, and often make use of professionals to identify the projects to fund. Hall (1987: 11-13) explains the growth of these organizations in the US between 1900 and 1933 as the business community's response to socialism and its desire for a form of "welfare capitalism" that emphasizes improvements in the community and workforce. While most of these organizations operate in an open and professional manner, they pose the potential for conflict of interest, particularly if employed as devices to ensure control of for-profit corporations and/ or to extend the power of the individuals or families that established them. In 1969, the US expanded reporting requirements for these entities, set forth rules limiting foundation holdings of business entities, and placed restrictions on their control by family members (O'Neil, 1989: 78).

3.2   The Financial Environment

A second environment in which non-profits face challenges is the financial environment. This affects both how many and which new non-profits will be established, the sources of support for non-profits, their financial health and stability, and their chances for survival and growth. This section considers several issues that arise during a transitional period from a command economy to a market economy with an active non-profit sector. These include where funds will come from to create new non-profits, how governments should treat donations and bequests for tax purposes, the conditions under which government grants are made, the other sources of funding that governments can make available to non-profits, and the access of non-profits to capital markets.

3.2.1 Provision of Seed Capital

Non-profits acquire the capital necessary to begin operation from several sources including organizations interested in seeing a service offered, donors with a commitment to a particular mission, governments interested in seeing private provision of a public good, and entrepreneurs determined to run an organization that fulfils a purpose they believe in. When a non-profit is organized in the corporate form, capital can also be raised from the issuance of stock by the founders of the organization. However, in contrast to the for-profit form, such stock does not represent a claim on the profits that the non-profits take in or on its assets. If it did, this claim would violate the prohibition against distribution of profits. Hence, investors can be expected to be reluctant to invest in the stock of a non-profit enterprise.

In a NEME wishing to develop a non-profit sector, an issue arises as to whether government should subsidize the creation of non-profits and, if so, under what conditions. The early history of non-profit organizations in the US suggests that, even when these organizations were founded by private individuals, government support was important in insuring their success. For example, O'Neill (1989: 24) reports that, because of its mixed funding, it took 200 years for Harvard College to figure out that it was a private institution and not a public one.

The question of whether government should provide funds to speed the development of its non-profit sector is less important than the terms under which such funding is provided. Government provision, particularly in economies where capital is scarce, can have an important impact on the growth of the non-profit sector. However, such financing should be limited to permissible charitable purposes and subject to minimal government interference. Young (1989: 189) argues that in the early stages of an industry, non-profits are highly experimental. To foster the development of a non-profit sector, "... all that is required is that participant organizations find some viable group of constituents to support them, whether by grants, donations, volunteer labour, member fees, and the like". Excessive government regulations can destroy the flexibility of these organizations and reduce their effectiveness as providers of social services. The challenge is to find a way to provide funding with minimal constraints on organizational activity while ensuring that public funds are used for their intended purposes.

3.2.2 Policies Towards Donations and Bequests

Donations and bequests are a prime source of financing for many non-profits. The amounts provided from these sources are affected by many factors including: the laws governing the disposition of estates at time of a donor's death, the attitudes of society towards charity, the age and wealth of the population, and tax treatment of gifts and bequests for tax purposes. Laws that permit creation of charitable foundations and trusts strengthen the non-profit sector. Because individuals are free to bequest funds and donations are tax-deductible, these laws can lead to the development of a diverse and numerous non-profit sector that is not heavily dependent on government support. It can also lead to considerable loss of tax revenue to the government. A NEME must make a decision regarding how much tax subsidy it is willing to allow for its non-profit sector. This is not easy to do, particularly in the early stages of development when reliable data on the amount of charitable giving and on sensitivity of giving to changes in the tax laws are not available.

A second potential problem arises because charitable giving tends to be uneven across activities. A consequence is that an unequal distribution of assets develops with a few organizations in possession of a large proportion of the wealth of the non-profit sector. Wealth may also be concentrated in one geographic area and hence may benefit only one part of the population. Moreover, the activities with the largest amount of funding may not be those most highly valued by society as a whole. NEMEs must to some degree accept these difficulties as a necessary outcome of a process that reflects free choice. If government were to try to change the priorities of donors, it would create a disincentive to donate.

Because public trust is necessary if a non-profit is to receive funding, marketing of a non-profit's mission can be extremely important. Non-profits in NEMEs can benefit from fund-raising strategies and techniques to raise funds from individuals and businesses (Seymour, 1988). Moreover, because many non-profits seek dona-tions at any given time, fund-raising campaigns are often characterized by competition among them for the limited supply of funds. In recognition of this problem, some communities establish an umbrella organization to raise funds for a host of non-profits in the hope that a coordinated effort will reduce competition and ease the burden of solicitations on the public. In the US, United Way or-ganizations have been highly successful in raising funds although they have not entirely succeeded in eliminating competition among non-profits for funds. Particularly, in areas where the need for social services is great, the wealth of the population is limited, and/or where non-profits prefer to raise funds on their own, competition for funds will be keen.

Economists have devoted considerable attention to the question of whether government tax and spending policies affect charitable giving. Most studies suggest that government policies do impact on the amount that individuals and businesses give. Schiff's (1990: 76-77) study, typical of the research in this area, suggests that charitable giving responds to changes in the price of giving (the amount of donation net of tax breaks) and in incomes of businesses and individuals. It also finds that contributions are "quite responsive" to changes in income tax laws and in gov-ernment spending in the social welfare area.

These findings suggest that NEME governments wishing to strengthen their non-profit sector can do so through tax law changes to make it attractive for individuals and businesses to donate to non-profits. At least three types of choices may be made. The first involves the types and amounts of tax deductions provided to individuals and businesses who donate to non-profits. The second involves whether government should leave donors free to contribute as much as they wish. It can be argued that in a market economy, donors should be free to provide as much charity as they wish since charitable giving is just one more way that a consumer can use his/her funds. The problem is the revenue loss to the government that accompanies tax subsidy. In the early stages of emergence as a market system, it may be necessary to control the revenue loss that might occur if unlimited contributions were allowed by placing a cap on the amount of giving that is tax deductible. Alternatively, the amount of the subsidy can be lowered if the revenue loss proves to be too great. The third choice involves which non-profits should be eligible for favourable tax treatment. It might be required that an organization must provide social services such that the benefits to society exceed those to the donors. However, such a requirement is difficult to administer and enforce.

3.2.3 Conditions Under Which Government Grants Are Made

Government grants are an important source of funding for non-profits in a market economy. Through its taxing power, government has the capacity to direct large sums of money to the non-profit sector. Because its resources are considerably greater than those of other financiers, it is an attractive party for non-profits to approach for funding. In theory, government will make grants that fulfil national priorities or to meet national goals.[13] In practice, politics play a strong role in influencing which grants are made at what levels. All governments must make decisions regarding which grants will be made to non-profits, the types of grants to offer, the arrangements for service delivery, the penalties for failing to deliver contracted services, and the restrictions, if any, to place on service delivery.

The dynamic tension that exists between government and the recipients of its funds must be recognized as an inherent part of an arrangement where third party payments are involved. Researchers have examined the impact of government funding on the operations of non-profits. Their findings highlight several problems when government provides grants to non-profits. For example, Salamon (1987) notes that when government funds external organizations, it is held accountable by the electorate for the use of these funds. This creates a need to oversee the activities of the non-profit, to insist on accountability of funds, and to set performance standards. Thus, governments often require elaborate proposals from the requesting organizations to justify funding, impose guidelines and rules for service implementation, require evidence or certification that contracted services are delivered, and insist on audits by outside parties. These requirements imposes a cost on non-profits in terms of money and other resources. They also limit the flexibility and ability of non-profits to respond rapidly to changes in the marketplace.

Non-profit decision makers are aware of these constraints and they face a decision as to whether to take government funds. Some fear the loss of autonomy that occurs when government creates extensive requirements for service delivery. Others fear that government requirements distort a non-profit's mission, turning it to activities preferred by the government and away from the purposes for which funds were requested. Still others express concern about the cost of doing business with government and the effects of the bureaucratization that accompanies government demands for accountability. The tension between the two parties can be reduced if planners in NEMEs recognize the need to balance between accountability and flexibility.

3.2.4 Other Government Funding

Government has several vehicles available to finance the non-profit sector. (1) Contracts are issued to purchase specific services and these can be designed to specify the amounts, kinds, and time periods for delivery of social services. (2) Government can provide grants to non-profit organizations to develop and implement specific service plans. (3) Reimbursement of third parties for services is normally used where a non-profit is providing a service that government wants to purchase for a specific target group. The critical issue here tends to focus on the amounts that government must pay and whether the services meet government specifications. (4) Government grants to community or private foundations are usually made to facilitate the setting of priorities on funding regional and local projects. No single approach to funding is best and the method adopted depends on the nature of the services provided, objectives of government, trust placed in the deliverer of the service, and cost-effectiveness of each vehicle.

3.2.5 Access to Capital

A problem common to most new non-profit organizations is the lack of adequate capital to finance operations. In the rare case where a non-profit is founded by a bequest from a wealthy donor or a large gift, this may not be a problem. However, new non-profits do not have the means and time to accumulate a large asset base and their initial revenue is likely to be primarily derived from their founders. A question arises as to how non-profits can establish a pool of funds sufficient to finance their operation for the first few years. We have noted that because non-profits cannot distribute their assets, stock issuances are not likely to be a large source of capital. Moreover, capital from banks or bond markets is, at best, limited because in a market economy loans are made only if adequate collateral is available to assure a lender that the capital will be returned in the event of financial failure. Few new non-profits have assets of sufficient value to provide this level of security to lenders and hence few have access to the credit market.[14]

Non-profits can acquire capital several ways. One approach is to engage in capital campaigns designed to raise funds from businesses and the public. This is a major source of finance for non-profit organizations (Hodgkinson and Weitzman, 1989). Another is to secure loans guaranteed by members of the Board of Directors. This is feasible when board members have sufficient assets and reputation to convince a bank to make the loan. A third approach is to seek funding from private foundations or trusts. Commercial non-profits (namely, those that earn a large proportion of their revenue from sale of their services) may, in certain cases, be able to secure a loan if they can offer evidence of a reliable and reasonably secure revenue stream. Moreover, some non-profits may be able to secure capital by joint venturing with for-profit enterprises. For many new non-profits, financing is likely to be difficult in the first few years. Government assistance may be critical to insure the rapid development of a strong non-profit sector.

3.3 The Market Environment

Non-profits in Western Europe and North America operate in a market environment. Depending on the nature of their services, they may compete with each other, with for-profits, and/or with government organizations. In this section we consider the challenges that arise in the markets for products, for the inputs of production, and in establishing effective strategic planning techniques.

3.3.1 Product Markets

Non-profits produce and deliver services in what economists refer to as the "product markets". Like for-profit managers, non-profit managers must have a thorough understanding of the market in which they operate because conditions in the marketplace affect non-profits' ability to produce and deliver services. For example, Steinberg (1987: 122) argues that solicitation by donative non-profits (namely, those that finance their operations by donations) is conceptually similar to the marketing and advertising done by for-profits and that "... the criteria for maximizing the surplus generated by a fund-raising programme are identical to criteria for maximizing the profits generated by production and marketing".

Similarly, increases in the number of suppliers can affect price and output decisions of non-profits, just as these variables affect for-profits. Those that produce in industries with limited competition have greater control over what and how they produce than those producing in industries where many non-profits compete. Some commercial non-profits apply their market power to charge high prices for the services they offer and use the resulting profits to "cross-subsidize" production of other services. Others use their power to upgrade the quality of services they produce while still others choose not to exploit their market power.

In sum, non-profits operating in a market environment face a number of challenges. Competition affects the number of people who want to purchase a service (or to donate), the quality and number of services profitable to offer, costs of production, profitability, and ability to grow. Operation in a market environment involves an understanding of the forces that cause market conditions to change, competitor behaviour, the regulatory environment, own goals, and production techniques. It also requires attention to consumer satisfaction.

3.3.2 Input Markets

Separate markets exist for the inputs that non-profits use in the production of services. In most market economies, non-profits hire paid employees in several labour markets and compete for voluntary labour in the markets for volunteers. Similarly, non-profits acquire capital in several capital markets and compete with other non-profits for grants, donations, and bequests. Challenges arise in determining which inputs to use in production, choosing an appropriate mix of voluntary and paid labour, and forecasting changes in the price and availability of labour and capital.

Management challenges also arise because non-profits compete in the marketplace for skilled and professional labour. Because the salary and fringe benefits offered are important in attracting highly-skilled labour, non-profits must find resources to finance their recruiting efforts. Competition for labour also may be based on such things as capital equipment, location, quality of existing staff. In non-profits concerned with research, for example, quality of the environment can be as important as salary in determining which researchers are attracted to a facility.

3.3.3 Role of Strategic Planning

Non-profits in Western market economies often utilize strategic planning to structure their decisions and account for threats and opportunities in the competitive marketplace. Strategic planning involves the use of concepts, tools, and techniques that help managers and administrators to understand and master the environment in which they operate for the purpose of realizing established goals and objectives. The key function of strategic planning is to enable decision makers to think strategically; that is, to develop strategies for systematically coping with their operational environment. Strategic planning involves a set of steps that integrate analytic thinking with specific actions. It may also involve organizational changes that provide better interface of the non-profit with its market environment (Bryson, 1988). The process involves clarification of organizational mission, evaluation of threats and opportunities in the external environment, analysis of organizational strengths and weaknesses, identification of strategic issues, and design of implementation plans. The technique is familiar to business managers in the West and it deserves the attention of non-profit decision makers who operate in changing and turbulent environments of NEMEs.

3.4 The Internal Environment

A key challenge facing non-profits in NEMEs is the need to develop efficiently managed organizations. Among other things, this involves the development of quality leadership, appropriate governance mechanisms, effective financial controls, and standards for performance evaluation. The challenges in each area are briefly considered below.

3.4.1 Quality of Leadership

Most non-profits in America utilize a governance system involving a chief executive and a Board of Directors. This arrangement is usually specified by the statutes that establish non-profits in most states. Some scholars argue that the Board is pre-eminent because it has the power to hire and fire the chief executive (Herman and Heimovics, 1991: Ch. 2). In recent years, however, observers of non-profit behaviour have argued that assignment of responsibility and accountability in a non-profit is more complex than this model suggests. Young (1987: 168) sees the chief executive as an entrepreneur who seeks to define the direction of the organization. He or she recruits productive employees, assumes risk, raises capital, takes responsibility for marketing, deals with the political environment, and exercises other management and leadership skills. Drucker (1990: 13) believes that a well-functioning non-profit assigns responsibility for effective governance to its chief executive. Herman and Heimovics (1991: 128) argue that the position of chief executives is based on "a leadership of responsibility rather than a leadership of formal authority".

A major problem facing NEMEs is to find persons with leadership skills willing to operate as chief executives in a non-profit setting. At least two problems are involved. The first involves creation of a pool of talented non-profit leaders. This is not difficult where a society has a tradition of entrepreneurship but it can be a problem where central planning and dictatorship have discouraged entrepreneurial activity. Deficiencies of this type can be overcome through education, exposure to the market-place, and the creation of incentives that reward entrepreneurial behaviour.

The second challenge is to attract well-paid executives from the for-profit to the non-profit sector. A significant part of the motivation for talented leaders to run non-profits is non-monetary. The challenge is to create public policies that encourage (or at least do not discourage) the decision to enter the non-profit sector. Young (1986: 180) argues that government policies that dictate what services to be provided in the non-profit sector can have at least two detrimental consequences. First, they can discourage certain entrepreneurial types of individuals from entering a field or industry thereby reducing the supply of leaders available to non-profits. Second, they can result in a heterogeneous entrepreneurial mix within the non-profit sector because a screening process takes place that causes different types of leaders to seek careers in the non-profit sector depending on the rewards that are offered. His analysis suggests that governmental actions can impact on both the number and types of leaders available to the non-profit sector.

3.4.2 Non-profit Boards and Governance

Non-profits in the US have been required to have Boards of Directors or their equivalents since the end of the 1700s, the precedent having been first established by Harvard College in 1636. Middleton (1987: 142) suggests that the legal responsibilities have not been well defined in the US, particularly with respect to accountability. Nonetheless, these Boards play an important internal role in fundraising, establishing operating procedures, enlisting public support, budgeting and fiscal control, and representing different perspectives as to what a non-profit should be doing. Middleton (1987: 143) also emphasizes several external roles of the Board including, development of exchange relationships that facilitate a flow of resources into and out of the organization, processing of information that provides the feedback needed to make internal adjustments, protection of the organization from external interference, and reduction of environmental constraints.

The American-style board structure has had a mixed record of success. On the one hand, assignment of hiring and firing functions to the Board of Directors has provided a means for overseeing the non-profit and opening it to external scrutiny. On the other, aloofness, paternalism, disinterest, and lack of adequate training and skills have limited the extent to which Board of Directors can exercise control over the organization (Herman and Heimovics, 1991). Policy makers in NEMEs considering the American model might wish to examine the alternative ways that internal oversight can be structured.

3.4.3 Financial Control Systems

Tight financial control is important to the establishment of a productive and responsive internal environment for non-profits. The fact that a non-profit is engaged in charitable enterprise does not absolve it from the need to be business-like in accounting for its resource use. Financial control systems provide a record of the transactions that a non-profit makes, offer assurance to those who support the organization and to those who receive its services that funds are properly used, and provide the basis for developing information that can be used to evaluate financial performance (Cleverley, 1986).

At the heart of financial control is an accounting system that matches the costs and revenues of non-profits for the purpose of accounting and for acquisition and disposition of resources. Some non-profits use fund accounting under which the resources of the organization are placed into self-balancing funds designated for specific purposes. For example, non-profits earmark funds for building, capital replacement, and/or provision of care to the poor. The funds in each of these accounts can only be used for specified purposes. Funding accounting facilitates fund-raising because it provides a guarantee to donors that funds will be used for the purposes that they wish. However, even in cases where non-profits use only one fund to store funds, their Boards can vote to restrict funds for specific purposes (Cleverley, 1986). Provisions should also be made for periodic audits of a non-profit's accounting records. An audit is an investigation, normally conducted by an external party, of the reliability of the financial statements developed by an organization. Its goals are to: (1) safeguard a non-profit's resources from waste and fraud, (2) promote accuracy and reliability in accounting data, (3) provide reasonable assurance that Board policy is implemented, and (4) facilitate the evaluation of performance.

The adoption of Western financial systems poses several problems for NEMEs. Differences exist between the accounting systems used by countries in Eastern Europe and those in the West. A decision to move to the Western systems would require retraining. Training will also be required of personnel in existing and new non-profits to insure that the records of these organizations are kept in acceptable form. It will take time to acclimate to the requirements of an effective financial control system and outside help may initially be needed to provide feedback on the effectiveness of the new financial systems.

3.4.4 Performance Evaluation

Kanter and Summers (1987: 154) argue that the centrality of social values over financial values makes it difficult to measure the performance of non-profits. The fact that these organizations provide services involving intangible benefits complicates the problem. Moreover, conflicts among goals make measures of goal attainment difficult to construct. One consequence is that scholars of non-profit performance tend to focus on inputs rather than outputs and another is that inefficiencies may develop because of the difficulties inherent in determining which evaluation methods are most effective. These problems may be overcome, to some extent, by establishing systems to create feedback to administrators on how well their non-profit is fulfilling its goals. Examples of feedback mechanisms are surveys of employee and clientele satisfaction, letters from donors or community leaders, and periodic visits from members of the Board to observe service delivery. A common practice is also to provide data at each Board meeting on population served, projects performed, and related activities. It may be important in the early stages of developing the non-profit sector to place emphasis on feedback mechanisms, particularly on the importance of satisfying consumer and donor needs.

3.5   The Regulatory Environment

The regulatory environment determines the number of non-profits able to enter and leave an industry. It also affects the extent to which non-profits can exercise market power, engage in behaviour judged to be unfair, take on unrelated businesses, and disclose information to the public and to donors. This environment is shaped by the legal statutes that govern behaviour, tax and subsidy mechanisms that create incentives and disincentives, and reporting structures, and agencies that enforce the statutes. The NEMEs face challenges in assuring that adequate laws are on the books to govern non-profit operation and in designing systems to police non-profit behaviour. We deal with some of these issues below.

3.5.1   Entry and Exit

The extent to which government should regulate entry and exit of non-profits represents another issue that must be confronted by NEMEs interested in developing a robust non-profit sector. Since the public sector provides subsidies and special treatment to non-profits, it has an interest in insuring that this sector does not expand at a rate that strains available resources. It also has an interest in making sure that services are distributed efficiently between the public, private, and non-profit sector (Weisbrod, 1988: Ch. 9). Government planners have difficulty devising criteria for determining when the optimal number of non-profits has been reached. This leaves open the question of whether it is better to allow individual decisions to determine the number of business organizations that incorporate as non-profits each year or whether a cap on non-profit growth should be established by government. While Hansmann (1981: 516-527) argues that it is sufficient to limit non-profits by policing the constraint against the distribution of profits, most governments have found ways to restrict the number of non-profit organizations formed each year.

3.5.2 Exercise of Market Power

A second issue relates to whether non-profits should be subject to antitrust laws. If a country chooses to enact laws to deal with abuses of market power by large for-profits then it is likely that a question will arise as to whether to subject non-profits to these regulations. The rationale in favour of this is that non-profits can engage in price fixing, acquisition of competitors, price discrimination, and other practices that may be deemed unlawful and the purpose of antitrust laws is to limit the extent to which these activities are allowed. However, Steinberg (1990: 28) makes the case that non-profits should be treated differently than for-profits when antitrust issues arise. Not only should non-profits be allowed some degree of isolation from competition but there also may be some situations where price discrimination is beneficial (e.g. lower fees for poor patients at a non-profit clinic). However, he distinguishes the behaviours of donative non-profits and commercial non-profits and argues for separate treatment of the two under antitrust laws. Commercial non-profits price their services and users pay for the privilege of receiving them. Donative non-profits finance their operations by donations and deliver them in the market-place.

The issues that face those who design these laws in NEMEs include: (1) whether to exempt non-profits from existing antitrust statutes or to create special statutes that apply to them; (2) which practices are illegal and which are not; (3) how to enforce antitrust laws; and (4) what penalties to impose on violators.

3.5.3 Policing the Market Boundaries

Simon (1987: 68) refers to the border patrol function of public policy as the regulation of the extent to which non-profits can "operate in the business and public sectors by competing with, controlling or influencing, the behaviour of commercial or governmental entities". The question of where the border between two non-profit industries (e.g. hospitals and nursing homes) lies poses a major challenge to policy makers. Of particular interest is the extent to which non-profits should be allowed to engage in activities unrelated to their primary mission. For example, should a non-profit museum be allowed to sell T-shirts to tourists in direct competition with private vendors? Government grants to non-profits have diminished in the US and, as a result, non-profits have increasingly engaged in business activities not directly related to their missions to offset declining government revenues (Weisbrod, 1988). These unrelated business activities have helped non-profits in the US to survive major cut-backs in government funding. They also have caused complaints from for-profit enterprises affected by this competition and charges that non-profits are not pursuing their missions (Swain, 1983). Weisbrod (1988: Ch. 6) has summarized the pros and cons of unrelated business activities. The advantages are that they stimulate efficient production, diversify revenue sources, and may stimulate creativity. The disadvantages are that they pose administrative and managerial problems for the chief executive and Board and they may divert resources and energy from an organization's principal purposes.

The revenues of new non-profits are low in NEMEs and, consequently, pressures may develop to allow non-profits to engage in unrelated business activities. The challenge is to define acceptable limits on this type of behaviour. Four approaches are most likely to be considered: (1) Prohibit non-profits from performing any unrelated business. (2) Cap the amount of revenue earned from unrelated businesses. (3) Allow the right to engage in any amount of unrelated business activity but impose a tax on this revenue source. (4) Allow non-profits to engage in any unrelated activities that are allowed for for-profits. Scholars of the non-profit sector have not reached unanimity on which approach is best but little support exists for the fourth option.

If statutes are adopted to limit the unrelated business activity of the non-profit sector then a question arises as to how to police non-profit behaviour. At a minimum, non-profits should be required to file annual reports with the government and data should be collected at the national level to enable researchers and policy makers to evaluate the financial health and performance of the non-profit sector. Reporting of unrelated activity might also be required and penalties can be established for non-profits that exceed allowable levels of unrelated business activity. Enforcement might be assigned to a central authority that has the authority to enforce statutory requirements. However, to preserve the flexibility of non-profits, limits should be placed on the ability of this authority to interfere with operational decisions and with the carrying-out of permissible non-profit missions. The goal should be to insure compliance with the law rather than to micromanage individual organizations.

3.5.4 Public Disclosure

Hansmann (1981: 615) maintains that for non-profits to function properly in situations marked by contract failure, information about how funds are used should be made available to patrons. It can be argued that such information should be made disclosed to the general public, particularly in NEMEs that lack a tradition of disclosure. At a minimum, information should be available on revenue sources, asset holdings, debt, equity position, administrative costs, and the costs of fund raising. Adoption of this recommendation would require a government to design a reporting form, a procedure for collection and computerization of these reports, and a means for their dissemination. A procedure is also needed for insuring that organizations that fail to file a report are identified and penalized. This process is important, not only to insure a data source that can be used to monitor the operation of the non-profit sector but also to insure that the public can learn about the activities and operations of the non-profit sector. The Federal Form 990 that tax-exempt non-profit charitable organizations file with the US Internal Revenue Service can serve as a model for NEMEs, although suggestions have been made for its improvement.

4   Conclusions

Many options are available to governments that wish to finance social service delivery. They can produce and deliver these services themselves, finance them through regulated or unregulated for-profits, quasi-governmental agencies, joint ventures between themselves and other sectors or between the for-profit and non-profit sector, or finance and/or encourage producer or consumer cooperatives. Examples of the use of more or more of these approaches can be found in Canada, England, France, Germany, Sweden, the US and other countries. Given the complexities inherent in delivering such services, it is not clear that any one approach is best for the delivery of all types of services.

Non-profit organizations enjoy an advantage where: (1) the goal is to encourage individual participation, (2) flexibility is needed, either to allow rapid growth of a programme or to insure that it can be terminated if it fails, (3) it is difficult to police delivery of an intangible service, (4) delivery of a service is controversial and for-profits might have problems providing the service, (5) it is important to "relieve some of the natural tension between powerful institutions and individuals" (O'Neill, 1989: 177). Since NEMEs face many of these situations as they shed the vestiges of a centrally-planned economy, it behooves policy makers in these countries to take the time to construct a framework supportive of their growth. Careful attention to the five environments described in this paper now can lead to more effective delivery of social services for many years into the future.

Notes

1   This paper uses the terms "non-profit" and "voluntary" interchangeably.
2   For convenience, the term "services" is used to refer to both goods and services.
3   An externality is a benefit or a cost that is experienced by a person who is neither a producer nor a consumer of a service. It occurs when a party who is not a part of a transaction is either positively or negatively affected by it.
4   Producer and consumer cooperatives can also be used for this purpose.
5   The term "financier" refers to anyone who provides funds that assist in the operation of a non-profit.

6   It should be noted that this figure would be lower if all religious activities were accounted for. Many churches, temples and mosques are exempt from filing a tax return under IRS regulations.

7   It is likely that assets are understated since they are based on book value instead of market value.

8   It should be noted that the history of charitable trusts in some countries indicates that they were conceived with the goal of providing a vehicle for devoting assets to a particular use in perpetuity.

9   While many pro and con arguments can be made, it is important to note that where the purposes of non-profits are not restricted a danger arises that society's wealth can be tied up in pursuits which do not meet public needs.

10 Section 501(c) (3) of the Internal Revenue Code sets forth the rules and regulations governing the granting of tax-exempt status to non-profit, charitable organizations in the US.

11 For a discussion of legitimacy issues that this raises, see Estes at al. (1989).

12 Self-dealing may take many forms including inflated contracts for services, land purchases, and/or consulting services.

13 It should be noted that the experience of the US suggests that large charitable foundations may also be able to set and realize national goals (Smith, 1989).

14 In some industries, a similar problem also exists for mature non-profits. Without an asset base, it is difficult to secure bond finance.

References

Bator, F. (1958) 'The Anatomy of Market Failure', *Quarterly Journal of Economics* 72: 351-379.

Buchanan, J.M. (1968) *The Demand and Supply of Public Goods*. Chicago: Rand McNally.

Bryson, J.M. (1988) *Strategic Planning For Public and Non-profit Organizations*. San Francisco: Jossey Bass.

Committee on Implications of For-Profit Enterprise in Health Care (1986) *For-Profit Enterprise in Health Care*. Washington: National Academy Press.

Estes, C.L./Binney, E.A./Bergthold, L.A. (1989) 'How The Legitimacy of the Sector Has Eroded,' in Hodgkinson, V.A./Lyman, R.W., and Associates *The Future of the Non-profit Sector*. San Francisco: Jossey Bass.

Douglas, J. (1987) 'Political Theories of Non-profit Organization.', in Powell, W. (ed.) *The Non-profit Sector*. New Haven: Yale University Press.

Hall, P.D. (1987) 'A Historical Overview of The Private Non-profit Sector', in Powell, W. (ed.) *The Non-profit Sector*. New Haven: Yale University Press.

Hansman, H. (1981) 'Reforming Non-profit Corporation Law', *Pennsylvania Law Review* 129 (3): 497-623.

Hermann, R.D./Heimovics, R.D. (1991) *Executive Leadership in Non-profit Organizations*. San Francisco: Jossey-Bass.

Hodgkinson, V.A./Lyman, R.W., and Associates (1989) *The Future of the Non-profit Sector*. San Francisco: Jossey-Bass Publishers.

Hodgkinson, V.A./Lyman, R.W./Weitzman, M.S. (1989) *Dimensions of the Independent Sector*. 3rd ed. Washington: Independent Sector.

James, E. (1987) 'The Non-profit Sector in Comparative Perspective', pp. 397-415 in Powell, W. (ed.) *The Non-profit Sector*. New Haven: Yale University Press.

Kanter, R.M./Summers, D.V. (1987) 'Doing Well While Doing Good: Dilemmas of Performance Measurement in Noprofit Organizations and the Need for a Multiple Constituency Approach', in Powell, W. (ed.) *The Non-profit Sector*. New Haven: Yale University Press.

Middleton, M. (1987) 'Non-profit Boards of Directors: Beyond The Governance Function', in Powell, W. (ed.) *The Non-profit Sector*. New Haven: Yale University Press.

Musgrave, R.A./Musgrave, P.B. (1984) *Public Finance In Theory and Practice*. 4th ed. New York: McGraw-Hill Book Company.

O'Neill, M. (1989) *The Third America*. San Francisco: Jossey-Bass Publishers.

Salamon, L.M. (1987) 'Partners in Public Service: The Scope And Theory of Government Non-profit Relations', in Powell, W. (ed.) *The Non-profit Sector*. New Haven: Yale University Press.

Schiff, J. (1990) *Charitable Giving and Government Policy*. New York: Greenwood Press.

Scitovsky, T. (1971) *Welfare and Competition*. Homewood: Irwin-Dorsey.

Seymour, H. J. (1988) *Designs For Fund-Raising*. Rockville, MD: Fund-Raising Institute.

Smith, J.A. (1989) 'The Evolving Role of Foundations', pp. 61-74 in Hodgkinson, V.A./ Lyman, R.W., and Associates *The Future of the Non-profit Sector*. San Francisco. Jossey Bass.

Steinberg, R. (1987) 'Non-profit Organizations And The Market', in Powell, W. (ed.) *The Non-profit Sector*. New Haven: Yale University Press.

Steinberg, R.. (1990) 'Antitrust and the Non-profit Sector'. Unpublished paper, Virginia Polytechnical University and State University, July.

Swain, F. (1983) *SBA News*: 83-41. Washington, DC: Small Business Administration.

Tuckman, H.P. (1984) 'Social Efficiency and the Provision of Collective Services', *The American Journal of Economics and Sociology* 43 (3): 257-268.

Tuckman, H.P. (1985) 'Alternative Approaches to Correcting Public Sector Inefficiency', *The American Journal of Economics and Sociology* 44 (1): 55-66.

Tuckman, H.P./Chang, C. (1991a) 'A Proposal to Redistribute the Cost of Hospital Charity Care', *Milbank Quarterly* 69 (1): 113-142.

Tuckman, H.P./Chang, C. (1991b) 'Non-profit Equity Accumulation and the Public Interest', in *1991 Spring Research Forum Working Papers*. Forum co-sponsored by Independent Sector and United Way Strategic Institute, Cleveland, Ohio.

Young, D. (1986) 'Entrepreneurship and the Behaviour of Non-profit Organizations', in Rose-Ackerman, S. (ed.) *The Economics of Non-profit Institutions*. New York: Oxford University Press.

Young, D. (1987) 'Executive Leadership in Non-profit Organizations.' in Powell, W. (ed.) *The Non-profit Sector*. New Haven: Yale University Press.

Young, D. (1989) 'Beyond Tax Exemption: A Focus on Organizational Performance Versus Legal Status', in Hodgkinson, V.A./Lyman, R.W., and Associates *The Future of the Non-profit Sector*. San Francisco: Jossey Bass.

Weisbrod, B.A. (1988) *The Non-profit Economy*. Harvard University Press.

CHAPTER 7

Non-profit Organizations: The Market within the Bureaucracy. The Case of Sporting Leagues

Bernard Ramanantsoa
Bertrand Moingeon

Introduction

This presentation is one part of a research project concerning the sporting leagues that we have been conducting for several years.[1]

This research project was done in two stages:

- The first stage dealt with the understanding of the relationship between the sporting leagues and their environment. The subject of our research was to discover if it is nowadays possible to consider this type of organization as an enterprise – and more specifically, if it is possible, and if so to what extent, to talk about sporting leagues in terms of *strategy*. The main results of this operation are restated in the first part of this document. We showed that these organizations are constrained (in strategic terms) to position themselves at the same time in two fields, to play a kind of double game. Having received a delegation from the State Office for Youth and Sports, they are a public organization having public protection and guaranteeing a mission of public service (Hage, 1984). Thus, the state provides them with both human resources (it appoints the functionaries responsible for the Technical Direction) and financial means.

But their legitimacy also comes from their capacity to develop themselves – in other words, to attract permit-holders by offering them products and services. There, we can already see a source of ambiguity which will grow because its clients, due to the associative nature of the sporting leagues, are "internalized" upon becoming members of the organization (the clients therefore pass from the market to the hierarchy). Our principal conclusion is that the sporting leagues are hybrid structures, being at the same time bureaucratic extensions of the state, enterprises having to conquer a market, and associations of individuals united for a common ideological cause.

- A second stage studied, in connection with the first stage, the internal functioning of the sporting leagues. Our goal was to explore the previously-mentioned ambiguity and to see how it shapes the *identity* of the sporting leagues. We will see that, in order to understand the functioning and the identity of these entities, it is interesting to perceive the organization as another type of market, in which agents (internalized clients) confront one another, desirous of reaching high-level positions. After having recalled the fundaments of the theory of the *habitus* and the *field* of Pierre Bourdieu (Bourdieu, 1989, 1990a) and having described the methodology, we will analyse the mechanisms of the production of these executives of the leagues.

1   Summary of the First Results

1.1 The Sample Studied and the Procedure Adopted

Within the framework of this research, we studied 11 French sporting leagues.[2]

The study of the texts defining the field of legal functioning of these organizations (laws), as well as the analysis of their statutes and internal regulation, constituted the first source of data. In addition, 64 semi-directed interviews were conducted with national executives, technical managers, administrative staff of the sporting leagues, and the employees of the State Office for Youth and Sports. Finally, a list of ethnographic data (extended periods of time in the league structure) was compiled in five of these sporting leagues.

1.2 The Sporting Leagues: Extensions of the State?

Since the ordinance of 28 August 1945, the structure of public sporting facilities is defined by the state – which can, however, delegate its authority regarding the rules and the organization of competitions to the sporting leagues. These leagues can be considered to be public organizations providing a mission of public service. The study of their structure and their functioning reveals this overlapping of associative realm and the state (Thomas, Haumont and Levet, 1987). Actually the "delegator" state plays a key role because of its human resources (availability of technical managers), and by its presentation of budgetary and extra-budgetary grants.

1.2.1 The Technical Frames

The sporting leagues function according to an associative model in which the leading positions are obtained through elections. In addition to this associative structure – whose modes of selections we will study in the final part – there is a technical structure of public agents made available to the league. The mission of these employees is to give technical support to the elected leaders. Usually trained in state institutions, they bring with them work habits typical of state employees. They have a status of *"marginal sécant"* (Jamous, 1968; Crozier and Friedberg, 1978),[3] being at the interface between the state office and the sporting league.

The observation of how the sporting leagues function, reveals the existence of power struggles between the executives from the associative structure and the hired employees. Beyond personal conflicts, these struggles reflect the opposition between two systems of legitimacy. In fact, the technical managers base their legitimacy upon the possession of diplomas given by the state (attesting to a high level of mastery of sporting techniques) and upon their appointment by the state, while the elected executives consider their success in "democratic" elections more important, making them the legitimate representatives.

1.2.2 The Ministerial Subsidies

While the state provides manpower (technical managers) to the leagues which have received delegation from the state, it also gives financial resources by means of ministerial subsidies. The degree of relative autonomy of the leagues from the state can be measured by the ratio of the resources allocated by the state to the full budget of the leagues (Ramanantsoa and Thiery-Baslé, 1989: 60). This ratio varied considerably according to organization studied. However, even if certain leagues manage to obtain significant resources from sponsoring contracts, state subsidies represent an indispensable source of revenue for most of them. The majority of French sporting leagues are dependent on state resources. This can be considered as a kind of external control upon the organizations insofar as it is described by Jeffre Pfeffer and Gerald R. Salancik.[4] This situation of dependence raises the question of the strategic autonomy of these leagues.

Thus, the sporting leagues can in many ways be considered as para-administrative extensions of the State Office for Youth and Sports (Houel, 1988) and as bureaucratic structures providing a mission of public service.

1.3 The Sporting Leagues and Their Markets

Unlike many public administrations, the sporting leagues have to conquer a market. This one in particular is made up of all current potential clients: in other words, current and future permit-holders. They are in fact social agents ready to exchange money and time in order to undertake athletic training, to participate in competitions and to manage the leagues.

1.3.1 A Social Distribution of Practices[5]

Contrary to common belief, there is not only one athletic market but several. In fact, the work of sociologists interested in sport consumption (Pociello, 1981; Irlinger, Louveau and Métoudi, 1987; Michon, 1988) emphasized the existence of a social distribution of practices.

Practicing a sport constitutes an element of lifestyle, just like the consumption of food, of art, etc. (Bourdieu, 1978). The choice of sport which one practices works as an indicator of one's social position (Bourdieu, 1990b: 158). From this, it is then possible to distinguish different markets. For example, wrestling and golf do not have the same markets: the former addresses itself to the agents occupying a position dominated within the social space, while the latter recruits its members from the dominant class.

1.3.2 Internalization of the Client

If the consideration of different markets allows one to discriminate between different sporting leagues, the process of the internalization of the client is a common denominator at the root of the specificity of this kind of organization. Indeed, unlike in traditional enterprises, the client bases his/her status on the exterior from the instant that s/he decides to buy the services offered by the sporting leagues: that is to say, to become a permit holder. S/he then wholly becomes a member of the organization. This process is called "internalization".

This situation leads to a paradox: the person in question is in the league and the market at one and the same time. If, as the possessor of a permit, a person is a member of the organization, s/he is all the same free not to re-subscribe to the services of the sporting leagues, thus to leave the league.

This obviously leads to the problem of boundaries (Who is inside? Who is outside?) and, in the same way, to an identity problem (Reitter and Ramanantsoa, 1985).

Our interviews with numerous sporting executives confirmed the existence of a certain haziness surrounding the definition of the boundaries of these organizations.

Actually, we can identify several populations:
• the permit-holders, members of a club;
• the permit-holders elected to executive position at different levels: the club, the regional league, national committees;
• the employees of the national league: administrative personnel, accountants;
• hired teachers in the clubs;
• the technical managers made available by the State Office for Youth and Sports.
Beyond the unifying speeches held by the executives of the leagues, we noticed a variation in the definition of the boundaries according to the category of the person

questioned. In fact, the imposition of a legitimate definition of the boundaries is one of the stakes of the field studied.

One could think that the possession of a certificate from the league is proof of membership in the league. This definition would imply that the teachers of the club, technical managers and administrative personnel would be "on the exterior of the league". But things are not that simple. Certain people in nationally-elected positions put forward a much more restricted definition of the league: "the league, that's us". Here "us" should be understood as "us, the national executives". From this perspective, the clubs are seen as clients. On the other hand, one finds discussion at the level of the club which defines the league as a "big family made up of all the people to contribute to the life of local and national structures".

1.4 Towards a Typology of the Sporting Leagues

We saw that the leagues were bureaucratic extensions of the state and organizations confronted with the market at the same time. In certain ways, the leagues resemble public enterprises. They actually have to reconcile a mission of public service with a necessity to conquer a market. "The directors of the public enterprises thus have two constraints imposed upon them: a constraint of the market, of a classical kind, and a political constraint, very direct, although complex. In comparison with private enterprise, political constraints distinguish public enterprises. In comparison with the administrative public services, it is the opposite – the constraint of the market. (Anastassopoulos, 1990b: 46-47).

But, unlike public enterprises, the sporting leagues are associative structures. They are characterized notably by a system of democratic election. The executives are in fact permit-holders and volunteers, elected by their peers. These structures carry with them an associative culture placing their main importance on the value of amateurism, olympicism, a disinterest in profit and "free access to sports". This culture is expressed through speeches on the executives' devotion and full-fledged commitment or through long tirades defending the "league spirit" (Chifflet, 1988).

According to the leagues, one or the other of these logics will be more or less fruitful. Thus, ice hockey very clearly follows a managerial logic. As we will see in the last part, there is an overrepresentation of directors-in-chief among the national ice hockey executives. These agents are preoccupied by the search for financial means from the enterprises. They consider the process of professionalization of sports normal and speak in terms of "return on investments". At the top of this organization, there is a president manager, who is himself director of several enterprises.

Speed-skating is a perfect illustration of a structure dominated by an associative culture. Volunteerism, respect for fair play, the defence of amateurism, the refusal to compromise with the business world: all this is at the base of the identity of this organization.

Finally, the French league of physical education and gymnastics, in addition to being an associative culture, is strongly characterized by a public service culture. Its executives feel deeply involved in a mission of education. Among them, there is a great proportion of teachers of physical and sports education who are trained and recruited by the state.

2   The Internal Functioning of the Leagues or the Existence of Another Type of Market

Until this point, we considered links existing between the leagues and their environment. We were led to emphasize the specificity of this type of structure focusing on their strategy and touching upon their organization. In this section, we will deepen our analysis of their internal functioning: whether it concerns their organization or their identity, the "production" mechanism of the executives seems to us to be a significant analytical tool.

2.1   The Theoretical Frame

In this research project, we will use the theory of the *habitus* and the *field* of Pierre Bourdieu as a theoretical frame. Before discussing the hypotheses proposed, we will summarize the basic tenets of this theory.

Pierre Bourdieu showed that "the conditionings associated with a particular class of conditions of existence produce *habitus,* systems of durable, transposable dispositions, structured structures predisposed to function as structuring structures, that is, as principles which generate and organize practices and representations" (Bourdieu, 1990a: 53). Thus the *habitus* acts as a *generating grammar of behaviours* (in the meaning of Chomsky), social agents seeing the world through the spectacles of their *habitus*. "The cognitive structures which social agents implement in their practical knowledge of the social world are internalized, 'embodied' social structures" (Bourdieu, 1989: 468).

This concept of *habitus* allows us to explain the correspondence we find between the *space of social positions* and the *space of lifestyles*. The position occupied by the agents in the social space depends on the global *volume* of the capital possessed (expressing the entirety of the resources and powers at the agent's disposal) as well as its *structure* (this *structure* reflecting the different types of capital, that is the composition of the global capital). Bourdieu distinguishes *economic capital* (income, the possession of coinable goods), *cultural capital* (where the possession of a diploma constitutes the institutionalized state) and *social capital* (the network of relationships). The material properties are joined by symbolic properties (referring back to the systems of representations), from which the agents can derive benefits. In this way, we can speak about *symbolic capital*. Finally, in the world of the sporting leagues we are studying, we will be led to consider the existence of a *technical capital* reflecting the advantages that an athlete can derive thanks to his/her mastery of a sporting skill.

> To have as exact an idea as possible of the theoretical model that is proposed, it has to be imagined that three diagrams are superimposed (as could be done with transparent sheets). The first presents the space of social conditions as organized by the synchronic and diachronic distribution of the volume and composition of the various kinds of capital (...). The second presents the space of life-styles, i.e., the distribution of the practices and properties which constitute the life-style in which each of these conditions manifests itself. Finally, between the two previous diagrams one ought to insert a third, the theoretical space of *habitus*, that is the generative formulae (e.g., for teachers, aristocratic asceticism) which underlie each of the classes of practices and properties, that is, the transformation into a distinct and distinctive life-style of the necessities and facilities characteristic of a condition and a position (Bourdieu, 1989: 126).

The agents present in the social space are involved in different *fields*. These *fields* function as markets in which struggles between people endowed with capital are organized. In each *field*, there are things at stake and rules of the game. "In order for the *field* to work, it is necessary to have things at stake and people who are ready to play the game, endowed with the *habitus* which implies the knowledge, and acknowledgement of the immanent laws of the game, the stakes, etc. ..." (Bourdieu, 1984: 114). Beyond the struggles, there is an *objective complicity* between the agents of the *field*, a complicity which pertains to the existence of a consensus on the stakes.

In our research project, we consider that a sporting league functions as a *field* where one of the things at stake is in fact access to the positions of the national executives.

2.2 Hypotheses of Research and Methodology

2.2.1 Research Hypotheses

With reference to the systematic theory of the *habitus* and the *field* of Pierre Bourdieu, we propose to demonstrate that there are significant differences between the studied sporting leagues according to the volume and the structure of the capital possessed by their executives.

The study of the selection process of the national executives should allow us to clarify the existence of *elective filters* only allowing the agents endowed with certain properties considered important in the *field* to pass through. These filters reveal some of the rules of the game and, in the same way, the identity of the *field* studied.

Finally, we think that differences exist in the way the sporting leagues are managed, differences that are partially explained by the social characteristics of their executives.

2.2.2 Methodology

The Populations Studied

In the framework of this research, we studied four national sports committees. In each case, we collected information concerning *all of the candidates* in the 1988 sporting league elections. They are as follows:
– the national committee of figure-skating: 6 men and 13 women;
– the national committee of ice-dancing: 10 men and 8 women;
– the national committee of speed-skating: 12 men and 2 women;
– the national committee of ice hockey: 17 men and 1 woman.
These agents are all executives of local or regional structures and are candidates for a national post.

The Techniques of Data Collection

a) Candidates' Files
   We collected information relative to the sex, the age, and the profession of the candidates provided by these agents at the moment when their candidacy file was opened. These data were completed with the help of interviews with some of the league directors (notably concerning the academic diplomas possessed).
b) Investigation through Interviews
   We made the interviewing guidelines from a group of indicators reflecting the socio-cultural properties of the directors as well as the way they manage the committees of which they are in charge.
c) Minutes from Meetings
   In order to complete the information relative to the management of the different organizations, we collected the minutes of the executive committee meeting that summarize all the decisions made during such meetings.

2.3 Results Obtained

In order to bring out the volume and the structure of the capital possessed by the candidates, we were compelled to classify them according to the profession exercised. It would have been preferable, of course, to have had access to precise data concerning the size of their income and the diploma they possess. However, the knowledge of the profession exercised by the agent completed with the data relative to the level of education (data collected during the interviews) gives what is an apparently sufficient accuracy to the classification. For example, we noticed that most of the candidates who were executive directors did not have a higher education degree. This justifies the fact that "executive director" belongs to the category of "agents endowed with a structured, economically dominant capital".

Thus, we can make the following distinctions:
- For the "volume":
  High Volume: Executive directors, managers and highly-intellectual professions.
  Average Volume: Middle-level positions, craftsmen, tradesmen and the like.
  Low Volume: Employees.
  Not Defined: Retired people, people without a professional occupation.
- For the "structure":
  Economic Predominance: Craftsmen, tradesmen, executive directors.
  Cultural Predominance: Highly-intellectual professions, middle-level teaching positions.
  Balanced Structure: Managers, middle-level positions (except teachers and the like), employees.
  Not Defined: Retired people, people without a professional occupation.

Farmers and labourers do not figure into these groups since no candidates belonged to these categories.

2.3.1 The Figure-skating Executives: "Women in Power"

1) *The Candidates:* Figure skating is populated by women equally as much at the level of practice (81%)[6] as at the level of management. Indeed, 19 candidates announced their candidacy for the 1988 national elections, of whom 13 were women. Among these women, five do not have a profession.

As for the volume of capital, the figure obtained in high volume (9/19) is not in itself sufficient for us to draw any conclusions. However, the absence of agents endowed with a low volume of capital and the knowledge of the profession of the spouses of certain candidates allows us to consider the executives of figure-skating as belonging to a relatively wealthy social class.

The "balanced structure" category is the most important. Here again, we must take into account the "not defined".

Finally, we should mention that more than half of the candidates are figure-skating judges.

2) *The Elected Members:* In figure-skating, the possession of a high technical capital (i.e. being a judge) and a high availability seem to constitute the key factors to success.

Indeed, 7/9 of the committee members are judges, while only nine judges were candidates; and of the five candidates without a profession, four were elected. In addition, the committee has the particularity that the majority of the members are women (6/9).

2.3.2 Ice-dancing Executives: "A Double Filter"

1) *The Candidates:* Among the 18 candidates, ten of them are men – although 77.3% of the permit-holders are women.

The population is characterized by a lack of agents endowed with a low volume of capital.

Eight out of 18 are in the average volume category, and seven of the 18 possess a high volume of capital.

The structure of the capital reveals a relatively high number of agents endowed with a culturally-predominant capital (almost 1/3 of the candidates, the highest percentage of the four committees studied).

As in figure-skating, numerous candidates are judges (8 out of 18).

2) *The Elected Members:*   The election results favour men. Indeed, one out of two men is elected, while only one out of four women is elected. The average age of the elected members is clearly less than that of the candidates (40.5 as opposed to 46 years old).

The candidates/elected members comparison emphasizes the existence of a social selection. The agents most heavily endowed with capital obtained the best results. In fact, five out of the seven agents with a high volume of capital are elected, while only one out of eight agents with a low volume of capital are elected. Judges jump the hurdle of the elections quite easily as 62.5% of those who were elected (as opposed to the average success rate of 38.9%).

Therefore, it can be said that there is a double filter, both "technical" and "social", in ice-dancing.

2.3.3 Speed-skating Executives: "Volunteer Coaches"

1) *The Candidates:*   Four out of ten permit-holders are women, while this proportion is considerably lower among the candidates: two out of 14.

As for the volume of capital possessed by the candidates, none have a "high volume". Eleven out of 14 have an average volume of capital, and two out of 14 have a small volume.

Among these 14 candidates, six volunteer as coaches in a club.

2) *The Elected Members*:   Here again, the average age of the elected members is less than that of the candidates (40.7 rather than 43.5 years old).

It is interesting to note that the two candidates endowed with a low volume of capital were both elected.

In addition, out of the six coaches who were candidates, four became committee members.

Thus, in speed skating, belonging to a socially-dominated category does not seem to constitute an obstacle on the road to a position as a national executive. The favourable results obtained by the coaches betray the existence of a technical filter.

2.3.4 Ice Hockey Executives: "A Business of Men and Money"

1) *The Candidates:*   In comparison to the other disciplines, these are the oldest candidates: their average age is 48.5.

Among the candidates, 94.4% are men, a proportion comparable to that of the permit-holders (95.5%).

The most highly-represented socio-professional category is that of the executive directors, with one third of the candidates.

Considering the volume of capital possessed by the agents, we find that the percentage of high-volume capital-holders is greater than in the other disciplines.

As for the structure of the capital, the percentage of agents with economically-predominant capital is higher than in all the other committees (one third of the candidates). Most of them are self-taught executive directors.

Finally, among the 18 candidates, seven declared themselves as being former players or referees.

2) *The Elected Members:* The average age of the elected members is essentially identical to that of the candidates.

The national committee is exclusively made up of men. The only woman who was a candidate had apparently a smaller chance of being elected because she belongs to a socioculturally-dominated category (employee).

Actually, among the elected candidates, seven out of the nine are endowed with a high volume of capital; and a third of the committee is made up of chief executives. Unlike the other disciplines, technicians do not form the majority.

2.3.5 The Management of the National Committees: Some Significant Differences[7]

After having looked at the selection mechanisms of the executives, we studied the way these elected members managed the organization of which they were in charge. We thus conducted some interviews with the presidents of the organizations and analysed the minutes of the executive committee.

In these associative structures, the elected president, in accordance with the regulations, enjoys considerable power. By fixing the agenda, he defines the themes that must be addressed and thus exercises a very strong influence over the development of the organization's strategy – as is emphasized by the administrative director of one sporting league. "The president is not the president for nothing. He is the strongest personality, he has made a name for himself. He is the one who calls the shots and makes the decisions. The minutes established by the president reveal what he is up to during a meeting."

Revealing differences appeared between the organizations concerning their resource allocation. It is in ice hockey where we see an overrepresentation of company directors (agents endowed with a large volume of capital of economic importance) and an underrepresentation of players and referees (agents endowed with a specific technical capital), that we can find real strategic links with external economic partners.[8] The president of this organization (who never played hockey) is a self-made man, the son of a tradesman who became a company executive: "All my life I had to fight. It is not by making hesitant choices that you can hope to win. You have to go for it and win. He who tries nothing has nothing!" His predecessor did not have the same viewpoint concerning management according to the national technical director (a high-ranking civil servant appointed by the ministry and at the service of a sporting league): "The main concern of the current president was to find sponsors, to be on TV and to valorize his sport. He is for "exteriorization", business. His predecessor was an agent of a territorial group. He managed rather as a civil servant (...), he had a better knowledge of the rules, but was a little hesitant. Now we have a man belonging to the private sector who has a different vision. With him we charge ahead, we commit, even exceed the budgets but we hold in there by finding external finance. He does not talk about training methods or selection. He has a national coach for that." When questioned about his major goals, the president said, "The first priority is to sell ice hockey. In hockey, we are naturally men of tremendous drive. Either I manage to change things or I leave".

On the contrary, in speed-skating – where the organization is led by former skaters, most of them endowed with a moderate economic and cultural capital – we can notice a critical attitude towards the bringing together of sport and enterprise. The president is a craftsman and coaches voluntarily in a club. He is married to a physical education teacher who also teaches speed-skating. He considers that "money spoils sport. The more sponsors there are, the less free the sporting leagues will be". His concerns are more oriented towards the training of executives and towards sport technique. He has created different committees in order to study these problems and spends a large part of the budget of his organization on the training of the teachers and executives. He is convinced that the managers of sporting leagues must not model themselves after company managers: "A person who takes care of sportsmen should not consider his job as he would in an enterprise. A company manager who is involved in sports will have a tendency to think about the sport as an enterprise and the sportsmen as employees. I am uncomfortable when I talk sports with such people because something utterly different is in question. I am more of the type who practiced on the field, the one who knows what being an athlete means".

In ice-dancing, the president, a former high-ranking athlete is the financial manager of a small family business. The way he manages reveals an accountant's rigor. Unlike the president of the ice hockey league, he will not commit himself to action until after he has made sure he has enough money to finance it. The resources are mainly granted to top athletes with whom the president is willing to sign a true "moral contract". According to him, "A good manager is a clear thinker, he looks for equality at all cost and, when in doubt will give the benefit of the doubt to sportsmen".

Finally, in figure-skating, the president has no profession; she devotes all her time to figure-skating. She has no special knowledge of administration. She believes a national organization can be managed like a local sporting club. This organization is handled according to the traditional associative pattern in which a clear distinction is made between amateurs and professionals. The members of the leading committee of this sporting league are, in the majority of cases, international figure-skating judges. In the words of the president, "to be a good manager, one must first be an excellent technician".

These few examples show that the consideration of *social properties*, the *trajectory* and the *habitus* of the agent as well as the *characteristics of the field* allow a better understanding of some strategic choices.

3   Conclusion

By means of this research, we think that we have contributed to a better understanding of the functioning of sporting leagues.

The notion of *elective filters* that we proposed demonstrates the selection mechanisms of the executives. The nature of the filters reveals the logic of the *field* and in the same way the culture of the organizations studied.[9]

The consideration of the social properties and the *habitus* of the social executives, as well as the consideration of the characteristics of the *field,* allow to partially explain the strategic choices made.

In the comparative perspective adopted, the size of the sample was a limiting factor. Further research should permit us, through a wider scope of study, to propose a typology of the sporting leagues according to the social properties of their executives (*the space of the sporting league executives*). Moreover, it should be possible to create a *space of management styles* of the federations from a comparison of the ways the executives manage the organizations that they are in charge of. We therefore verify the existence of a homologous relationship between these two spaces.

Notes

1   See notably Ramanantsoa and Thiery-Baslé, 1989. Moingeon, 1991.
2   We studied the following sporting leagues: The French Equestrian League; The French Volleyball League; The French Soccer League; The French Tennis League; The French Table-Tennis League; The French Golf League; The French Physical Education and Gymnastics League; The French Figure-skating League (part of the French Ice Sports League); The French Ice-dancing League (part of the French Ice Sports League); The French Ice Hockey League (part of the French Ice Sports League); The French Speed-skating League (part of the French Ice Sports League).

3   This concept was proposed by H. Jamous and taken up again by M. Crozier. A *"marginal sécant"* belongs to several systems of actions. He can be an interpreter between the logics of different actions. See notably Jamous, 1968; Crozier and Friedberg, 1978.

4   In their work, Pfeffer and Salancik describe the mechanism which drives the organizations to be dependent on their environment. According to them, in order to acquire the resources that are indispensable to their functioning, all organizations must interact with their environment. Because it is dependent on its imported resources, the organization is dependent upon its environment (Pfeffer and Salancik, 1978).

5   See the graphic representation of the space of social positions and the space of life-styles proposed by Pierre Bourdieu (Bourdieu, 1990: 128-129).

6   The data relative to the permit-holders comes from league data (the1988 season).

7   The results communicated in this section were already communicated at the time of the IAREP/SASE conference: Ramanantsoa and Moingeon, 1991.

8   These strategies of alliances differ from the relational strategies put into action by the leagues during their interventions with the state. See Ramanantsoa and Thiery-Baslé, 1989.

9   For a detailed account of the relationships between culture and leadership, see Schein, 1985.

References

Anastassopoulos, J.P. (1980) *La stratégie des entreprises publiques.* Paris: Dalloz.

Bourdieu, P. (1978) 'Sport and Social Class', *Information sur les sciences sociales* 17 (6).

Bourdieu, P. (1984) *Questions de sociologie.* Paris: Ed. de Minuit.

Bourdieu, P. (1989) *Distinction. A Social Critique of the Judgement of Taste.* London: Routledge (Originally appeared in 1979).

Bourdieu, P. (1990a) *The Logic of Practice.* Stanford: Stanford University Press (Originally appeared in 1980).

Bourdieu, P. (1990b) *In Other Words. Essays towards a Reflexive Sociology.* Stanford: Stanford University Press (Originally appeared in 1987).

Chifflet, P. (1988) 'Les fédérations sportives, politiques et stratégies', in Michon, B. (ed.), op. cit.

Crozier, M./Friedberg, E. (1978)*Actors and Systems.* Chicago: University of Chicago Press (Originally appeared in 1977).

Houel, J. (1988) 'La politique du sport', in Michon, B. (ed.), op. cit.

Irlinger, P./Louveau, C./Métoudi, M. (1987) *Les pratiques sportives des français.* Paris: INSEP.

Jamous, H. (1968) *Contribution à une sociologie de la décision: la réforme des études médicales et des structures hospitalières,* Paris. Copédith.

Meynaud, J. (1966) *Sport et politique.* Paris: Payot.

Michon, B. (ed.). (1988) *Sciences sociales et sport, état et perspective. Actes des journées d'études de Strasbourg de novembre 1987.* Strasbourg: Labouratoire APS et sciences sociales.

Moingeon, B. (1991) *Contribution à une socio-économie des organisations. L'exemple d'un univers associatif.* Thèse de Doctorat de sociologie, Université de Franche-Comté.

Pfeffer, J./Salancik, G. R. (1978) *The External Control of Organizations. A Resource Dependance Perspective.* Harper and Row.

Pociello, C. (1981) *Sport et société: approche socio-culturelle des pratiques.* Paris: Vigot.

Ramanantsoa, B./Moingeon, B. (1991) *Contribution to Socio-Economics on the Strategic Approach.* IAREP/SASE Conference on Interdisciplinary Approaches to the Study of Economics Problems, Stockholm School of Economics (June).

Ramanantsoa, B./Thiery-Baslé, C. (1989) *Organisations et fédérations sportives, sociologie et management.* Paris: PUF.

Reitter, R./Ramanantsoa, B. (1985) *Pouvoir et politique. Au delà de la culture d'entreprise.* Paris: McGraw-Hill.

Schein, E.H. (1985) *Organizational Culture and Leadership. A Dynamic View.* San Francisco: Jossey-Bass.

Thomas. R./Haumont. A./Levet, J.L. (1987) *Sociologie du sport.* Paris: PUF.

Part IV

INDUSTRIAL DISTRICTS AND REGIONAL COMPETITION

CHAPTER 8

Contemporary Relationships Between Firms in a Classic Industrial District: Evidence from the Social Change and Economic Life Initiative

Roger Penn*

1   Introduction

This paper examines the relations between firms across a wide spectrum of industrial sectors in Rochdale. The analysis is set within the recent renewal of interest amongst economic sociologists and economic geographers in the notion of the industrial district.[1] Rochdale can be examined both as a local industrial district with a distinct network of interrelated firms and also as a part of a wider metropolitan district in and around Manchester. In the latter case, we can compare contemporary Rochdale with the situation in the latter nineteenth and early twentieth centuries, when the town formed an element within the wider industrial district of south-east Lancashire. Indeed, this historic industrial district formed the exemplar for Marshall's (1923) original classic economic analysis of industrial districts.

Marshall argued that Lancashire in the period before 1914 could "be seen perhaps [as] the best present instance of concentrated organization"[2] in the world and that the high levels of specialization amongst the large number of small and medium-sized textile firms in the area represented "more than one million [employees] in a composite business". For Marshall the external economies achieved by this highly differentiated but spontaneous network of firms far outweighed any likely advantages accruing from possible coordination by a small number of large producers. The present paper presents a re-examination of the structure of firms within textiles, amongst other industrial sectors, in Rochdale during the 1980s, thereby providing an interesting counterpoint to Marshall's classic analysis.

Furthermore, there has been considerable recent international research that has suggested that *cooperation* is a major feature of the normal relations between small and medium-sized firms in a range of spatial contexts (see Pyke et al., 1991). The International Labour Office (1987) reported that small firms were likely to perform particularly well in localities where they were embedded in social structures that encouraged continuous cooperation. Raveyre (1986) demonstrated that there has been a significant growth in France of cooperative relations of interdependence between large manufacturing companies and smaller supplier firms, particularly in the area of transferring technological expertise. Saglio (1984) and Pyke (1987) have shown how networks of firms have developed in association with a mixture of cooperative and competitive practices. Checkland (1981) utilized the metaphor of the Upas tree[3] to explain how the large metal-working firms in Glasgow acted as a barrier to the development of smaller firms in his historical analysis of employment change on the Clyde. Other commentators[4] have focused on the role of Japanese-owned firms, both in Japan and, more recently, in Britain, in combining conventional competitive behaviour within product markets alongside strong cooperative relations in the spheres of research and development.

The most influential analysis along these lines, however, has been Piore and Sabel's *The Second Industrial Divide* (1984). Relying considerably on Bagnasco's (1977) earlier exposition of the characteristics of the "Third Italy", Piore and Sabel argued that the present era was witnessing a conflict between two axial forms of economic activity. The first involved large-scale manufacturing firms utilizing mass production and competitive marketing techniques to supply mass consumption goods. The alternative pattern, revealed in its classic form in the Emilia-Romagna region of Italy in and around Bologna, involved the use of flexible manufacturing systems to provide customized products for a differentiated range of consumer demands. Such firms are portrayed as predominantly small or medium-sized and as operating within a close network of cooperative relations in localized industrial districts. These ideas have enjoyed considerable popularity recently within certain political circles in Britain, particularly those on the left of the political spectrum. Murray (1985) advocated the sponsorship of such networks, a viewpoint incorporated both within the Labour Party's Draft Programme for the 1990s and the Communist Party's *Manifesto for New Times* (1988). Indeed, part of the thrust of the present paper is to provide an empirical analysis of *existing relations* between firms in a classic industrial district with a view to the creation of a clearer picture of how, in fact, firms do interrelate in the present conjuncture in Britain.

The present paper focuses primarily on the existence of and possible growth of subcontracting relations amongst firms in Rochdale in the 1980s. Both Murray (1985), in his discussion of Benetton, and Atkinson and Meager (1986), in their analysis of flexibility in Britain, and Piore and Sabel (1984), see this area of cooperative inter-firm relations as central to their prognoses of structural transformation. Murray cites the example of the clothing industry in northern Italy where most workers manufacturing Benetton clothes work not for Benetton itself but for small, independent, subcontracting firms. Murray proclaims, on the basis of this evidence, that in Britain "in industry after industry a parallel restructuring has been taking place". Atkinson and Meager also see subcontracting as an essential element of rational corporate action in the contemporary period since in their view, it reduces labour costs significantly by permitting firms to minimize their direct dependence upon external market fluctuations. Recently, these ideas have become enmeshed in eschatological claims about the transformation of modern capitalist societies from a Fordist to a post-Fordist stage of development (see Aglietta, 1979; Murray, 1988; and Harvey, 1989). The present paper provides a systematic assessment of sub-contracting relations between and amongst establishments in Rochdale and should be seen both as a contribution to the operationalization of these recent ideas and as an antidote to the rather speculative mode of analysis now prevalent amongst many writers in this area.

2   The Development of Rochdale as an Industrial District

We can identify three historical stages[5] in the development of Rochdale as an industrial district (Figure 8.1). Each subsequent stage can be conceptualized as overlaying the former. Indeed, by the mid-1980s the structure of industrial interconnections within Rochdale manufacturing industry had become highly complex. The first stage in the development of the local industrial district centred upon the rise of textile production in Rochdale. By 1860 Rochdale was a classic urban example of early industrial capitalism, dominated by factory production and containing a large number of mainly manual working-class occupations in textiles (Penn, 1985). The dynamic behind this social transformation was undoubtedly the general rise of the British textile industry after 1780 (see Penn, 1985, for further details). By 1851 there were over 13,000 people employed directly in textiles in Rochdale. Furthermore, within the wider south-east Lancashire belt, of which Rochdale formed a key element, a large number of other industries developed in a symbiotic relationship to textiles. These included clothing production, chemicals for use predominantly in textile finishing activities and paper manufacture.[6] The latter was located close to textile production since at that time it was manufactured mainly from cotton waste. Furthermore, there were almost 1,000 workers employed by "machine-makers" in Rochdale in 1851, almost all of whom were engaged in the manufacture of textile machinery (Penn, 1985). By the mid-1860s, the classic bifurcated structure of manufacturing output in Rochdale, which was also typical of the wider south-east Lancashire industrial belt, had been formed around the two core activities of textile manufacture and machine making.

Figure 8.1: The Development of Manufacturing Industry in Rochdale, 1800-1986

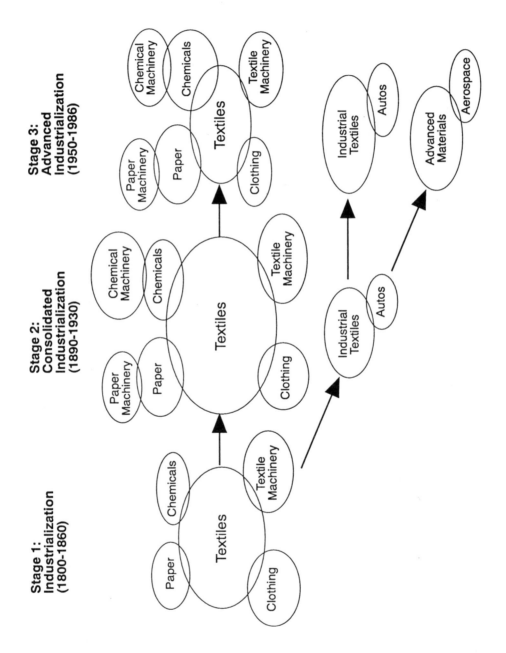

*   The area of the ellipses in the diagram is approximately proportional to the numbers employed in the industrial sector.

These two sectors have continued to dominate employment in the town :

Table 8.1:   **Numbers of Workers (Male and Female) Employed in the Textile and Engineering Industries in Rochdale**

	Textiles	Engineering
1861	11,584	930
1891	14,311	1,461
1911	23,816	5,632
1931	18,655	4,265
1961	9,481	5,060
1981	6,000	6,500

Sources: Penn, 1985; Haughton, 1985.

The second stage in the development of manufacturing industry in Rochdale witnessed the growth of industrial textiles. The classic nineteenth-century textile industry had been based exclusively upon the manufacture of cotton, most of which was designed for direct consumption by households in the form of such items as clothing, curtains and tablecloths. Industrial textiles, on the other hand, involved the manufacture of specialist fibres that had direct industrial uses. In the case of Rochdale, the initial rise of industrial textiles was centred upon asbestos production.

By the early 1920s Turner Brothers Asbestos (TBA) had become the largest local employer, employing well over 1,000 people. In the 1920s, TBA formed the cornerstone and provided the headquarters site of Turner and Newall, the newly-formed British multinational conglomerate. In this period Turner and Newall's worldwide operations were centred at the Rochdale asbestos plant. The output of the Rochdale plant had many uses, including conveyor belts in steel plants, fire-safety curtains and shed roofing. However, the most significant use was as a core element within the composites used for brake-linings and gaskets in the burgeoning automobile industry.[7] As we shall see, the close connection between industrial textiles and automobiles continues to be of considerable significance in contemporary Rochdale.

The newly emergent industrial textile sector *overlaid but did not replace* the earlier classical structures of industrialized employment. Cotton textile production continued to be of major significance, although its long-term secular decline can be dated from the early 1920s. The local paper industry also flourished in the inter-war period but became more independent of cotton waste as a source of materials.

Chemicals likewise became more differentiated, with the development of such specialized activities as the production of paints and industrial inks. Nevertheless, there remained a close symbiosis between chemicals and textile finishing (the latter being itself a Rochdale specialism).

The engineering industry remained heavily focused on the manufacture of textile machinery. Nevertheless, there was a parallel growth of the manufacture of paper and chemical machinery. Since the 1860s, machine-making in Rochdale had developed into an international industry with considerable exports of equipment. Nevertheless, many local textile, paper and chemical firms purchased locally manufactured machinery. There were many advantages for both machine-using and machine-making firms in these local links. The users of the machinery could call upon expert advice concerning their equipment close to hand, whilst local machine-makers themselves could learn about new market needs by observation and discussion within these local manufacturing plants.

The third stage in the development of Rochdale manufacturing industry witnessed the emergence of an advanced materials sector. This has grown out of industrial textiles in the period since 1950. Rochdale firms such as TBA and Fothergill and Harvey pioneered the manufacture of carbon and glass fibres, kevlar and boron filaments.[8] These fibres are often combined with other materials like rubber or plastics to form composites. Rochdale has become a centre for both the manufacture and the engineering of such composites. Interestingly, the paper industry has also become linked into this newly emergent sector via the route of non-woven fabrics. Indeed, non-wovens should be seen as textile fibres manufactured utilizing paper industry processes of production.

There is an intimate link between these advanced materials' firms and the aerospace industry. Aerospace itself is not a significant employer within Rochdale itself but there are several very large plants within ten miles of the town centre, notably at Chadderton and in Oldham. A series of examples illustrate the nature of contemporary linkages. The nose-cone of Concorde is made from carbon fibres. Contemporary missiles have specialist papers within their structures to deflect and confuse radar scanners. The cabling in modern warships is surrounded by textile materials that can withstand the kind of high temperatures generated by explosions and fires, particularly those seen during the Falklands war in 1982.

Advanced materials, industrial textiles and standard consumer textiles are all present within contemporary Rochdale.[9] Indeed, they are often undertaken by the same firm within the same plant. Each sector of textiles and advanced materials has close links with other industrial sectors. The overall set of industries forms an integrated network of firms within the locality that intersects with a wider network of such firms throughout the south-east Lancashire belt of industrial towns.

Clearly, this analysis of the emergence of contemporary industrial patterns in Rochdale suggests the likelihood of a closely interdependent set of local firms.

Indeed, there remained around 100 textile mills and over 350 engineering plants today within the Rochdale travel-to-work-area in 1986. A main aim of the empirical research undertaken by the Lancaster Social Change and Economic Life Initiative[10] team in the period between 1986 and 1989 was to develop an empirical analysis of the internal and external relations within and between these firms, particularly between relatively large organizations and smaller putative subcontracting firms. The data in this paper have been derived primarily from two sets of sources: a survey of 32 establishments undertaken in 1987 and 1988, and a series of intensive case-studies completed between 1986 and 1989. Both analyses covered organizations in textiles, engineering, paper, chemicals, public services, telecommunications, financial services, retailing, transport and distribution. The 32 establishment data were collected by two members of the Lancaster research team in face-to-face interviews with managerial representatives at these establishments. Supplementary data were subsequently provided by letter and/or by telephone. Additional information was then obtained from relevant trade union officers. The case-studies were undertaken by the same two researchers. They utilized either a postal questionnaire or a parallel questionnaire left with respondents depending upon the sector involved. These questionnaire data were supplemented with semi-structured interviews with other managerial respondents, pertinent trade union officials and, wherever possible, workforce representatives.[11]

3 Forms of Relations Between Large and Small Firms

There are at least four forms of relationship between large and small firms that can be identified theoretically. The first involves the classic *satellite* relationship between large firms and a series of independent, unrelated, smaller firms. Such smaller firms can provide a series of functions for large firms ranging from the supply of components to the production of entire machine modules. These relationships are coordinated by market relations between the firms involved.

However, there are two new forms of relations between large and small firms that are thought to have emerged in recent years and that are central to recent debates in economic sociology and economic geography. The first involves a much stronger interaction between the larger and smaller firms whereby the large firm actively engages in the internal functioning of small firms. The classic examples of these types of development are found in Japanese plants, notably those owned by Nissan and Komatsu in north-east England. In these well-publicized instances, the large firm actively penetrates the internal structures of the small components' firms both to ensure adequate quality control and to sponsor technological innovation directly. Of course, such relations can also exist between large firms, as was illustrated by the links between Thames Board and Kelloggs over the development of improved cartonboards for cereal packaging in the mid-1980s (see Penn, 1988). We can label this mode of relationship as *active engagement*. The second new form of relationship between small and large firms can be illustrated in its purest form in the contemporary clothing industry. Two developments in the retailing of clothes have affected small producers of such clothing.[12] Retailing in Britain is dominated by a small number of large companies, of which Marks and Spencer is the most famous. In addition, there are now five distinct phases to the clothing year in terms of sales. This means that clothing suppliers must react swiftly to the ebbs and flows of customer demand in the shops since retailers do not wish to hold large stocks. Pyke (1987) has shown how small clothing firms in Macclesfield – itself part of a clothing district comprising Macclesfield, Congleton and Leek – have entered into cooperative relations in order to supply these large orders from the large clothing retailers. Pyke's research revealed that local clothing firms, which for many years had kept their businesses closely guarded, were now openly engaged in discussions as to how they could cooperate together in order to respond to orders which were too large for any individual firm to take on. Pyke has shown in detail the contours of such cooperation. For example, firms may lend each other scarce skilled workers; a firm might have a specialized machine which it allows another firm to utilize from time to time; firms may recommend one another to customers; information on new technology or new market possibilities might be exchanged and assistance with storage might be given. Nevertheless, such cooperation between independent small firms is undertaken under the aegis of the large retailing corporations which intervene to structure these cooperative relations. Crucially, it is they who decide upon the presence of specific small firms within these cooperative relations. Such a pattern of inter-firm relations can be termed *subordinate cooperation*.

The final form of relations between small and large firms is one where small firms acting in concert create an alternative mode of producing to the classic satellite relationship of dependency. Such *independent cooperation* between small firms has been portrayed in detail by Brusco (1986) in Italy and Ravèyre (1986) in France. It is central to the general imagery of post-Fordism and the "second industrial divide" discussed earlier.[13] However, there has been little rigorous empirical research to determine the salience of this model in Britain. Whilst our data cannot present an exhaustive test of these models, they can provide a partial examination of them within the context of a more general analysis of relations between employers in Rochdale.

4   Subcontracting in Rochdale

Our data from 32 establishments collected in Rochdale during 1987 and 1988 examined details both of the use of subcontractors by firms and whether the firm itself acted as a subcontractor. Respondents were also asked whether subcontracting at the establishment was increasing or decreasing, whether it was a new phenom-

Table 8.2: Use of Subcontractors by Firms and Whether the Firm Itself Acts as a Subcontractor (32 Establishment Data)

Variable	Textiles		Engineering		Other Manufacturing
	Industrial	Consumer	Machine-makers	General	
Use of Sub-contractors	Y X X	X X X	Y Y Y Y X	X Y X	Y X X
Subcontractor	X X X	X X X	Y Y X Y X	X Y Y	X X X
Size of Work-force	1,200 47 100	200 310 90	100 220 120 61 245	61 24 40	76 200 34

Variable	Professional Services	Government Services	Retail, Distribution, Transport	Financial Services
Use of Sub-contractors	X Y	X X X Y Y X	X X Y X Y	X X
Subcontractor	X Y	Y X X X Y X	X X X X X	X X
Size of Workforce	2 18	154 23 23 378 206 4	48 35 281 66 960	10 4

Key: Y = YES; X = NO.

enon and the proportion of output or services affected. We also asked respondents about the advantages and disadvantages of subcontracting and, where relevant, their objections to its use. These answers provide a comprehensive picture of key aspects of current managerial orientations towards the fundamentals of economic organization in the town.

The 32 establishments were located across a wide range of industrial sectors. They included three consumer and three industrial textile firms, five machine-makers and three general engineering firms, including one specialist fabricator. The sample also included three other manufacturing plants – a paint manufacturer, a chemical firm and a firm producing components for the textile industry made from paper. We also examined two establishments in professional services, two in financial services, six in government and public services and five establishments in retail, distribution and transport.

As is clear from Table 8.2, *the use of subcontractors is concentrated overwhelmingly within specific industrial sectors,* and in particular within engineering. Four of the five machine-makers used subcontractors, as did the specialist fabricator (itself a subcontractor for larger firms). Three of the five machine-makers acted as subcontractors themselves as did two of the three general engineering firms. Clearly, therefore, subcontracting was pervasive amongst engineering companies in Rochdale. Elsewhere in manufacturing, however, it was very uncommon. Only two of the eight textile or "other manufacturing" plants utilized sub-contractors. They were only used for specialist engineering activities such as the installation of machinery or machine maintenance at periodic shutdowns. In the latter case, a paper-related plant, this is a common and long-standing practice within the industry (see Penn and Scattergood, 1985 and 1988).

Furthermore, it is evident from Table 8.3 that these subcontracting relations are *long-standing* features of metal-working in Rochdale. None of the subcontracting relations in this sector was reported as new to the 1980s and in most cases they amounted to less than 10% of overall output. In only one manufacturing plant were these relationships increasing in the 1980s. There was little evidence that subcontracting had increased significantly in the service sector in Rochdale during the 1980s. Five service sector establishments reported a use of subcontractors. Within government services these involved specialist (not routine) vehicle maintenance at a Local Authority depot and fabric maintenance at a school. Respondents in these establishments reported that it was the policy of the Local Authority to avoid using subcontracted labour wherever possible. Within retailing, we discovered the use of subcontractors for major (not routine) cleaning at a very large retail store. However, this was new only in so far as the firm had opened its establishment in Rochdale during the 1980s. In addition, a large distribution centre used the British Legion for providing security personnel at their premises.

Table 8.3 : Use of Subcontractors in Rochdale (32 Establishment Data)

Sector	Use		Proportion	Increasing/ Decreasing	New to 1980s
A) *Manufacturing*					
Textiles (1/5)	Structural Maintenance Installation Equipment		Small	Decreasing	No
	Sheetmetalworking/Welding		1%	Decreasing	No
Engineering (5/8)					
(a)	Machining	(1)	10-30%	Constant	No
	Production small machines	(1)	10%	Increasing	No
	Machining	(1)	10%	Decreasing	No
	Fabrication/Machining	(1)			
(b) General (1/3)	Machine Maintenance/ Machining	(1)	7%	Constant	No
Other Manufacturing (1/3)	Machine Maintenance at Shutdowns		1%	Constant	No
B) *Services*					
Professional Services (1/2)	Specialist Professional Services		5%	Constant	No
Financial Services (0/2)	None		–	–	No
Government Services (2/6)	Specialist Vehicle Maintenance	(1)	1%	Increasing	No
	Fabric Maintenance	(1)	1%	Constant	No
Retail, Distribution, Transport (2/5)	Major cleaning		10%	Constant	Yes (Firm new)
	Security		–	Increasing	Yes

Overall, then, we found little evidence to support the notion that subcontracting was increasing in the 1980s. It only existed significantly within machine-manufacturing plants. Even here it generally accounted for a small proportion of output. Furthermore, it was a long-standing feature of the industry. The advantages adduced for such subcontracting were traditional examples of economic rationality. The one textile plant employing some subcontractors (itself the largest manufacturing employer in Rochdale) used them for certain specialized ancillary engineering tasks. This had been common practice since at least 1945 and eliminated the need for the firm to train or possess such expert workers. The rationales provided within engineering centred upon the ability of the firm to cope with peaks in demand. The manufacture of machinery, in particular, is both cyclical and intermittent. One firm may have excess skilled labour that can be put to work on subsystems for another local plant. However, this was never the latter management's first choice of action. Only when their domestic skilled workforce could not cope was work contracted out.[14] This was because the firm under pressure could neither directly control the output of the firm to whom work was sent, nor could they be sure about delivery dates. These increased uncertainties meant that firms had to expend greater managerial efforts of control and coordination whenever work went outside the plant.

Similar opinions were expressed about the relative advantages and disadvantages of subcontracting within the service sector (see Table 8.4). Indeed, the overwhelming lack of subcontracting and the powerful objections provided against it suggest that Atkinson and Meager's prognosis is highly misleading. Far from improving efficiency or profitability, the extensive use of subcontractors would create major managerial difficulties in most Rochdale establishments. Indeed, the kind of extensive use advocated by Atkinson and Meager would almost certainly increase inefficiency and would probably put most private sector operations out of business!

5   Relations Between Firms in Rochdale

If relations between firms (and *pari passu* between large and small firms) are not characterized by any significant degree of subcontracting, how are such firms connected in contemporary Rochdale? Our research has identified the following patterns.

5.1   Cooperation Amongst Firms

We discovered a degree of cooperation amongst firms in the locality. This was strongest within the two core areas of manufacturing: textiles and engineering. There were 52 engineering firms within the Rochdale District of the Engineering Employers' Federation (EEF). These included almost all the major engineering firms

Table 8.4: Advantages, Disadvantages and Objections to Subcontracting in Rochdale (32 Establishment Data)

	Advantages	Disadvantages	Objections
A) Manufacturing			
Textiles	Specialized skills in ancillary areas (1)	–	Quality Control (3) Cost (1)
Engineering			
• Machine-makers	Cope with peaks in demand (4)	Quality of work worse (4) Need for tight control (3) More administration (1)	Quality of Work (1)
• General	Reduce training costs (1) Avoid purchase of machinery (4) No need to hold staff with knowledge that has only limited use (1)	Deliveries often late (1)	–
Other Manufacturing		–	–
B) Services			
Professional Services	To provide complete service (1)	Lack of control	–
Government Services	Cost of employing specialists who would not be fully utilized (1) Useful for intermittent needs (1)	Costs	–
Retailing, Transport, Distribution	Machinery supplied by contractors (1) Ability to employ people at short notice (1)	Control of quality Cost	– –

in the town. The Federation provided continuous, local data on wage rates and assisted with wage bargaining with the local Engineering Union (AEU). This high level of cooperation extended also to apprenticeship training. Local engineering firms funded the Rochdale Training Association which undertook the selection and training of craft and technician apprentices (Bragg, 1987). All major local employers except Renold (who have their own training school) participated in this training programme. It was also clear that the local EEF was dominated by its larger local members. Few small firms were members and this applied to almost all the small fabricating firms. We found no evidence that these collective forms of organization extended beyond wage information and training provision into specific market relations between firms. Indeed, it was unlikely that the informal contacts between EEF members could have facilitated significant subcontracting relations.

Most of the largest local textile firms were members of the Oldham and Rochdale Textile Employers' Association. The Association had 38 members, some of whom, like Courtaulds, had a multiplicity of plants in the area. Thirteen member firms were located in Rochdale. They included a preponderance of the larger industrial textile producers. Three member firms manufactured tyre cords and two others were both industrial textile and advanced materials' manufacturers. However, the largest textile employer in Rochdale – TBA – was not a member. There was less evidence of significant economic effects resulting from such collective organization amongst local textile producers than had been the case within engineering. Membership of the Association centred upon the supply of general information, particularly concerning local wage patterns.

We concluded that there was considerable generalized cooperation between manufacturing firms in Rochdale but this centred overwhelmingly upon issues of general concern such as wages and training. Local employer associations were dominated by larger firms which displayed a strong sense of local identity. This was supported in many cases by the fact that many firms have been located in Rochdale for at least 80 years and many have remained with local managements. The intense localism of Rochdale employers was thrown into relief in recent months when they successfully rejected attempts by the Training Agency to force them into either Oldham or Bury and Bolton for the purpose of organizing the new employer-led Training and Enterprise Councils within the region.

5.2   Market Relations Between Firms

The overwhelming relationship between firms in Rochdale was characterized by classic external market linkage. Indeed, there were at least three processes currently under way in Rochdale that have increased the dominance of these external market relations. Firstly, fewer local plants utilized local machinery in production. There has been a significant expansion of foreign-made equipment within Rochdale plants. In a postal survey of 71 textile and engineering plants in 1986, it was revealed that half of the advanced manufacturing equipment used within these plants had not been manufactured in Britain and the proportion was even higher in the areas of the most sophisticated machinery. Textile production in particular had witnessed a significant utilization of Swiss and West German equipment. One large industrial textiles producer reported that they had abandoned purchasing locally-made equipment because local textile machinery manufacturers had not kept up sufficiently with their needs for advanced equipment. This view was confirmed when we examined the destination of much of the machinery exported from Rochdale machinery-making plants. A great deal of it was destined for China, the USSR and Eastern Europe where the demand was mostly for relatively unsophisticated equipment. Many Rochdale machine-makers have become less and less prominent within the most advanced markets for equipment.

Secondly, subcontractors were used less frequently in manufacturing industry. A subcontractor was used as long as his product proved reliable in terms of quality and delivery. There was little internal monitoring of such contractors' activities and few attempts to promote internal changes within these subcontracting firms by larger firms in the locality. Our research at a specialist fabricator provided further confirmation of this. Only one customer firm had insisted on the fabricating firm obtaining the newest British Standards Institute (BSI) Quality Standard. This firm was a relatively new customer and was engaged in the nuclear power industry where high standards of contract work are the norm.

Finally, various large firms in Rochdale have restructured their operations during the 1980s, creating a series of sub-businesses from their previous monolithic structures. Other large firms have instituted decentralized financial regimes of control that have produced parallel results. In both instances, we discovered that traditional internal linkages within such firms have been externalized. For example, at a large metal-working firm, adjacent plants became separate businesses and each had to contract competitively for any work in the other. More often than not in recent years each had been unsuccessful with the other. Likewise at a large industrial textile producer, three vertically-integrated plants were turned into separate businesses and the material imputs down the chain of production were subject to competitive tendering.

5.3 The Situation of Independent Small Firms in Rochdale

Our research revealed a clear picture amongst small independent firms in Rochdale. They were isolated, highly dependent on larger firms and financially precarious. There was little evidence of extensive local networks amongst small independent firms. There was no evidence of any collective organization by small firms within the locality. Such firms simply did not feature greatly within organized employers' collectivities. Indeed, this pattern proved a serious problem for the Department of Trade and Industry (DTI) Inner Cities Task Force in the town when they initially tried to contact small firms. The general lack of collective representation amongst small firms has been a long-standing feature of British societal relations and renders suggestions of any competitive advantage to networks of small firms largely irrelevant in most current situations in Britain. Small independent firms in Rochdale were overwhelmingly dependent upon larger firms. Their relations with these larger dominant firms were largely coordinated through the external market. Such an articulation was financially precarious and there has been a large failure rate amongst such businesses in the town during the 1980s.[15]

6   Conclusions

Our research revealed a dense set of interrelated industries located in contemporary Rochdale. This pattern had evolved progressively since the advent of industrialization in the early nineteenth century. There was a close symbiosis historically between textile manufacture and textile machinery-making in the town which was parallelled by similar relations within chemicals and paper. Such a dense yet differentiated structure of employers in the locality suggested the possibility of extensive inter- and intra-industry linkages. The SCELI research focused particularly on subcontracting between firms in the town. The results revealed that subcontracting was far from pervasive. It was concentrated within the machine-making sector of engineering and was used as a *strategy of the last resort* by employers when they encountered surges in production that were beyond the capacities of their domestic workforces. Such subcontracting was a traditional feature of inter-firm relations in this part of engineering and was by no means new to the 1980s. Overall our survey revealed the general absence of subcontracting as a form of inter-firm articulation in the present era in Rochdale.

There was evidence of an industrial district in Rochdale. There existed a series of interlocking industries that have emerged progressively over a long period. However, there was strong evidence that the relations between firms within the locality were becoming less integrated. The machinery-makers were far less connected in either market or non-market terms with local manufacturers in their field of equipment-making.

Many machine-makers had become isolated from the most advanced markets for their products. Ironically some of these advanced markets were located within a few miles of their own manufacturing plants in the 1980s. Local employers in engineering and textiles did cooperate in employers' associations. However, this cooperation was mainly centred upon matters of wages and, less often, training. These organizations were dominated by the larger firms in these two sectors of manufacturing.

We found little or no evidence of extensive networks of small and medium-sized employers in Rochdale. Neither did we find much evidence of the other much vaunted new forms of inter-firm relations that were characterized earlier as either active engagement or subordinate cooperation. *The overwhelming impression of links between small and large firms in Rochdale was one of a classic satellite relationship. Relations between firms were overwhelmingly coordinated by external market relations.* Paradoxically, the pattern was therefore, in certain respects, similar to that portrayed by Marshall in the 1920s. However, in certain key respects it was different. In the earlier period there was an extensive subdivision of firms which were linked in a complex web of interconnected specialisms. In the modern era, there is the form of such a pattern but its content is quite different. Our evidence suggested that the historic residue of inter-industry linkages remained a significant feature determining the kinds of firms still located in Rochdale. However, there has been a progressive uncoupling of the constituent parts. Today we find a series of large manufacturing firms located in the town which have very limited connections with other such firms in the locality. These large manufacturing plants in engineering do use subcontractors *in extremis* but it is very much a solution of the last resort. The links between these subcontractors and the main contractor are determined overwhelmingly by external market relations and decreasingly by informal or formal networks of inter-firm relations.

Notes

* I would like to thank Frank Wilkinson of the Department of Applied Economics, Cambridge University, for his comments on an earlier draft of this paper, and also Brian Francis of the Centre for Applied Statistics, Lancaster University, for his assistance with the production of Figure 8.1.
1 See, for example, E. Goodman et al. (1989) *Small Firms and Industrial Districts in Italy* in the forthcoming collection of papers from the 1990 BSA Conference edited by N. Gilbert (1991).
2 A. Marshall (1923), pp. 600-601.
3 The Upas tree of Java was thought to have the power to destroy other plant growths for a radius of 15 miles.
4 See, for example, the special issue of the *Industrial Relations Journal* in Spring, 1988, on "Japanization".
5 These stages are heuristic.
6 In the mid-nineteenth century, coal was another important local industry employing almost 1,000 men in Rochdale in 1851. Most of this local coal was used to generate power in local textile and metal-working plants. However, most seams were worked out by the last quarter of the nineteenth century.
7 Turner and Newall also owned Ferodo, the major supplier of such products to the British motor industry.

8   See Penn and Scattergood, "Corporate Strategy and Textile Employment", Lancaster University Social Change and Economic Life Initiative, Working Paper 12, 1987.
9   It is clear that this model of industrial development could not be generated inductively from any available sets of official data. Nevertheless, the model is critical for any adequate understanding of the dynamics of industrial development in the town.
10 Social Change and Economic Life Initiative. ESRC Grant No. G13250011.
11 The various research instruments used are available from the Social Change and Economic Life Research Project, Department of Sociology, Lancaster University, Lancaster LA1 4YL.
12 "Changing needs and relationships in the UK apparel fabric market", London, NEDO, 1982; and "The cotton and allied textiles industry : A report on the work of the Cotton and Allied Textiles Economic Development Committee", London, NEDO, 1983.
13 This imagery often goes under the name of flexible manufacturing systems (FMS). For a cogent discussion of this notion, see A. Pollert, 1988.
14 Management preferred to use overtime by existing employees to cope with peaks in demand. Only when this proved insufficient would they contemplate subcontracting work to another plant.
15 Data provided to the author in confidence by the DTI Inner Cities Taskforce.

References

Aglietta, M. (1979) *A Theory of Capitalist Regulation*. London: New Left Books.
Atkinson, J./Meager, N. (1986) *Changing Working Patterns: How Companies Achieve Flexibility to Meet New Needs*. London: NEDO Books.
Bagnasco, A. (1977) *Tre Italie. La Problematica Territoriale dello sviluppo italiano*. Bologna: Il Mulino.
Bragg, C. (1987) 'Apprenticeship Training in the contemporary Rochdale Engineering Industry', *MA Thesis*, Lancaster University.
Checkland, S.G. (1981) *The Upas Tree: Glasgow 1875-1975*. Glasgow.
Brusco, S. (1986) 'Small Firms and Industrial Districts: The Experience of Italy', in Keeble, D./Weever, E. (eds.). *Regional Development in Europe*. London: Croom Helm.
Gilbert, N. (ed.) (1991) *Fordism and Flexibility: Divisions and Change*. London: Macmillan.
Goodman, E./Bamford, J./Saynor, P. (1989) *Small Firms and Industrial Districts in Italy*. London: Routledge.
Harvey, D. (1989) *The Condition of Postmodernity*. Oxford: Basil Blackwell.
Haughton, G. (1985) 'The Dynamics of the Rochdale Labour Market'. Lancaster University Social Change and Economic Life Initiative. Working Paper 3.
Hirst, P./Zeitlin, J. (1989) *Reversing Industrial Decline? Industrial Structure and Policy in Britain and her Competitors*. Oxford: Bragg.
International Labour Office (1987) 'Smaller Units of Employment: A Synthesis Report on Industrial Reorganization in Industrialised Countries'. Geneva: ILO.
Marshall, A. (1923) *Industry and Trade: A Study of Industrial Technique and Business Organization*. London: Macmillan.

Murray, R. (1985) 'Benetton Britain: The New Economic Order', *Marxism Today*, November.

Murray, R. (1988) 'Life After Henry (Ford)', *Marxism Today,* October.

Penn, R.D. (1985) *Skilled Workers in the Class Structure*. Cambridge: Cambridge University Press.

Penn, R.D. (1988) 'The Internationalization of the Contemporary Paper Industry', Lancaster University Paper Industry Research, Working Paper No 1.

Penn, R.D./Scattergood, H. (1985) 'Deskilling or Enskilling?: An Empirical Investigation of Recent Theories of the Labour Process', *British Journal of Sociology* XXXVI (4), December.

Penn, R.D./Scattergood, H. (1988) 'Continuities and Change in Skilled Work: A Comparison of Five Paper Manufacturing Plants in the UK, Australia and the USA', *British Journal of Sociology*. XXXIX (1), March.

Piore, M./Sabel, C. (1984) *The Second Industrial Divide*. New York: Basic Books.

Pollert, A. (1988) 'Dismantling Flexibility', *Capital and Class* 34.

Pyke, F. (1987) 'Industrial Networks and Modes of Cooperation in a British Context', North West Industry Research Unit, Manchester University.

Pyke, F. (1988) 'Cooperative Practices among Small and Medium-Sized Establishments', *Work, Employment and Society* 2 (3).

Pyke, F./Becattini, G./Sengenberger, W. (eds.) (1991) *Industrial Districts and Inter-firm Co-operation in Italy*. Geneva: International Institute for Labour Studies.

Ravèyre, M. 1986. 'Small and Medium-Sized Firms in Saint-Cobain'. Intermediate Report. GLYSI. University of Lyons.

Saglio, J. 1984. 'Les systèmes industries localises', *Sociologie du Travail* 2.

CHAPTER 9

Is a Diamond a Region's Best Friend? Towards an Analysis of Interregional Competition

Max Boisot

1   Introduction

The neoclassical firm, that elusive dot on a production function that knows neither spatial nor temporal constraints, would have been a source of considerable puzzlement in fourteenth-century Florence or Venice. There, and at that time the only SBUs (Strategic Business Units) worth talking about, were the guilds; and the only corporate strategy on offer was that of the local authority. Within the urban polity, economic relations were hierarchical and cooperative; and between different urban polities, there prevailed a climate of unbridled competition.

The belief that economic competition was nothing but an expression of a competitive relationship between territories survived the emergence of the nation-state and gave rise to physiocracy and mercantilism (Blaug, 1985). Earlier forms of competition between neighbouring cities or city-states was then attenuated in favour of rivalry, military as well as economic, between larger territorial units. According to mercantilists, the key to successful rivalry was a positive balance of trade which would allow the accumulation of bullion and this would be achieved by importing as little as possible and exporting as much as possible. Since the state controlled the territorial boundaries over which trade flowed, i.e. the physical barriers to entry, it wielded considerable power over what was to be produced domestically, what was to be imported, and what would be allowed abroad.

In the late eighteenth century, at about the time that Adam Smith was writing the *Wealth of Nations*, the concern of political economy shifted from exchange to production, from spatio-temporally constrained trading regimes to production activities energetically constrained by the availability of physical capital and labour power. In the liberal scheme of things, the government was consigned to a passive regulatory role. Mill's "nightwatchman state" was a very different animal from the strategic actor of former years – in economic terms, at best a parameter; and at worst, an afterthought. Government put in a brief appearance in Anglo-Saxon thinking with Keynesian economics – but this time on the demand side, only to be once more relegated to the role of stage hand by the so-called neoclassical synthesis which, freshly armed with Arrow-Debreu general equilibrium models, showed that the presence on stage of government actors was, if anything, detrimental to the plot.

Yet the issue of government's role in economic affairs will not go away. If anything, it is becoming more pressing. Like firms, governments are institutional creations that can be conjured up or away at will. The dissolving Soviet empire has seen the creation of several potentially viable nation-states. The EC's "Project '92", conversely, might witness the voluntary merging of several national sovereignties into a supranational political entity. Eastern (now Central) Europe is today being pulled simultaneously in opposite directions: on the one hand, towards a supranational EC; and on the other, towards a fragmentation into feuding regional entities. One reason why this is happening is that there is little consensus on what the role of government should be in the economy to help overcome the pain of necessary adjustments.

In Eastern Europe, as in many other parts of the world today, concern with the role of government has two distinct facets:
1) What scope does it have to legitimately intervene in the economic process?
2) At what institutional level should intervention, if any, take place?
The first question invites replies that range from an unshakable proclamation of faith in the self-regulating power of markets with monetarism as its servant, to an unyielding belief in the value of impartial welfare-maximizing plans and a *dirigiste* order. Of course, many possibilities lie between these two extremes, fed by the power of government to tax and to "guide" and, more generally, to persuade.

The second question is inevitably linked to the first since intervention – in theory, at least – could occur at the level of the economy as a whole, of specific sectors, of regions or of firms. The ways that possible answers to these two questions combine, are indicated in Figure 9.1. Recent history suggests that the position chosen by the now-defunct USSR in this space is not viable and that bounded rationality and opportunism rapidly take their toll of government ambitions to intervene in a Laplacian fashion. The current debate has thus focused on the two other points on the scale: one proclaiming an Anglo-Saxon belief in self-regulation, the other casting the state in a more mercantilist role.

In nearly all cases, however, the nation-state is taken as the territorial unit for which the governance issue is posed.

Figure 9.1: Intervention Options

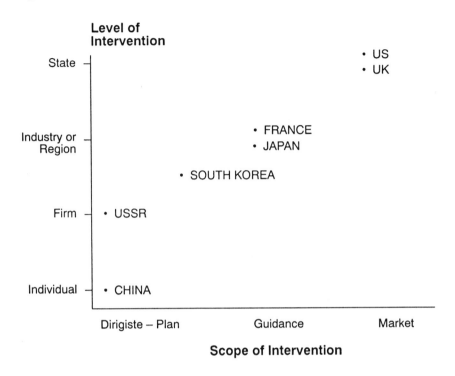

Scope of Intervention

In certain quarters, nevertheless, the assumption that the state – like the firm – is a natural unit of economic analysis, is coming under scrutiny. Keniche Omae, for example, noting the inexorable trends towards the globalization of markets, argues in favour of supranational territorial entities, macro-regions of which the three most important – the US, Europe and the Far East – form what he terms a "triad" (Omae, 1985).

Michael Porter, by contrast, in his *Competitive Advantage of Nations* (1990), takes the nation-state as his natural unit of analysis. Porter, however, is at pains to point out that his analysis also holds true for territorial units below the level of the nation-state. Thus, he somewhat undermines his argument in favour of the nation-state by drawing his most telling examples from a regional level.

In fact, a growing body of researchers now focus explicitly on the region and its potential for economic governance. Reviving Marshall's notion of the industrial district, both Piore and Sabel (1984) and Best (1989), for example, explore forms of economic organization that do not require a rigid institutional separation between territorial and economic governance. With the work of Jane Jacobs (1984) the wheel comes full circle; and we find ourselves once more with the city as a natural economic unit just as it was in the Middle Ages. Indeed, Jacobs actively recommends the pursuit of mercantilist policies at the urban level as those most likely to achieve local competitive success.

Although – in the interest of advocacy – the issue of territorial governance has sometimes been framed as a choice between levels, it need not be. A more encompassing view would acknowledge these different levels as being each viable in their own right within certain limits, and it would see them as both competing and collaborating with each other at the same time. Over what do they compete or collaborate? The answer is, over the value generated by economic agents such as firms within their territory.

Competition and collaboration by territorial units over the value generated by firms is both vertical – between different levels of governance covering the same territory – and horizontal – between different territorial governance structures on the same level. The phenomenon, however, cannot be grasped from a neoclassical perspective, for one simple reason: in the neoclassical scheme, there exist neither firms nor the territories in which they operate.

In this paper, I shall argue that a Schumpeterian rather than a neoclassical perspective is the one required for understanding the nature of territorial governance, territorial competition, and the role played by firms in this competition. I will proceed as follows: in the next section (2), I will present a conceptual framework – the C-Space – that will serve the purpose of giving a spatio-temporal dimension to Schumpeterian economic processes. In section 3, I will apply this framework to a dynamic analysis of what Best (1990) has described as the "New Competition", the arena in which issues of territorial governance are currently emerging. In section 4, I will apply the framework to an institutional analysis of the industrial district as an example of the new competition, operating as it does below the level of the nation-state. Finally, in the concluding section (5), I will briefly explore the theoretical and policy implications of the exercise and compare them with those derived by Porter in the *Competitive Advantage of Nations* (Porter, 1990).

2   The C-Space

The C-Space (Boisot, 1986, 1987) explores the relationship between the structuring and sharing of information in a given population – whether it be made up of cells, individuals, firms or larger entities. The way in which information and knowledge are structured and shared, give a culture its particular signature, since the two activities are intimately related: the codification of knowledge (structuring) facilitates its diffusion (sharing) to ever larger populations; and conversely, the inability to codify such knowledge – to put it into words, to set it down on paper, etc. – limits its diffusion to small face-to-face groups in time-consuming communicative exchanges. This situation is depicted schematically in Figure 9.2, in which the top right-hand corner of the C-Space is populated by stockbrokers engaged in

Figure 9.2: The C-Space

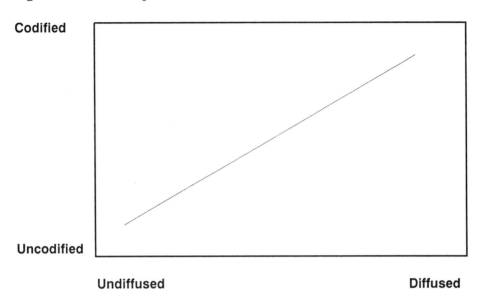

Codified

Uncodified

Undiffused   Diffused

screen-based trading, sharing well-codified prices with thousands of market participants instantaneously and on a global basis. The lower left-hand corner is populated by Zen Buddhists, each living in an intimate and durable relationship with a small group of trusting and loyal disciples. The latter spend their time trying to figure out by means of direct observation and imitation, sometimes spread over years, what their respective master's uncodifiable message might be.

As Polanyi well understood (Polanyi, 1962), one always pays a price for codifying one's knowledge and for rendering it communicable. The process of cognitive structuring is an act of selection (Shannon, 1948) in which much uncodified knowledge that has not been so selected, gets left behind, inhabiting the outer fringes of consciousness and eventually putting itself beyond the reach of unaided recall. The challenge in such cognitive structuring – as in any act of codification – is to shed data without, at the same time, losing useful information. Selection has to be judicious if it is to be knowledge-preserving; and for this reason, codification has an irreducibly hypothetical character (Gregory, 1981; Bruner, 1957). It is a risky act which, like a scientific hypothesis, is constantly open to revision or sometimes outright refutation (Popper, 1959).

Figure 9.2 depicts the size of the audience that can be reached in a given unit of time by a message as a function of its degrees of codification. This is a static picture that assumes that the message content already exists as knowledge. The C-Space, however, can also be used more dynamically to analyse the way in which new knowledge is created and acquired by a given population – which, as we have

Figure 9.3: The Social Learning Cycle (SLC)

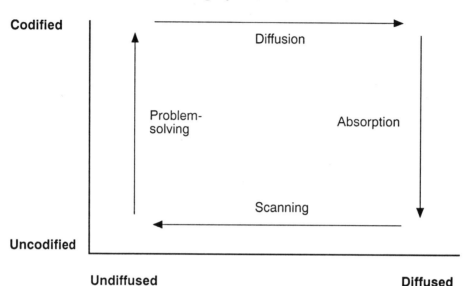

seen, could be taken as the cells that make up an individual, the individuals that make up a firm, the firms that make up an industry, the industries that make up a national economy or the economies that make up the global trading system. Boisot (1986) hypothesizes that social learning – knowledge acquisition and diffusion – is a cyclical phenomenon in the C-Space, and that it can be schematized as the four-step process depicted in Figure 9.3.

Step 1: Scanning. Weak and often ambiguous signals are extracted from uncodified data that is already diffused and generally available to a population located on the right of the space. In spite of their availability, these diffused signals are usually ignored or misunderstood. They form part of a "life-world" (Schutz, 1962) that is taken for granted and only registered implicitly. Occasionally, such weak signals become "impacted" (Williamson, 1975) on the left of the space, lodging themselves in what appears to be a random fashion in a few minds that interpret them – often idiosyncratically – as expressing threats or opportunities in the wider environment. The resulting insight tends to escape the larger population group also in possession of the relevant data; or it may be rejected by that group as incompatible with its dominant beliefs.

Step 2: Problem-solving. Where the threats or opportunities registered by individuals on the left of the space are experienced as sufficiently pressing, they trigger a problem-solving activity in which the vague intuitions and insights generated by the scanning process are given contour and structure. Choices are made between competing interpretations of the phenomena under consideration; and where these choices are well made and information is preserved, uncertainty is gradually reduced. As suggested above, this process of selection and codification is a risky business: the weak signals that initiated the problem-solving effort, might either turn out to be will-o'-the-wisps or suffer distortions through poor structuring, i.e. a false hypothesis being built up.

Step 3: Diffusion. As new knowledge emerges from efforts at codification, it moves up the C-Space where it becomes more easily diffusible beyond the face-to-face group. At the same time, increasing codification, by reducing the uncertainty and hazards of using such knowledge, increases its utility and extends it appeal to a wider audience. This codification invokes both "push" and "pull" factors to explain the diffusion of new knowledge. The push factor is associated with the increased communicability of codified knowledge; the pull factor, with its enhanced market appeal.

Step 4: Absorption. The diffusion of newly codified knowledge in a given population, usually provides opportunities for using and testing it in a variety of different circumstances unanticipated by its creators. Possible domains of application are identified and explored in a process of "learning by doing" in which the relevant structures or codes are gradually internalized by users over time. Such internalization gradually builds up an intuitive "feel" for the possibilities and scope of the new knowledge, a "feel" which is itself inarticulate and uncodified – hence, the downward movement in the C-Space – and which acts as a potential source of further weak signals calling for adjustments to what has been learned. In this way, a new learning cycle is initiated.

The Social Learning Cycle (SLC) just described, can be thought of as a large communication feedback loop linking together members of a given population. It is subject to blockages of a cognitive or of a sociological kind which either confine its operations to certain regions of the C-Space – and hence, to subgroups within the population (see Figure 9.4) – or act to halt its progress altogether. A major influence on the path taken by new knowledge in the C-Space, is the prior distribution of existing knowledge in the space, knowledge that exists in either a collaborative or a competitive relationship with what is emerging from the cycle – thus facilitating or impeding its further evolution. Existing knowledge benefits from a certain inertia in the C-Space by virtue of the institutional structures in which it becomes embedded. In turn, the internal operations and nature of such structures reflect the nature of the information environment in the region of the C-Space to which they are assigned on account of their knowledge-bearing capacity. Figure 9.5 identifies a number of such institutional structures, locating them at different points on a hypothetical SLC; and Table 9.1 briefly outlines some of the key information-related characteristics of these structures. Clearly, if we take a cultural order as expressing the way in which knowledge is structured and shared within a given population (Kroeber and Kluckhohn, 1952) then the role of institutions in mediating such an order in a patterned way, becomes apparent.

Figure 9.4: Blockages in the SLC

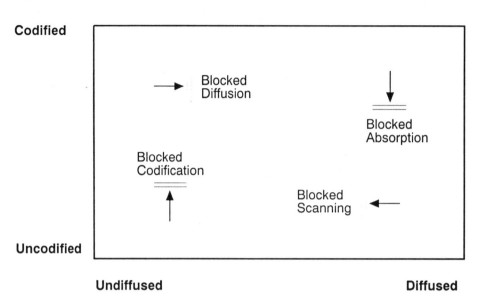

Codified

Uncodified

Undiffused   **Diffused**

Our conceptual scheme allows us identify two very different orientations to the social learning process that will become helpful to our subsequent discussion: the neoclassical orientation and the Schumpeterian one. How are they distinguished?

Neoclassical learning takes the region of the C-Space labelled "markets" in Figure 9.5 as an "absorbing" state, so that – following the codification and diffusion of new knowledge, i.e. of prices – a market-clearing equilibrium is achieved and the SLC effectively comes to a halt in that region. Both spatial and temporal constraints on institutional processes disappear, since well-codified information becomes ubiquitous on account of its diffusibility.

Schumpeterian learning, by contrast, takes the SLC as continuing beyond market equilibrium with new opportunities for learning arising from the "noise" generated by the equilibrating process itself (Stiglitz, 1989). Yet when such learning occurs, it gradually moves the system *away* from equilibrium, as publicly-available knowledge is absorbed by individual actors and, following a scanning phase, is once again affected by some of them in idiosyncratic ways (Shackle, 1972). Thus, to borrow a mathematical concept, noisy markets generate singularities rather than equilibrium, thus becoming sources of dynamic transformation for which neoclassical learning cannot account.

In sum, neoclassical learning is an equilibrating process that terminates with the attainments of market equilibrium, i.e. with the complete diffusion of new knowledge fully captured and codified through the price mechanism – whereas

Figure 9.5: Institutional Structures in the C-Space

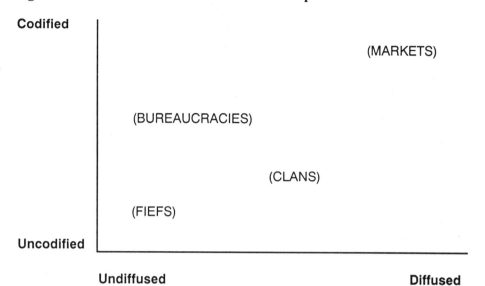

Codified

(MARKETS)

(BUREAUCRACIES)

(CLANS)

(FIEFS)

Uncodified

Undiffused   **Diffused**

Table 9.1:   Institutional Profiles in the C-Space

	Undiffused Information	Diffused Information
Codified Information	*2) Bureaucracies* • Information diffusion limited and under central control • Relationship impersonal and hierarchical • Submission to superordinate goals • Hierarchical coordination • No necessity to share values and beliefs	*3) Markets* • Information widely diffused, no control • Relationship impersonal and competitive • No superordinate goals – each one for himself • Horizontal coordination through self-regulation • No necessity to share values and beliefs
Uncodified Information	*1) Fiefs* • Information diffusion limited by lack of codification to face-to-face relationships • Relationship personal and hierarchical (feudal/charismatic) • Submission to superordinate goals • Hierarchical coordination • Necessity to share values and beliefs	*4) Clans* • Information is diffused but still limited by lack of codification to face-to-face relationships • Relationship personal but not non-hierarchical • Goals are shared through a process of negotiation • Hierarchical coordination through negotiation • Necessity to share values and beliefs

Schumpeterian learning is alternately an equilibrating and disequilibrating process in which codification and diffusion are followed by absorption and scanning. Both of these latter processes, taken together, constitute the entrepreneurial phase of the SLC and must be considered to be the ultimate source of Schumpeter's "Creative Destruction" (Schumpeter, 1934). The new knowledge that will emerge from the entrepreneurial phase of the SLC, now threatens to dislodge existing knowledge distributed throughout the C-Space, together with the specific institutions in which it has been embedded.

Schumpeterian learning, unlike neoclassical learning, requires a complete SLC, one operating continuously and having market equilibrium as but one phase among others. It is thus led to accept disequilibrium as an essential complement to equilibrium processes. Since the scope for disequilibrium will be at a maximum in the lower left-hand corner of the C-Space following the entrepreneurial phase, the singularity that will initiate creative destruction will take place in an information environment that is the antithesis of efficient markets and that will consequently be suffused with bounded rationality, opportunism, and strategic behaviour – the very characteristics that, according to Williamson, the modern enterprise was designed to avoid (Williamson, 1985).

Not only does Schumpeterian learning, then, accommodate forms of economic behaviour that are frowned upon by neoclassical learning; it also activates institutional structures – clans, fiefs, and bureaucracies – in a collaborative way rather than the competitive one demanded by, say, transaction costs economics. They are all deemed to be at least as necessary to the continuing functioning of the SLC as market institutions themselves. The neoclassical orthodoxy is not, institutionally speaking, such a broad church. Its commitment to a market order leads it to view movements through the SLC as inefficiencies to be temporarily endured on the way to equilibrium in the top right-hand region of the C-Space rather than as being inherently beneficial to the learning process. More importantly for our purposes, by constantly seeking out the market region of the space, the neoclassical orthodoxy is seeking to escape the physical constraints of space and time – whereas the Schumpeterian approach, by moving down the space and to the left, seeks to exploit them. It places economic processes in historical time and in real spaces subject to territorial governance.

3   The New Competition

In this section, we apply the conceptual apparatus of the C-Space – and in particular, the SLC – to an analysis of what Michael Best (1990) calls the "New Competition". To do so, we draw quite heavily from his book by the same name.

In order to understand the salient features of the new competition, we need to look first at the old competition. It has its origins in an engineering or mechanistic conception of organization which gradually gives way to an organic one. In both cases, however, the concern is with efficiency as evidenced by productivity figures. The focus is not necessarily on production, however, since it is also acknowledged that an effective marketing orientation can lead to productivity gains through the agency of the experience curves and a large market share. With the old competition, however, the logic of success is a logic of ever-increasing size. The large firm secures technical and administrative economies of scale which gives it an absolute competitive advantage over its smaller rivals. It can routinize and standarize production runs and substitute capital for labour, which can then be de-skilled; it can then deploy analytical and data-processing powers far beyond what is available to the small firm.

Alfred Chandler is the undisputed champion of the large firm. His carefully-researched history of the rise of the modern corporation (1977) traces its development from single-unit family enterprises which are gradually brought under single ownership to become managerially coordinated and which, under the pressure of continued growth, are led to divisionalize their operations by introducing internal capital markets within the enterprise in order to further decentralize decision-making. Chandler's description of enterprise evolution can be captured by the C-Space (see Figure 9.6). The owner-managed firm is a fief in which authority is personalized and based upon the owner's intimate knowledge of the business. With the growth of the owner-managed firm, or its integration in a larger multi-unit

Figure 9.6: Enterprise Evolution in the C-Space

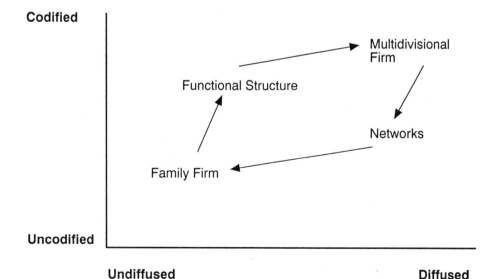

business, the fief bursts its banks. Task complexity and the number of employees to be coordinated both exceed what can be achieved by a personal management style. Bounded rationality and opportunism now threaten. In order to maintain his organizational effectiveness, the owner-manager is forced to structure and codify what were hitherto informal practices. As he does so, he moves the organization up the C-Space towards bureaucracies, towards a specialized and rational functional structure that can coordinate larger numbers on the basis of standardized and routinized procedures. Gains in efficiency translated into higher profitability, compensate the owner-manager for the "routinization of his charisma", as Weber termed it (Weber, 1965) and the consequent loss of personal power.

With further growth of the firm, earlier efficiency gains become once more eroded by resurgent problems of coordination. The pursuit of efficiency and cost competitiveness now calls for a decentralization of strategic decisions to autonomous operating divisions that are closer to "the action" and the problems to be coordinated. The multidivisional structure in effect decentralizes strategic decisions by internalizing a capital market that substitutes itself for a bureaucratic allocation of resources (Chandler, 1962). In the C-Space, this can be described as a move from left to right in the upper reaches of the diagram in Figure 9.6.

To summarize, the Chanderian thesis is that the large multidivisional enterprise was a two-step creation. In the first step, personal authority is replaced by impersonal authority through a process of *formalization*. In the second step, hierarchical control is partly relinquished in favour of market control through a limited *decentralization*. Both steps, taken together, move the firm from the fief region of the C-Space to the market region passing through bureaucracies.

It would appear that, in a logic of growth, firms could in theory go on moving diagonally up the C-Space, accommodating ever-larger internal populations through evermore sophisticated acts of formalization. One would then end up with a Walrasian equilibrium inside the firm. It is clear from Chandler's most recent book, *Scale and Scope* (1990), that this logic does not appeal to him. In the book, he identifies three different brands of capitalism: *personal capitalism*, as practiced in the UK; *managerial capitalism*, as practiced in the US; and *cooperative capitalism*, as practiced in Germany. Personal capitalism is the least effective in Chandler's view, reflecting a reluctance by owner-managers to relinquish personal power. They wish to remain in fiefs and consequently keep most of the organization's transactional style there with them. Managerial capitalism is judged to be effective and is of the kind that was described by Chandler in his earlier work. But with cooperative capitalism, Chandler finds himself suddenly in the clan region of the C-Space through a process that involved a limited decentralization but comparatively little formalization of managerial practice at the top of the enterprise.

Cooperative capitalism stresses interfirm collaboration rather than competition, based on a shared set of supraorganizational goals and vision. Chandler sees such interfirm collaboration as delivering effective performance. What he fails to see is that, if this is the case, then the logic of organization – that the advocates of growth see as a unique response to the challenge of economic coordination – will lose much of its force.

The New Competition, by contrast, if anything pursues a logic of shrinkage, of downsizing, of personalized organizational and interorganizational relationship regulated by trust and cooperation rather than by "command and control" (Best, 1990). It is therefore more comfortable in the lower regions of the C-Space, among transactional structures, that Chandler – in spite of his views on cooperative capitalism – would label "pre-modern" in his scheme.

Best distinguishes between the old and the new competition along four dimensions:

1) The Firm: Collective Entrepreneur. In opposition to the hierarchical firm, the new competition characterizes the entrepreneurial firm. Its competitive advantage is not secured by cost reductions or low prices, but rather by innovation in products and processes, by continuous innovation based on incremental improvements and by adjustments. The entrepreneurial firm shuns the stability and static efficiency yielded by the standarization and routinization of production. It is above all a learning organization committed to the pursuit of change and adaptability in a turbulent environment. To achieve this flexibility, the entrepreneurial firm must integrate thinking and doing rather than keeping them hierarchically separated, and it must consequently be open to new ideas – whatever their origin, whether from inside or outside the enterprise, whether from the top or the base of the organization. In other words, and in the language of the C-Space, the entrepreneurial firm is concerned to maintain a rapidly-moving SLC and cannot afford to have it blocked or distorted by managerial practices that keep information flows overly codified and formalized – and hence, confined to the upper regions of the space. The lower regions of the C-Space may threaten opportunism, but they also promise opportunities; they may be a cause of bounded rationality, but they are also a source of boundless entrepreneurial insight.

2) Production Chain: Consultative Coordination. Under the old competition, successive steps in the production process are either coordinated externally through markets on the basis of price, or internally through hierarchy and managerial fiat. Relative transaction costs dictate the choice (Coase, 1937; Williamson, 1975). Efficiency criteria predominate in drawing the boundary beyond which the firm comes to a stop and the market takes over.

The new competition, with a broader agenda for the firm than efficiency narrowly construed, affords a wider choice of coordination mechanisms. Best and I differ in our description of these: he cites what he calls hierarchical-bureaucratic and hierarchical-clan (what I have termed a "fief") as internal coordinating mechanisms, and markets and consultative-cooperative arrangements (what I have termed "clans") as external coordinating mechanisms. Although I find it gratifying to discover that we have both singled out similar transactional structures – in spite of differences in the way we label them – I see no reason to assume that they help to distinguish between internal and external transactions. Just as markets can be internal to firms (see above), so can fiefs be external to them – as, say, in the relational contracting arrangements of the Japanese *Kaisha* (Abbeglen, 1985).

It is clear that it is the entrepreneurial firm's concern with those segments of the SLC located in the lower, uncodified regions of the C-Space, that activates clans and fiefs as viable and legitimate transactional options – whether these be taken as internal or external.

3) The Sector: Competition and Cooperation. As we move outside the hierarchical firm into its relevant environment, the old competition invites us to dichotomize it into *macro* and *micro* regions. In the macro-region, the state as a regulatory agent is all but invisible to firms; and reciprocally, since these populate the micro-region, firms are invisible to the state. Economic governance thus operates on two distinct levels which treat each other as parametric.

The new competition interposes a third level of governance between these two which acts to mediate the relationship between them and thus sets up potential lines of communication where none existed before: sector institutions, or what Piore and Sabel have aptly termed "extra-firm infrastructure" (Piore and Sabel, 1984). This might consist of industry associations, research networks, marketing consortia, joint purchasing organizations, training establishments and so on. Through such an infrastructure, economies external to firms but internal to an industry are captured and work to crystallize a common interest. Under the old competition a "common interest" that links firms together is considered collusive and anti-competitive, hence hardly something to be fostered.

It may well be. Adam Smith's "conspiracy against the public" is an ever-present danger under such arrangements. But interfirm collaboration only effectively becomes anti-competitive if the clan region of the C-Space has itself become an absorbing state that effectively brings the SLC to a halt there. As long as information keeps flowing in the space, carrying new opportunities and forcing either adaptation or creative destruction, clans – like any other transactional structure – are kept permanently on their toes. The trick then is to maintain the flow, not to prohibit the clan. The SLC will see to the rest.

4) The Government: Strategic Industrial Policy. The old competition is first and foremost about, well, competition. Any institutional arrangements that move the system away from neoclassical competitive outcomes – cartels, industry association, excessive market shares – are discouraged or disallowed. Those that encourage competition – the SEC, the GATT, etc. – are actively supported.

The new competition is about balance: not a denial of markets, nor a pursuit of the planned economy as the critics of industrial policy have argued, but a set of measures designed to keep the SLC functioning and functioning fast. This, after all, is what economies of time are all about. In the new competition the prizes go to the fast learners, the ones who scan, problem-solve, diffuse, and absorb faster than others. Those who get stuck in an absorbing state – whether it be a bureaucratic version as in the Soviet Union, a fief version as in China (Boisot and Child, 1988) or a neoclassical market version as sometimes happens in the US – are doomed to fall further behind.

We conclude this section with the observation that the new competition is concerned with the SLC as a whole and not simply those segments of it that codify and diffuse. As a consequence, the new competition is led towards the lower regions of the C-Space where relations are personalized, where trust and shared norms and experience matter, and where valuable tacit knowledge does not travel very far. Here, we must note that effective transacting is facilitated by spatial concentration, so that competition between firms translates by degrees into competition between territories. The advent of the multinational corporation has attenuated but not done away with this reality. Howard Perlmutter's "geocentric" manager, committed only to his firm and equally at home in Manhattan and in Jeddah, remains – as Perlmutter himself has now acknowledged – a pipe dream (Perlmutter and Heenan, 1974). Firms, like people – as Porter has pointed out – have home bases. Outside them they begin to feel homesick.

Territorial loyalty, like brand loyalty, is a major competitive asset for the new competition.

4   Institutional Analysis

The old competition is a presumption in favour of internalization based on the assumed efficiency properties of hierarchy. Yet, as we have seen, internal transactions are not necessarily hierarchical; and today, we are witnessing a search inside organizations for new ways of integrating clan- and fief-like transactions with bureaucratic and market ones. The imperative of the SLC is asserting itself through a new-found concern with internal venturing, entrepreneurship, and those uncodified managerial processes described by Peters in *Thriving on Chaos* (Peters, 1987).

Yet if we are prepared to abandon the idea that internal transactions have to be conducted through hierarchy – whether of the informal kind such as fiefs or of the formal one such as bureaucracy – on what grounds do we then assume that external transactions have to be confined to markets?

The neoclassical reply to this question is that internal organization is management business and that economists have nothing to say about the comparative efficiency properties of alternative transactional styles within an enterprise. For them, the firm is still a dot on a production function in abstract space. Outside the firm, however, the contingent properties of different transactional style crystallize into absolute institutional choices that permeate the social order as a whole. Historical examples of such institutional choices are given by way of illustration in Figure 9.7. Once transactional issues have been framed in such exclusive terms, all that is left for the neoclassicist to do is to demonstrate the superior efficiency properties of the market option when ranked against competing institutional alternatives. Policy implications follow naturally from this line of thinking: the role of the state is to devise regulatory policies designed to maintain an impersonal market order as an absorbing state in the C-Space. This was the course of action pursued by the British government in the eighteenth century with consequences that were described in Karl Polanyi's *The Great Transformation* (Polanyi, 1944).

A Schumpeterian approach to the question, by contrast, would accept a contingent institutional order outside the firm for the same reason that it accepts contingent transactional styles inside it: both are necessary to the maintenance of the SLC. From this perspective, the choice between external and internal transactions is not reduced to one between markets and hierarchies but rather is framed in terms of alternative ways of managing the SLC. The crucial point is that *all* transactional

Figure 9.7: The Institutional Order

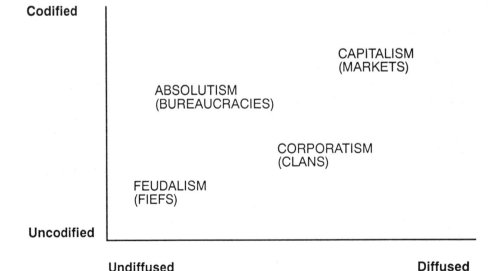

structures participate in a collaborative and complementary fashion, whether the SLC is internal or external to the firm.

The policy implications of the Schumpeterian perspective differ radically from those of the neoclassical one, as might be expected. For if the light regulatory touch of the "nightwatchman state" is necessary to safeguard the integrity of markets – and who would dispute this? – quite different forms of economic governance are required when the SLC has generated a sufficient fund of either tacit collective learning to move into clans, or of individual idiosyncratic learning for opportunistic entrepreneurial moves into fiefs to occur.

The effective maintenance of the SLC in the lower part of the C-Space requires spatial concentration and forms of economic governance – whether internal or external to firms – consistent with such concentration. The Chandlerian firm, quintessentially American, escaped the constraints of spatial concentration by moving up the C-Space towards a highly-codified management style that could impersonally control and coordinate over large distances. The success of this strategy today is evident: witness the global reach of the transnational corporation. But the shift up the C-Space, when it was too complete, exacted a price from the firm by robbing it of its entrepreneurial capacities further down the space, in clans and fiefs. Those firms that remained invested in the lower regions discovered that spatial concentration was essential to the success of their activities there, and that the crucial links to be preserved were those between strategy, research and development – i.e. those typically located in the lower reaches of the SLC on account of their lack of codifiability. These remain the elements of a firm's activities that add most value and constitute what Porter calls its "home base" activities. Inside the firm they call for a highly-supportive corporate culture. Japanese firms, for example, derive much of their effectiveness as innovators both by their skills in the clan region of the C-Space and by their ability to exploit collective learning. Outside the firm, they require the building-up of a supportive territorial culture based on shared norms, mutual dependency, and the kind of trust that can only arise from the personalization of relationships.

A regional culture, as we shall call this, is not necessarily the fruit of territorial governance as such. Many large Japanese firms, for example, have proved to be effective coordinators of regionally-based supplier networks. But such supplier networks are beset by power assymetries that effectively convert them into fiefs of the large firms that direct them. Industrial districts, on the other hand, of the kind to be found in the "Third Italy", are more loosely coupled, voluntaristic, and hence more plausibly located in the clan region of the C-Space.

How, then, does such a regional culture function?

The Third Italy is located in the North-Central part of the country and at some distance from its industrial heartland of Milan-Turin-Genoa. One of its regions, Emilia-Romagna, has been the fastest-growing region in all Italy. In 1980, Emilia-

Romagna had a population of 3.9 million, an economically-active population of 1.7 million, and 325,000 firms having an average of about five employees per firm. Ninety per cent of its manufacturing firms employed under 99 persons and accounted for 58% of its total workforce. Over a third of the workforce is self-employed (Best, 1990; Hatch, 1986).

The manufacturing centre of Emilia-Romagna is the province of Modena, with a population of around 600,000. Per capita income in the province ranked 17th in Italy in 1970; but by 1979, it had moved to second place (Brusco, 1982). Intriguingly, since the end of World War II, the municipality of Modena has been governed by the Italian Communist Party. In the same way that Marx fulminated against monopoly capital but kept a place in his heart for "petty commodity traders". Thus, the Italian Communist Party could rail against big business at the national level while attracting the small business vote at the municipal level, by creating the closest thing that the twentieth century has to medieval guild socialism: the industrial district. To quote Best,

> In localities governed by the Italian Communist Party the notion of free enterprise has taken on a new meaning. For nowhere is small business more ably attended to by government than in Communist-Party-governed provinces such as Modena (Best, 1990: 209).

The role of the local authority covering an industrial district is to nurture a collective identity and a sense of shared vision and purpose that productively channel the external economies generated by interfirm collaboration while minimizing the "free-rider" problem. The challenge is a subtle one, for it consists not so much in getting rid of opportunism as in harnessing it to acceptable entrepreneurial ends. Yet, one might reasonably ask, who is responsible for establishing the network norms and purposes that define free-riding and opportunism in a particular case?

In clan transactions, these emerge by negotiation and consensus among local players; and to the extent that the local authority acts as a catalyst in this process, it acts as an agent of local rather than national interests. In a sense, the industrial district becomes a territorially-based strategic business unit, a community of fate that is brought into a competitive relationship with other territorially-based communities. Self-awareness enhances the community's strategic potential. Best illustrates the point with an example: the eclipsing of North London furniture-makers in the 1980s by furniture-manufacturers from the Third Italy and from German industrial districts. The North London manufacturers, far from perceiving themselves to be a community of fate and acting accordingly, pursued purely competitive strategies in relation to each other, with each choosing to "go it alone". Not only was the local authority not involved, but under a Thatcherite dispensation, local government – acting as an agent of central government – had no mandate to do so.

When local government acts on its own account or that of its client network, it becomes the regional equivalent of what Chalmers-Johnson in an East-Asian context has called a "developmental state" (Chalmers-Johnson, 1982), entering into explicit competition with other units of territorial governance both at the regional and at the national level. If national governance structures are weak, the outcome is potentially fissiparous. The inability of the Chinese government in recent years, for example, to impose its will on provincial or municipal governments has resulted in rampant protectionism between provinces and frequent conflicts at municipal boundaries. Guanzhou province has on occasion found its exports to neighbouring provinces blocked by their local militia (Boisot and Child, 1988). In China, regional sentiment is much stronger that national sentiment – and it was greatly strengthened in the mid-1980s by the economic decentralization that followed the country's attempts at economic reforms. Although a limited amount of decentralization to enterprises themselves occurred, most of it took the form of a delegation of hitherto central-planning powers to provincial and municipal authorities. What prevented different Chinese regions from building up viable industrial districts under their care – certain localities in South China, it should be said, may be close to achieving this – is a feudal legacy that transformed devolved firms into fiefs to be exploited rather than resources to be nurtured by consensus. Therefore, hierarchy prevailed, albeit a more personalized one. The Chinese lesson seems to be that developmental states or regions may not be pure markets, but they are not pure hierarchy either. They are nimble managers of the SLC across a whole range of institutional structures.

The sterile nature of interregional competition in the People's Republic of China could usefully alert us to a number of unresolved problems with the European Community's project for the single market after 1992, problems that have a direct bearing on how we think of both the new competition and industrial districts.

A limited transfer of national sovereign power to Brussels and to other supranational institutions – the ERM, the Strasbourg Parliament, the European Court of Justice, etc. – will make it more difficult in the future for member states to cope with regional disparities within their borders. A good example of this are the tensions created between Germany and its European trading partners by its efforts to incorporate the old East Germany in ways that are not too destabilizing. With the protective mantle of the nation-state now being removed in the interest of impartial market integration, many regions of Europe are going to find themselves on their own – and, compensations from the FEDER (The European Regional Fund) notwithstanding, they will face the need to act both autonomously and strategically rather than merely as local extensions of central government.

Only those regions capable of adequately conceptualizing their new role are likely to succeed. Casual empiricism – as well as a reading of Piore and Sabel – suggest that the "late developers", i.e. Germany and Italy, are likely to fare quite well. Why?

The late developers grew to full nationhood at a time when the sun was setting on the absolutist state. They thus inherit an institutional memory of regional structures better adapted to the strategic role they will be called upon to play in the new Europe. In some parts of Europe, such as Catalonia or Scotland, market integration and the weakening of national government may well foster latent or not-so-latent separatist tendencies. Some regional governments, most notably Catalonia's, are already seeking independent access to the Brussels Commission and other supranational institutions. In these cases, the regional strategy – more often implicit than explicit – consists in substituting the regional government for the national government wherever possible, thus creating a competitive rather than a complementary relationship between different levels of territorial governance.

One suspects, however, that in many cases – perhaps the majority – the response of local governments to any intensification of territorial competition unleashed by the advent of the single market will be passive incomprehension. This is not to say that, in these cases, local government is wanting in vigour or dedication. Rather, it is to point out that, in the absence of an adequate concept of its strategic role in the new Europe, whatever vigour and dedication is possessed cannot be properly directed. I believe that the concept of the industrial district, the regional SBU – animated and monitored by a local government capable of fostering and managing a competitive territorial culture – points the way forward.

5   Conclusion

In his *Economic Institutions of Capitalism* (1985) Williamson takes large multidivisional corporation as an organizational response to the transactional problems created by bounded rationality and opportunism. As Figure 9.6 indicates, that response moves important elements of the firm's managerial style up the C-Space and towards the right. Efficient markets are assumed to constitute external responses to the same problems and, unsurprisingly, they are located in the same region of the C-Space. Indeed, where efficient markets are to be found in practice, internal organization is deemed to be unnecessary – which is possibly why it has been so long neglected by neoclassical orthodoxy.

Schumpeterian learning, in contrast to neoclassical learning, does not seek to do away with bounded rationality and opportunism so much as put them to good use. The challenge is to regulate rather than suppress them. Who shall be allowed to move opportunistically towards the left of the C-Space on the basis of an idiosyncratically perceived opportunity? What support will be given to risky problem-solving processes and on what terms? How far should one allow joint investments in collective learning – the fruit of knowledge absorption – to yield opportunistic outcomes individually pursued? In short, from a Schumpeterian perspective, what is needed are clear "rules of the game" for managing the segment of the SLC located in the lower region of the C-Space, rather than unrealistic attempts to confine the learning process to the market region alone.

Our discussion of the New Competition and its associated institutions point to common socialization processes, trust, shared values, and personal inter-dependencies, as important ingredients of the rule-making process in the lower part of the C-Space. And for these, spatial concentration will be an important requirement.

Micheal Porter (1990) intuitively appreciates this, pointing out that his "diamond of National Advantage" – a coherent integration of factor conditions, demand conditions, related and supporting industry characteristics, and firm strategy, structure, and rivalry – is likely to work better under conditions of spatial concentration than otherwise. But he fails to draw the inevitable lesson from this simple observation: namely, that only when the nation-state is small enough to operate as a *regional* government, does one find the appropriate level of governance for addressing problems of territorial competition. Of the ten countries that Porter studied for his book, only Singapore meets this requirement. Nevertheless, Porter is often led to draw his most telling examples from the regional level in the countries he discusses.

Porter, being wedded to the idea that nation-states are the natural unit of analysis, offers many prescriptions that are inevitably redolent of the old competition. Their flavour can be sensed from his comments that "Governments cannot create competitive industries, only companies can do that". It is quite possible to subscribe to the view that national government is too remote from the competitive market-place to effectively "pick winners" through an industrial policy and, simultaneously, to argue that local government is often quite well equipped to do so. In order to act credibly as an impartial macro-economic regulator, national and supranational government must subscribe to universalistic values, whether these are expressed hierarchically through a plan or through the invisible hand of the market. Local government, by contrast, is a much more particularistic affair, in which individual actors are identifiable both at the industry and at the enterprise level; and local welfare is as likely to be maximized by pursuing group goals and reciprocal commitments as it is by market clearing. The industrial district, for example, is built up from a web of transaction-specific investments (Williamson, 1985) that act to bind economic actors to each other and to a region. The local authority may not be directly picking winners in the sense of deciding what goods and services will be produced locally and by whom; but it is intimately involved in the process through which winners may be finally selected.

Our conclusion has potentially important implications for Europe's post-communist economies. Their rejection of four decades of Marxist-Leninist mediocrity, has rendered them particularly open to the remedies of the old competition. And the witch doctors of the old competition are prescribing some pretty strong medicine – in many cases, strong enough to kill the patient before it cures him. Most of it is macro-economic; micro-economics, it is blithely assumed, will take care of itself following large-scale privatization. In no case, to my knowledge, has local government been given an explicit economic role in enterprise reform. Internal organization remains, as always, an internal matter beyond the reach of policy makers.

This is a pity. The particularism associated with socialist practice may be distorting and debilitating when applied to national economies; but, as the experience of the Third Italy indicates, it may be well adapted to the emerging strategic mission of local or regional government. Strange as it may sound to the ideologically overcommitted, the capitalist road passes through Modena. Eastern Europe should plan a stopover and visit the place on its way to Washington.

References

Abblegen, J./Salk, G. (1985) *Kaisha: The Japanese Corporation*. New York: Basic Books.

Best, M. (1990) *The New Competition: Institutions of Industrial Restructuring*. The Polity Press.

Blaug, M. (1985) *Economic Theory in Retrospect*. Cambridge: Cambridge University Press.

Boisot, M. (1986) 'Markets and Hierarchies in Cultural Perspective', *Organization Studies*, Spring.

Boisot, M. (1987) *Information and Organization: The Manager as Anthropologist*. London: Collins (Fontana).

Boisot, M./Child, J. (1988) 'The Iron Law of Fiefs: Bureaucratic Failure and the Problem of Governance in the Chinese Economic Reforms', *Administrative Science Quarterly*, December.

Bruner, J. (1957) 'On Perceptual Readiness', *Psychological Review* 64: 123-152.

Brusco, S. (1982) 'The Emilian Model', *Cambridge Journal of Economics* 6.

Chalmers-Johnson (1982) *MITI and the Japanese Miracle*. Stanford, California: Princeton University Press.

Chandler, A. (1962) *Strategy and Structure*. Cambridge, Mass.: M.I.T. Press.

Chandler, A. (1977) *The Visible Hand*. Cambridge, Mass.: Harvard University Press.

Chandler, S. (1990) *Scale and Scope*. Cambridge, Mass.: Harvard University Press.

Coase, R. (1937) 'The Nature of the Firm', *Economica* 4 (4).

Gregory, R. (1981) *Mind in Science: A History of Explanations in Psychology and Physics*. London: Weidenfeld and Nicholson.

Hatch (1986) *Italy's Industrial Renaissance: A Strategy for Developing Small Manufacturing Business*. New York: Port Authority of New York.

Jacobs, J. (1984) *Cities and the Wealth of Nations*. Middlesex: Penguin Books.

Kroeber, A./Kluckhohn, C. (1952) *Culture: A Critical Review of Concepts and Definitions*. Papers of the Peabody Museum of American Archeology and Ethnology XLVII, I. Cambridge, Mass.: Harvard University Press.

Ohmae, K. (1985) *Triad Power: The Coming Shape of Global Competition*. New York: Free Press.

Perlmutter, H./Heenan, D. (1974) 'How Multinational Should Your Top Managers Be?', *Harvard Business Review* 52 (6): 121-132.

Peters, T. (1987) *Thriving on Chaos*. New York: Alfred A. Knopf.

Piore, M./Sabel, C. (1984) *The Second Industrial Divide*. New York: Basic Books.

Polanyi, M. (1962) *Personal Knowledge: Towards a Post-Critical Philosophy*. New York: Harper Torchbooks.

Polanyi, K. (1944) *The Great Transformation*. New York: Rinehart.

Popper, K. (1959) *The Logic of Scientific Discovery*. London: Hutchinson.

Porter, M. (1990) *The Competitive Advantage of Nations*. The Free Press.

Shannon, C. (1948) 'A Mathematical Theory of Communication', *Bell System Technology Journal* 27: 379-423.

Schutz, A. (1962) *Collected Papers* (edited by Mavria Nathanson). The Hague: Martinus Nijhoff.

Stiglitz, J. (1989) 'Information and Economic Analysis – A Perspective', *Economic Journal*, pp. 21-41.

Shackle, G. L. (1972) *Epistemics and Economics*. Cambridge: Cambridge University Press.

Schumpeter, J. (1934) *The Theory of Economic Development*. Cambridge, Mass.: Harvard University Press.

Weber, M. (1965) *Economy of Society* (edited by G. Roth and C. Wittich). New York: Bedminster Press.

Williamson, O. (1975) *Markets and Hierarchies: Analysis and Antitrust Implications*. New York: Free Press.

Williamson, O. (1985) *The Economic Institutions of Capitalism: Firms, Markets, Relational Contracting*. New York: Free Press.

Part V

MANAGING THE ECONOMIC TRANS-FORMATION IN CENTRAL-EASTERN EUROPE AND CHINA: TOWARDS POST-SOCIALIST GOVERNANCE

Chapter 10

Problems in Making the Transition to a Market Economy in Czechoslovakia*

Ota Šik

In order to save time, I will refrain from discussing *why* the transition to a market economy in Czechoslovakia should occur as quickly as possible. The majority of both politicians and the population agree that this transition must be accomplished in the next few years, even if it means a temporary lean patch ahead. In the setting of such a general goal, almost no political disagreements have arisen, and even the revamped Communist Party – whether in full sincerity or not – claims to be in favour of introducing a market economy.

However, even in defining what a market economy is, as well as setting out concrete steps to achieve it, widely opposing viewpoints exist among the various parties and movements. Before presenting these, I would like to give an outline of the current situation, the starting point for our efforts at transition, in order to clarify the objective difficulties posed by the transition process.

1   Structural and Technical Changes Needed in Czechoslovakia

Prior to World War II, Czechoslovakia had a well-developed market economy with a strong industrial basis and ranked sixth in the world in per capita productivity. Its living standard and work productivity matched Germany's at that time. The worldwide economic crisis of the early 1930s did, however, affect Czechoslovakia to a very perceptible degree; and the rate of unemployment rose to 15%, resulting in strong politicalization – both to the left (Communist Party) and to the right (especially with the *Henlein* Movement in Sudetenland). Nevertheless, the economy recovered towards the end of the 1930s and suffered only to a limited extent during the war and the German occupation.

It was during the postwar years when the Communists seized power and during the transition to a socialist economic system modelled entirely on the Soviet system, that the development of the Czechoslovakian economy increasingly stagnated and began to fall far behind the developments in the West. Right from the beginning, however, the rather fast, quantitatively extensive growth was characterized by an ever-increasing lagging behind the West in terms of qualitative, innovative and technical development.

The primitive planning and accounting procedures, the absence of a market mechanism as well as efficiency criteria, the lack of interest in qualitative and technical innovations and the non-existent pressure to compete, all contributed to the growing inefficiency of productive facilities and to an ever-dwindling investment productivity. The basic productive assets were constantly required to increase more quickly than the gross domestic product (GDP), simply in order to maintain a slackening rate of growth in production. The GDP, in relation to capital assets (basic funds), dropped from 58.4% in 1980 to 42.25% in 1989.

Czechoslovakia trailed more and more behind the developments in Western Europe and, to the present day, has been overtaken by many developing countries in Europe. If production per capita of the population is converted to dollar income per capita, according to purchasing power parity, then Czechoslovakia is currently just behind Spain; and in 1985, it occupied the 45th place in the world in terms of per capita consumption.

The production basis in Czechoslovakia is particularly and crassly outdated. The average age of the machinery is 20 years, and it is clearly impossible to achieve any real improvement in work productivity with such old equipment. The statistics concerning the increase in work productivity – issued officially by the Communist regime – were fabricated *de facto* from undetectable price increases in the plants and based on the ever-increasing production of unneeded goods kept in stock, as well as a growing amount in storage. This is therefore a case of a pro forma increase in work productivity.

The technical and technological backwardness in production, the relatively high importance placed on heavy and defence industries, and the distorted attitude – rooted in planning – of the plants towards the squandering of materials, energy and investments resulted in a disproportionately high amount of production goods being used per final unit of consumption. Hence, it was at the beginning of the 1980s that the use of production goods per unit of consumption in Czechoslovakia was 45.3% higher than in the FRG. For many comparable products the figures for the consumption of raw materials and energy even amounted to more than 50-60% higher than in the FRG.

From this emerged a production structure in which an excessively high portion of the production industry and an excessively low portion of the consumer goods industry, figured in the entire production process. In the early 1980s, the share of consumer goods production relative to the entire production in Czechoslovakia, was approximately 31% lower than in the FRG. If Czechoslovakia wanted to achieve the same portion of consumer goods industry to overall production as in West Germany, its consumer goods production would have to grow much more quickly than the manufacture of production goods. However, not only would this take many years, but it could only be achieved in conjunction with an improvement in quality and in the technical standard of the production basis – which would lead to long-range growth in investment productivity. Only by means of continuous advancement in the technical standard and efficiency of the machinery, would it be possible for the consumer goods industry to grow faster than the production of machinery etc. required for this purpose.

A structural, technical and qualitative transformation of this kind will take years to accomplish – my estimation is 10 to 15 years, provided no crass errors are committed in economic policy. In addition to needing imaginative, innovative interest on the side of the enterprise and management, accompanied as far as possible by technical and innovative interest on the part of the employees of these firms, such a transformation also requires enormous capital and investment funds. The net investment quota (portion of new investments relative to the national income) of 12.3% on average to date during the period 1985-89 is difficult to surpass and will most likely be smaller. Nevertheless, new investments can be expanded by the inflow of foreign investment, which can then accelerate the structural transformation not only in a quantitative way, but also in a technical and qualitative one.

Nothing has been said yet about the environmental problems which are particularly critical in Czechoslovakia. It is one of the countries with the most horrific environmental pollution, affecting the soil, the forests, the water and the air. Enormous efforts will have to be made in the next few years to diminish the damage and later to bring about ecological recovery. These, in turn, will require further structural transformations in production, extremely costly changes in energy and transportation and innumerable clean-up and environmental protection facilities.

The entire productive, ecological, urban, educational, etc. transformation is only possible in tandem with a prodigious increase in capital and work productivity; and this is critically dependent on the rate at which the market mechanism and dynamic enerpreneurial activity can be set in motion, as well as on a fundamental change occurring in the behaviour of all elements of the economy.

The above can only be accelerated or slowed down and hindered by the introduction of a prudent or of an unsound economic policy on the part of the government or of the governments of the two republics (the Czech and the Slovak). This leads me to a description and critical analysis of the political and economic influence on the transformation process in Czechoslovakia; first, however, a few comments on the current political situation.

2   The Political Situation in Czechoslovakia

As the dominant political forces of the time exercise a decisive influence on the setting of political and economic goals, as well as on the way in which transformation evolves, it is essential before proceeding further to describe the political circumstances in Czechoslovakia.

In the spring of 1990, at the first free elections to be held, the Citizens' Forum headed by Václav Havel gained the absolute majority in Parliament. This movement started out in a social-liberal direction, ostensibly embedded in the political centre. Strictly speaking, it was supported by former members of Charter 77 and other underground organizations. However, most of these former resistance fighters acquired important political positions, becoming members of Parliament or the government, etc., and no longer concerned themselves with the Citizens' Forum movement.

One man, who seemed to have had great political ambitions right from the start, took advantage of this situation. Václav Klaus was never a member of the Charter movement nor of any other resistance group. In the last few years, he was a member of the Forecasting Institute headed by W. Komárek. He focused his attention particularly on finance and money problems and was an enthusiastic adherent of Friedman's monetarist theory. During the days of round-table negotiations between Havel's Citizens' Forum and the Communist government under Adamec, from which the new government emerged, Klaus was nominated by Havel as Finance Minister – even though the two men were not closely acquainted.

Klaus had ideas of his own about the transition to a market economy and its future character, and so he very soon encountered opposition from Komárek and the other politicians in the Citizens' Forum with socio-liberal leanings. He began to form his own group of followers within the Citizens' Forum, focusing on the base level. He was able to set up a rightist wing of the Citizens' Forum and finally his own right-wing party, the DDS (Bourgeois Democratic Party). Even though only half of the MPs in the Citizens' Forum took membership in the DDS, the rightist forces still have the majority in Parliament (together with the Christian National Party, among others).

The other, socio-liberal section of the Citizens' Forum, whose most well-known representatives include J. Dienstbier (the Foreign Minister) and P. Pitthart (Premier of the Czech government), also organized itself into the Citizens' Movement (OH) – which will most likely become a liberal party.

Nevertheless, Klaus was successful in gaining a strong organizational lead and, together with his closest supporters, has occupied many important economic positions. In fact, almost all economic functions in the federal and Czech government, the economic editorial departments of the most important publications, and many regional bureaus, etc., are now in the hands of supporters of Klaus. He is currently a powerful man in the government and has succeeded in enforcing his concept of economic reform.

Klaus and his editorial staff dismiss any outside suggestions, criticisms or opposing opinions as being the views of former Communists. Even the reformers of 1968 – to which I also belong – who fought against the communist Novotný leadership and ushered in the Prague Spring, were cast out of the party. Many of those who were persecuted as defenders of the Charter and who ended up in prison, are now labelled as "68ers"; all are considered former Communists and their current views and ideas are either ignored or rejected. Klaus's one-sided monetarist concepts in the prevailing political circumstances have not only had an impact on the re-form scenario, they have also exercised a critical influence on the concrete course of the entire economic development.

3   Problems of Privatization in the Transition to a Market Economy

The most decisive steps in setting up a market economy are the following:
1) the establishment of a strong sector of private companies, especially by priva-
    tizing state-owned enterprises;
2) the liberalizing of domestic prices and the setting up of competitive conditions;
3) the liberalizing of foreign trade and the establishment of a convertible currency;
4) social security in the event of unemployment, with retraining opportunities;
5) the introduction of an economic policy to complement the market mechanism.
All the various political forces agree on these steps to be taken, as long as they are formulated in general terms. However, since fairly basic differences do exist between supporters of neoliberal or monetarist theory and the supporters of Keynesian or social theory, opposing views will also be put forth by the rightist and the socio-liberal political forces concerning how to carry out these steps in a concrete way. Political differences are, at least, in part an expression of differing theoretical views of the market economy.

It must be stressed, however, that these differences have nothing to do with a conflict between the advocates and the opponents of the market economy, as Klaus supporters would have one believe. They indicate, as will be shown further on, differing views on the concrete ways to introduce a market economy.

The differences soon become evident in the *problems of privatization.*

In Czechoslovakia, privatization was divided into two categories, small- and large-scale. In the former, approximately 7,000 enterprises are affected (trade, restaurants, crafts), which can be sold directly at public auction to interested buyers. Basically there are no conflicts here, and this type of privatization has already begun throughout the country. By May of this year, 1,530 businesses had been sold; and a further 5,500 should be disposed of by the end of next year.

In the course of large-scale privatization, approximately 4,000 state-run enterprises are to be transformed into stock companies. At present, the exact figures are known only for Bohemia and Moravia, but not yet for Slovakia. In Bohemia and Moravia, 1,776 enterprises are to be privatized in a first stage and 1,118 in a second; 491 state-run enterprises will not be privatized, and approximately 41 are to be liquidated.

A great amount of discussion centres on how this change will be accomplished, as it is evident that the total value of the buildings and facilities far surpasses the financial resources that the population can spend at short notice to purchase shares. The estimated operating assets amount to approximately 1,800 billion *koruny* (Czechoslovak crowns) – whereas the people's available savings that could be used to purchase shares, so-called "hot savings", are about 250 million *koruny*. In other words, only 250/1,800 or 13.9% of the available productive value in the form of shares, can be purchased by residents.

There is no opposition to the sale to foreign buyers, nor are there any legal obstacles. However, interest by foreign parties to date is too slight, even if it could prove otherwise once the sale of shares begins *de facto* on the stock market and by the banks. The sale of shares is now being delayed by a method that Klaus thought up and which was actually intended to begin the entire process.

This is the so-called "Voucher Method", whereby a large portion of the shares are meant to be distributed among the population, basically at no cost (or at token cost). Every adult citizen receives a voucher booklet containing 1,000 investment points. These points may be exchanged for shares in the future stock companies of one's own choice. However, the number of shares that each person receives from the individual companies depends completely on the relationship between supply and demand; and in the event of imbalance, the point value of the shares changes accordingly.

It is expected that the process will occur in a number of rounds – so that in the event of an imbalance between supply and demand, the required amount of points per share of the company in question can change during a further round. This continues until a balance is reached. The hope is that a "rapid" privatization will thus be achieved, but there have not yet been any concrete indications of what amount of shares from the individual companies will be released for the Voucher Method. It has been assured in advance that those enterprises expected to be involved in joint ventures with foreign participation are exempted from the Voucher Method.

Many other economists, in addition to myself, have misgivings about this method and have expressed them in print. Yet as the Parliament of Czechoslovakia has taken the decision to employ this method, I will forebear describing my misgivings in greater detail here. Large-scale privatization based on the Voucher Method is scheduled to begin at the end of 1991.

A short summary will be given, however, of the reasons why I believe that this method cannot achieve what I consider to be of critical importance to the increased efficiency of the Czechoslovak economy. To begin with, I sincerely doubt that it is possible that there could arise from the ranks of the voucher shareholders – who risk none of their own capital and, for the most part, are absolutely inadequately informed – competent members of supervisory bodies and boards of directors as occurs when genuine shareholders make carefully considered share purchases. It is much more likely that a small minority of the well-off will buy up the shares of the great masses of disadvantaged voucher shareholders, thus driving up inflation. The socially disadvantaged voucher shareholders will then go to the consumer goods market with the money they receive, thereby boosting inflationary price increases. This will prompt the stock companies to stall for an extended period the issuing of new shares at favourable prices. Anyone who could purchase new shares will think twice about it, for s/he knows, firstly, that too many of the possibly anticipated, not very high profits will be passed on as dividends to the voucher shareholders; and secondly, that s/he can obtain shares much more cheaply from the voucher shareholders directly. These are also the main reasons why the Voucher Method should not be employed for companies for which a joint venture with foreign participation is expected. The majority of voucher receivers will not obtain shares in forward-looking companies anyway, due to a lack of information or the necessary connections. They will have to be satisfied with shares that do not generate dividends for a long time, or which may even be liquidated at a later date.

It is my conviction that privatization can be accelerated by initial sale to a minority of shareholders, as occurs in almost every Western country – and that this could have begun some time ago. With the aid of special credit intended only for the purchase of shares, at a low interest rate and modelled on the American ESOP Method (Employee State Ownership Plans), it would be possible to find more buyers for the initial purchase. This method would be particularly sound because, instead of boosting inflation, these credits would encourage saving and thus divert financial resources away from the demand for consumer goods.

Further arguments opposing the Voucher Method have been published, but there is little point in elaborating on them here. The fact that all important considerations were simply ignored in the decision-making process, reveals once more the critical impact which the political power struggle has on the economy. The large, monopolistic state-owned concerns have still not been dissolved yet; and the structure and efficiency of these enterprises, as well as their inability to compete on foreign markets, have not changed at all.

What does this mean for the other processes of change along the path towards a market economy?

4   On Problems Involved with Liberalization of Domestic Prices, and on Restrictive Money and Financial Policies

The economic reform imposed by Klaus as a form of shock therapy to be carried out in the shortest possible time (referred to in Czechoslovakia as the *"Velky tresk"* – that is, "Great Blow"), included the removal at short notice of state (administrative) price-fixing and of the state's (planned) stipulation of exports and imports – in other words, the liberalization of domestic prices and of foreign trade. The question arises as to whether the effect which this shock therapy had on true recovery from the economic backwardness caused by Communism was to accelerate recovery or to slow it down. My aim is to logically demonstrate that the latter is the case.

Critics from all camps warned against an immediate release (deregulation) of prices with a simultaneous liberalization of foreign trade. It was also contended that the *de facto* still existing absolute monopolization of most production sectors, would lead to galloping inflation if all prices were deregulated.

It was under these circumstances that the government attempted to retain certain types of price control while still releasing most prices.

There are:

1) commodities with fixed minimum prices (energy sources and basic foodstuffs);
2) products for which a price increase is approved only when proof is given of rising costs in the previous step in production (e.g. automobiles etc.);
3) products which require central authorization for price increases in every case. However, the official statistics claim that 80% of prices have already been deregulated.

In spite of partial price control, a strong increase in prices did occur. The major food price increases were made intentionally by eliminating the former state allocation (so-called negative tax). Due to this alone, food prices soared an average of 25% (this one-time increase was compensated for by a one-time cash reimbursement to all residents).

For other price increases enacted by the state – for example of all energy sources, i.e. coal, gas, electrical energy – there was no compensation. This also applies to the increased fares for public transit. The rise in rents, which has been delayed, will be substantial.

In actual fact, prices did rise much more than the government anticipated. This year's 30%-gain, when compared to last year, was far beyond the expectations:

• The price of consumer goods in April 1991 was already 65.4% higher than the figure for April 1990 – of these, foodstuffs rose by 58.5%.
• The greatest jump in prices occurred for consumer goods other than foodstuffs, at a rate of 80% compared with April 1990.
• The slightest of all price rises occurred in the service sector at only 29%.

- The price of the automobile known as *Skoda*, which even before the price increases amounted to approximately 25 times the average monthly income (in Western Europe, approximately 4 times), zoomed up to currently 45 times the average monthly income.

Wages improved, after agreement between government and the unions, at a much slower rate. Originally, an increase of 5% was negotiated for 1991; but this figure was increased in March, so that wages should have improved by an average of 9%. However, as many enterprises could not adhere to this figure at all (due to inability to pay), the actual wage increase over the previous year in the first quarter of 1991 amounts to only 6%. This translates to a 27%-drop in real wages compared with 1990.

By the end of the year, when all the promised social improvements are included in the figures, it is expected that large families and pensioners will feel a brutal financial pinch and that the income of approximately 15-20% of the population will sink below the so-called poverty level.

The situation will deteriorate more quickly towards the end of the year, as a sharp rise in the unemployment rate is to be expected. At present, the situation is not too bad; the unemployment rate is 2% in the Czech Republic and 4.6% in the Slovak Republic, or 2.9% on average. However, as the liquidation figures for numerous enterprises are not expected until the end of the year, an increase in unemployment by December of 600,000-1,000,000 persons is anticipated – which means an unemployment rate of 7.5 to 13%.

The country has already skidded into a true and proper economic crisis, characterized mainly by an unheard-of drop in production. In the first four months of 1991, industrial production sank by 13%; and by May of this year, it was already 27.2% lower than in May 1990. The figure for the Czech republic was 24.9%; and for Slovakia, 32.7%. Building activity declined a full 50% compared with May 1990.

This crisis has been caused in particular by massively shrinking markets and by the necessary rise in prices. The latter were initiated by enterprises to compensate both for the breakneck speed at which their input costs have risen and for the high interest rates.

Sales are dwindling, and decisively – both because of the shrinking domestic market (declining real income and diminishing government spending, i.e. restrictive policy) and because of the great decrease in foreign markets (meaning the Comecon countries and the disappearance from the scene of East Germany).

At the same time the input prices for enterprises are growing extremely rapidly, as a result of the surging prices of crude oil and especially of the strong devaluation of the *koruna*, which tremendously raises import prices for enterprises.

Furthermore, in addition to this, the restrictive money and financial policies have caused interest rates to shoot up drastically. As a result, costs also soar in the enterprises, with the result that they see no other way to avoid bankruptcy than to raise their own prices. And because the demand for their product slumps when the price rises, they react by cutting back production.

The outcome of all this is classical stagflation (stagnating production accompanied by rising prices), which until now has only occurred in industrial countries to this extent as a result of war. Growing problems with finding markets cause a slowdown in investment, which is an indispensible prerequisite for overcoming economic backwardness. The drop in investment is greatest in the machine and consumer goods industries, as well as in services: in other words, in those sectors in whose favour the production structure should change.

The question now arises as to what extent this development is the result of a defective economic policy.

It is undoubtably true that a restrictive monetary and financial policy was needed in the given situation of a large, inflationary surplus of money in the past both as a means of economic pressure on the enterprises and as a way of forcing them to increase their efficiency. The aim was, then, to achieve the most balanced state budget possible while sharply decreasing expenditures, particularly state economic subsidies. In addition, the volume of credits had to be diminished and the credits made more expensive. Interest rates were increased to 24%.

The purpose of the drop in subsidies – with the aim of eliminating them altogether – and of the high interest rates was to force the enterprises to rapidly boost their efficiency, trim their costs somewhat and achieve profitability by means of structural changes, innovations and gains in quality. This goal is in itself perfectly good; however, one tends to overlook the fact that the incentive and willpower of management alone are not enough to achieve it.

Of course, it is also true that the majority of the old management bodies are in no way capable of implementing new management techniques; therefore, they must be replaced.

However, the problem thus posed is threefold: first, the type of supervisory bodies that could enforce such replacements do not yet exist; second, it is questionable whether, in such a short time, many of the politically-compromised managing bodies could be replaced by new management personnel; and third – and this is the most important – even the most capable managers cannot bring about in a very short time the necessary structural changes and modernization which would render these enterprises able to compete on domestic and foreign markets and be profitable.

At the time of the Prague Spring, we figured that it would take us about five to seven years to achieve a level of economic efficiency comparable to Austria's. Now we realize that it will take – as already mentioned – approximately 10 to 15 years. Of course, it is possible for individual enterprises to institute progressive changes much more quickly than that, but this is absolutely not the case for the overwhelming majority of the large-scale enterprises.

All such modern and market-oriented changes require enormous investments which simply cannot be achieved in a short time. The mere transformation of large-scale armament factories into profitable plants producing civilian goods is an immensely difficult task! And because 70% of these armament factories – for which at present it is practically impossible to find a suitable new production possibility – are located in Slovakia, the slump in production and the surge in unemployment are greatest there. A natural consequence of this situation is a burgeoning of conflict between the Slovak and the Czech populations.

As a part of the national income, the scope of investments can only be enlarged to a tolerable limit – and with this given scope, only part of the necessary structural changes and technical modernization of the production basis can be carried out every year. This production-related background to reform developments is constantly overlooked by the monetarists, who are used to thinking only in monetarist terms.

It is clear that no central authority can conceive of all the possible and necessary changes in production, much less plan them. However, neither is it possible only to exercise market-oriented, economic pressure and think that production efficiency can be improved all in one stroke. A systems expert who recognizes the connection between market-oriented reforms and production possibilities, must also be capable of recognizing when, for example, the restrictive money and financial policy changes into a measure used not to exercise pressure to improve efficiency, but to slow down real structural changes.

From that point in time when, due to interest rate- and input-related price increases, costs begin to increase more quickly than earnings (approx. 34% of enterprises are insolvent) and gains in efficiency cannot be accomplished quickly enough, that is, when rates of profit drop or even disappear (with an additional deduction by the state of 50% of all existing profits), the enterprises cannot react otherwise than by sharply curbing production. In such a situation, the liberalization of foreign trade enforced through political means seems even more counter-productive.

5   On the Problem of Liberalizing Foreign Trade after Creating a Convertible Currency

Even with the idea that the quickest possible liberalization of foreign trade and the related creation of a convertible currency are necessary for the very swift emergence of a market economy, the fact is totally overlooked that it is *impossible to achieve* competitiveness of domestic production at short notice. This inability to compete must be taken as the starting point when considering the liberalization of foreign trade.

After eliminating the administrative planning of exports, with the unalterable need for such a high level of export with which to guarantee foreign currency earnings for the necessary import, it must be possible to motivate the enterprises to aim for the highest possible export level. Therefore, even the less efficient sectors and enterprises must be made capable of and interested in this goal, so that they nevertheless do engage in exportation – on their own, without a central mandate and with the grim prospect of achieving very unfavourable prices on the foreign market.

This requires at least the internal convertability of the currency for the enterprises – that is, a possibility both to exchange foreign for domestic currency and domestic for foreign currency at a market-oriented rate of exchange. *Internal* convertability is required because the domestic currency cannot yet be sold or traded on foreign markets. The earners of foreign currency (funds) must sell these to the state-owned banks at market rates. At the same time, a rate of exchange has to be fixed domestically which assures a sufficiently large inflow of foreign currencies (from exportation, tourism, etc.) to satisfy the anticipated demand by the importers for foreign currencies.

However, given the poor competitiveness of the Czechoslovakian products, this requires the domestic currency – that is, the *koruna* – to be devalued to such an extent to make it possible for even the barely efficient producers – who would in fact suffer losses if the *koruna* were "harder" – to export. Even though they receive only rather poor prices abroad for their goods, the *koruna* is devalued so much that they get back so many *koruny* in exchange for their marks or francs or dollars that they can cover costs and even make a profit.

If, therefore, a "softer" rate of exchange is fixed for the *koruna* – for example, 28 Kcs for a dollar instead of 17 (that is, strong devaluation of the *koruna*, which in no way corresponds to its stronger domestic purchasing power) – then even those producers are able to export who would not be able to cover their costs from the very poor prices received abroad, for example at an exchange rate of $1 = 17 Kcs (when buying *koruny*).

However, the consequences of these soft exchange rates run strictly counter to the aims of the restrictive policy. Instead of producing pressure for increased efficiency, the least efficient sectors and enterprises are also able to export – that is, sell and even make profits – without any particular effort. What is, then, the point of innovations and structural changes when a profit can be made without them?

On the other hand, soft exchange rates result in *imports* becoming more expensive. For every product with a foreign price tag, a relatively large amount of *koruny* must be paid to purchase domestically the currency required. The volume of import has to be reduced in part; and to some extent, the high import prices will have to be shifted to domestic products, even including consumer goods. Thus, the effect of devaluation is to strongly encourage inflation and to slacken the pressure on domestic production to perform efficiently.

A further important point is that after a certain time, when prices at home increase more quickly than the efficiency rate, the exporters' costs also rise again; and they cannot remain capable of exporting if the exchange rate is soft. If the export volume is to be maintained (to assure necessary imports), then devaluation must be carried out again. Hence it can be seen that devaluation reinforces inflation, and inflation brings about further devaluations.

In addition, it is clear that the cheap *koruna* leads to very unfavourable sale of plants or plant parts to foreign investors, and increasingly also to unfavourable prices for consumer goods and services being sold to foreign tourists.

It was necessary, of course, to move away from the administrative planning of foreign trade. However, the question is raised as to whether it was really necessary to switch over to a standard exchange rate so quickly, or whether this step could not have been delayed until there was a genuine increase in efficiency and in the competitiveness of domestic production.

Whatever the answer may be, the transition to a liberalization of foreign trade and to convertible currency is in any case not a process which should be carried out with no regard for domestic production possibilities and the realistic achievement of competitiveness on foreign markets. The losses which could be incurred, should these possibilities be ignored and purely theoretical monetaristic decisions carried out, are far too immense and critical for the Czechoslovakian economy to be passed over carelessly.

6   Which Market Economy is the Objective?

Czechoslovakia will of course achieve a market economy, for it has the best qualifications to do so (with the exception of the former GDR, which is a special case). Yet no matter how the economic policy is set up, the politicians will always be able to look back and say, "We have achieved our goal; therefore, our decisions were correct".

Economists can only reveal certain economic and social relationships within certain circumstances and attempt to demonstrate with which political-economic measures the optimal fulfilment of human needs might be achieved with the least amount of loss. However, they cannot conduct an economic experiment in order to prove the astuteness of their theories; it is only by means of logical argument and persuasive powers that they can exercise political influence. But the politicians, who have decision-making powers over economic policy, will always ignore the arguments of the economists which run contrary to their political prestige or their strivings for power.

My attempt here to show that there are possibilities for Czechoslovakia to achieve a market economy different from those promoted by Klaus and his followers, is motivated by the conviction that Klaus's method will cause not only unnecessary delays but – also and more importantly – excessive economic losses and social hardship.

Klaus has been able, using political slogans and with the broad-based support of his party members in many media, to build up the illusion among the populace that the way of "radical reform" is the fastest way to achieve widespread prosperity. His words, "The more we are willing today to bear difficulties and endure, the faster the conditions will occur under which we will be much better off", have had a broad impact.

All of his critics and the defenders of other scenarios for the transition to a market economy are branded publicly as opponents of such an economy, as socialists in disguise, as economists and politicians loaded down with old-fashioned Marxist ideology, and – in some media – are even prevented from expressing their opinions.

Klaus goes so far as to resist every *socially*-oriented attempt at transformation, to reject the term "social market economy" and to plead for a market economy with "no ifs or buts", totally stripped of adjectives. It is his theoretic conviction that the market economy has no need of economic policy-makers, which is completely in line with Friedman's monetarist theory. In his view, social aims have nothing to do with economics, and the market alone is in a position to maintain a balance in the economic development and set it up in the best possible way.

It is not possible here to elaborate on this monetarist theory and the relevant economic ideas; my thoughts on the subject can be found in various publications.

In conclusion, I would like to say that an economic system does insure the greatest efficiency in production with the help of the market mechanism; but the processes of distribution of the national income are also a characteristic of an economic system. I strictly reject an economic system according to the monetarists' model, whereby the distribution of income is to be subject only to the market mechanism.

In my view, in a market economy the state must have a say in the distribution of income; and this occurs *de facto* throughout the world. The state should strive to achieve this type of income distribution – over the longest possible term and on the basis of democratic decision-making – to satisfy as much as possible the social, cultural and ecological needs of society with no loss of production efficiency. The term I use for such a market economy is "social market economy"; the one used by the President of Czechoslovakia, Václev Havel, is "socially appropriate market economy". A fully-functional market mechanism should come into being as soon as possible, with legally-assured conditions for the import of capital and investments from abroad. For a market economy which is sufficiently secure in the social sense creates the necessary political conditions for the fastest, most efficient development possible.

Note

* Text of a German lecture given at the 10th EGOS Colloquium on "Societal Change between Market and Organization", Vienna, 15-17 July 1991. The reader is reminded of the fact that the given contribution analyses the situation in Czechoslovakia at the time when this colloquium was held, i.e. summer 1991. Hence, part of the information and analysis presented would now be subject to change and updating.

CHAPTER 11

Society and Enterprise Between Hierarchy and Market

John Child

1   Introduction

This paper focuses on one of the most remarkable contemporary instances of societal change between market and organization, namely the movement away from hierarchical governance in the post-socialist and reforming socialist countries (Eastern Europe and China). It endeavours both to analyse this change from an organizational perspective and to discuss its implications for the management of enterprises.

The perspective adopted here follows the tradition of Max Weber in several respects (cf. Weber, 1922/1964). In the first place, it is assumed that a framework of political economy has to be adopted to make sense of recent events in Eastern Europe and China. These have illustrated how the exercise of political will can reshape the conditions of economic behaviour, and at the same time emphasize that the legitimacy of political authority is often conditional on the delivery of economic performance. It was primarily an economic failure which prompted the political revolution in Eastern Europe, leading to a crisis of legitimacy for their communist governments. In China the democracy movement of 1989 was given considerable impetus by urban workers dissatisfied with falling real incomes. In Eastern Europe the crisis gave rise to a struggle – either within the ruling party as in Hungary, or between the party and an external popular force as in Poland – which led to a fundamental change in political power that now seems to be irreversible. The East European revolution has opened the way for the building of what George Soros (1991) has called the "Open Society" to replace the closed and hierarchical society of state socialism. This may yet happen in China.

The changes of political power in Eastern Europe have been sufficiently sweeping to usher in a new normative order. This order legitimates private property, institutional and political pluralism and open relations with other countries. It is giving rise to a radical restructuring of the economic and social context within which organizations operate, towards the "three D's" of (1) decentralization, (2) differentiation and looser coupling, and (3) diffusion of information and initiative. What is taking place is therefore an institutional change in the full sense of that term, embracing both societal values and structures.

This identifies the second Weberian strand, which Biggart (1991) has called a "Weberian institutional perspective". In addressing the problem of explaining East Asian economic organization, she concluded that this perspective can usefully build on analyses referring to market, cultural, and political-economic contexts while avoiding their limitations. In particular, an institutional perspective is helpful because it can accomodate the dynamics posited by other social theories while enriching an understanding of the connectivities between societies and organizations which incorporate those dynamics.

The third strand is a modernist orientation, in which organizations are regarded as the instruments as well as the products of societal development. In Eastern Europe, there are momentous societal changes underway. These are seen by most people living through them as constituting progress and modernization away from a condition and regime they have rejected. Organizations (especially economic ones) have been allocated a key role as agents of this transformation. It is appropriate therefore to embrace the Weberian pursuit of the theoretical connections between the organization as a technical device and its development and use within a wider context of political and cultural contest. This is, indeed, a tradition which Michael Reed has recently argued we should renew within organization studies (Reed, 1991: 30). In contrast to the post-modernist project of deconstructing organizational phenomena down to the existential world of individuals and their discourse, this approach seeks to theorize primarily in terms of collective units – particularly organizations and their leading groups – and in relation to their social environment (cf. Cooper and Burrell, 1988; Featherstone, 1988).

A final debt to Weber lies in the use of his method of constructing "ideal types", which provides a method for handling the broad analytical contrasts to be drawn between the centralized hierachical system of state socialism and the so-called market-based system.

There are several reasons for concentrating on the economic sector and its constituent enterprises. The first is that (as just mentioned) the economy is the strategic site for the politics of social control and the shaping of social change. Enterprises are the key category of organization both for demonstrating the new alignment of political forces at ground level and for providing the economic basis which will sustain societal reform and prevent it from collapsing into a chaos of material deprivation. Such deprivation would soon undermine the new-found faith in Soros's open society and may indeed yet do so in Russia.

The second reason is that there are considerable pressures for enterprises to change in the former socialist societies, and these provide an excellent opportunity for students of organization to observe the connections between organizational behaviour and the relevant institutional context – both the former and the newly emerging one. As Balaton and his colleagues (1990) put it:

> Contemporary Eastern Europe provides a natural experiment for studying how organizations adapt ... Recent events place Eastern European organizational structures and procedures under substantial pressure to change. The conventional litany is well-known: market relations are changing. New markets are being opened; old ones are disappearing. Monopolies are being transformed into oligopolies. Foreign trade restrictions are being changed. Sources of supply are changing. Methods for financing operations are changing. Marketing connections and the relations with customers are changing. The ways in which enterprises deal with the labor market and with individuals are changing. The organization of research and development, of production, and of management are all changing. Structures, power relations, and control are changing (pp. 2-3).

The third, and pragmatic, reason for concentrating on enterprises is that this is the field of organizational activity with which the author is most familiar in the societies we are considering. During the past few years he has worked in direct contact with enterprises in China, a location which illustrates a number of the problems which can arise in effecting the transformation being considered. He has also gained a limited familiarity with Hungarian enterprises through the opportunity of working closely with colleagues in that country and drawing on their insights.

Three specific issues are examined in turn. First, what are the organizational features of the institutional context for enterprises, referring both to the former centralized hierarchical system and the emergent market-based system? Second, given that context, what are the implications for enterprises of the societal change from hierarchy to market systems? Third, what problems arise from transition itself, especially in respect of its provisional nature and the presence of institutional lag?

2   The Institutional Context of Enterprises: Structural and Behavioural Comparison of Hierarchical and Market-based Systems

To contrast the organization of the hierarchical and market-based systems with the necessary degree of economy requires the use of ideal typifications. The danger, of course, is that this exaggerates the internal consistency, homogeneity and invariant character of each system in comparison to the reality. For example, the proportion of industry in state ownership differs considerably between China and

Hungary. The percentage of industrial employment accounted for by state enterprises was about 90% in Hungary at the beginning of 1991, but under 70% in China. Hungarian economic activity has also been far more concentrated in the hands of large enterprises than is the case with China. Thus socialist and former socialist economies could vary significantly even on criteria which had common ideological approval such as state-ownership and the development of large-scale industry.

The characterization of state socialist societies has been much influenced by what was actually their extreme form: that total and enclosed society achieved under Stalin and through his influence. (It should, however, be remembered that this system was in place in the USSR for a generation longer than in the rest of the postwar socialist world). All facets of life were dominated by political dogma and control, and the access of citizens to external ideas and contact was strictly limited. While this era established the institutional framework and the ideological values and structures of communist societies, the stereotype it furnishes obviously has to be qualified in the light of subsequent reforms.

Table 11.1: Structural Comparison of Hierarchical and Market-Based Systems

HIERARCHICAL SYSTEM	MARKET SYSTEM
Centralized	*Decentralized*
• State monopoly of material and intellectual property rights	• Wide distribution of private property rights
• Totalitarian system: stress on political compliance and a mix of political and economic goals	• Non-totalitarian system: stress on plural economic goals
Undifferentiated: tight coupling	*Differentiated: loose coupling*
• Bureaucratic coordination by state political and administrative bodies	• Coordination by connected institutional networks
• Concentration of institutional power: law, regulation and information	• Institutional differentiation of law, regulation and information
Concentration of information	*Diffusion of information*
• Information impactedness	• Information widely diffused through multiple sources
• Closed system	• Open system

Although Stalinist state socialism was at one time prototypical, this cannot be said of the many capitalist countries which have developed through their own diverse routes involving, *inter alia*, quite distinct patterns of state intervention in the market (cf. Littler, 1983). As Davis and Scase stated a few years ago, "if there is debate over the nature of East European countries, there is comparable dispute over the character of Western societies." (1985: 9). However, the same writers concluded that, despite these disputes, "if the countries of the West can be regarded as essentially capitalist, the countries of Eastern Europe can be viewed as over-whelmingly state socialist. " (1985: 9). It is with this justification, therefore, that the following characterization is offered.

The two systems can be compared in terms of key structural and behavioural features. The structural comparison is summarized in Table 11.1.

2.1 Structural Characteristics

2.1.1 Locus of Control – Centralized/Decentralized

Broadly speaking, the state socialist system was a centralized total system in which the state monopolized both material and intellectual property rights. It tried to enforce compliance with political norms in all walks of life; norms which were justified in terms of a dogmatic ideology. Rival ideologies such as religion were attacked. Consequently, the goals that enterprises were expected to pursue were informed by a mix of political and economic criteria. By contrast, the market-based system tends to be decentralized and to permit a spread of material and intellectual property rights. The role of the state varies considerably; though it is always greater at an informal level than is manifest, it does not endeavour to impose its own total framework on society. Enterprises are expected to pursue primarily economic goals; they are not expected to perform the functions of political control or social welfare, although their actions are tempered by political pressures to minimize external social costs.

2.1.2 Differentiation – Tight and Loose Coupling

Kornai (1986) distinguished between the bureaucratic and market coordination of the two systems. The state socialist system was tightly coupled by a centralized bureaucracy, in which political control is combined with administrative regulation. The regulation of economic transactions used to be through direct control by higher authorities, typically ministries or their bureaux, which by means of administrative fiat and/or legal sanction obliged lower-level units such as enterprises to accept commands and prohibitions from above. Although in many socialist countries state control became less direct in recent years, a strong vertical dependency was maintained by the need of lower-level organizations to rely upon higher authorities for the favourable redistribution of resources in various forms, including the allocation of funding for investment or subsidies, the approval of access to foreign exchange and the granting of contracts to trade with other socialist countries. Higher authorities also influenced, if not determined, the appointment of state enterprise chief executives.

Market-based systems are, by contrast, loosely coupled. There is no attempt to coordinate their transactions centrally; rather, this takes place through a large number of deals and contracts within distinct yet connected institutional networks. Under state socialism the same governmental framework (at national level in Eastern Europe and mainly at local level in China) would approve production plans, the sourcing of supplies, the funding of investment and the allocation of labour. Under a market-based system, the firm can take its own initiative on these matters, dealing with separate external parties – customers, suppliers, financial institutions, and the labour market – and would not necessarily involve the state. Moreover, in the market-based system economic structures are not normally politically determined.

Within particular industries or sectors, the looser coupling of the market-based system is normally also manifest in the presence of multiple competing players, whereas Eastern Europe was characterized by industrial monopolies which were in the past tied closely to their respective ministries. In China, given its huge size, the scope of these monopolies is more usually coterminous with the boundaries of provincial or metropolitan areas, within which they have been administratively protected. The rationale of planning, bolstered by the convenience of having single industrial units reporting to higher administrative bodies, led to monopoly and low substitutability. In other words, the socialist economic structure of industrial monopolies created asset specificity. This asset specificity has today given rise to economic mammoths which do not possess the inherent capacity to adapt to other markets, and this is why in Eastern Europe so much urgency is attached to their privatization as a means of de- and re-constructing them.

There is also a greater differentiation between the institutional segments of market-based systems than those of centralized hierarchical ones. In market-based systems, for example, different institutions take responsibility for the administration of law, the provision of economic resources and the sourcing of information. The legal process is institutionally separate from the executive process of government. Enterprises are scrutinized for the quality of their products by consumer associations as well as government inspectorates. The characteristics of markets themselves vary. Labour markets tend to be much more localized and poorly coupled in terms of information exchange than are capital markets. This pluralism was absent in state socialist society, although this is not to deny that conflicts could arise between different arms of the state governance system. Differentiation even extends to within particular institutional areas of the market-based system; finance may, for example, be obtained from banks, the stock market, retained profits, trade creditors, and so on.

2.1.3 Information – Concentration/Diffusion

Information is available in market-based systems from a wide range of sources, and is widely diffused as a consequence. As Boisot (1986) has pointed out, a condition for the efficient operation of markets is that relevant information is both highly codified and widely diffused. By contrast, the information available to economic units within a hierarchical system tends to be confined to vertical administrative channels and to be expressed through coded, but not necessarily codified, understandings between actors within the closed structure. This means that hierarchical social systems are characterized by what Williamson calls "information impactedness" to a greater extent than their market-based counterparts.

The relative pluralism of market-based systems lends them an open character internally. In reality, of course, the market-based system is a global one based on an international division of labour which is ideologically justified in terms of comparative advantage. So it is open across national boundaries, whereas state socialism was a relatively closed system in this respect as well. The international division of labour in Eastern Europe was administratively and politically planned within the COMECON framework, which itself encouraged the establishment of industrial monopolies within the countries selected to specialize on the production of particular product categories.

The combination of information impactedness and administrative closure did not provide the information, authority, or indeed motivation, for state enterprises to develop their own initiatives, such as diversification into new fields.

2.2 *Behavioural Characteristics*

Hierarchical and market-based systems tend to exhibit a number of characteristic behaviours which, it can be argued, derive directly from the ways that they are structured and, less directly, from the values of the regime which controls them. These behaviours are summarized in Table 11.2.

The adaptive problem-solving capacity of the hierarchical system is inhibited by a number of limitations which do not apply, at least in the same degree, to the market-based system. As just noted, its rationality is bounded by information impactedness and closure. Information tends to be stored within bureaucracies which regard it as a power resource and are therefore secretive. It is not widely dispersed and subject to the multiple analyses and interpretations of a kind offered by the plural, independent organizations of the market-based system. This is a contrast between particularism and universalism. The hierarchical system tends to give rise to an information hoarding society, whereas the market-based system encourages an information sharing society. In the former, political attempts to impose a monolithic ideology and the lack of stimulus from contacts across national boundaries further inhibit the free exchange of ideas, information and suggestions.

Table 11.2: Behavioural Comparison of Hierarchical and Market-based Systems

HIERARCHICAL SYSTEM	MARKET SYSTEM
Limited adaptation non-incremental learning via crisis and informal practices	*High adaptation* incremental learning and selection of organizations
Economic risk borne by state low motivation for organizational learning	*Economic risk borne by firm* high motivation for organizational learning
Supercriticality vulnerability to catastrophic failure	*Subcriticality* resilience to economic crisis
Opportunistic alawful behaviour	*Constraints on opportunism* from open accountability

The hierarchical system therefore exhibits non-incremental development. Instead, its changes tend to be explosive reactions to crisis. All of the state socialist societies experienced periodic, sometimes extreme, major policy shifts which affected the whole system. These changes were usually provoked by crisis and were often accompanied by a substitution of one leader for another within the same ruling party.

Market-based systems also experience crises, though since the Keynesian era few have been catastrophic. Generally speaking, however, they adapt to changing circumstances through incremental learning and through a process of selection both between political parties and within their population of organizations. Incremental learning is stimulated in the market system by competitive pressures – the fact that firms bear the risk of failure and are not normally protected by a soft budget constraint adds considerably to their managers' motivation to learn. Whereas risk is borne by the state in hierarchical systems, it resides with the enterprise in market systems. Learning can take place because firms are able to secure relevant external information and then, based on the analysis of this information, can launch new products, try new production methods, adjust prices or whatever, without restrictions from superior administrative authorities. The selection process takes place via entry and exit, which again is not generally countenanced in the hierarchical system. In the economic sphere, innovating firms, often new entrepreneurial entrants, point the way and are prepared to shoulder greater risks for the prospect of securing rent in the short-term. They draw forth followers and leave behind laggards. Selection is achieved through the entry and exit of organizations to and from the population of organizations in a sector or industry (cf. Hannan and Freeman, 1989).

A related consideration is that the centralization of initiative within a hierarchical system denied the opportunity for state-owned firms to develop their own set of adaptive routines for anticipating and adjusting to crisis. As noted below, there was some learning amongst those firms through the development of informal practices, but this tended to be concerned with "making do" operationally rather than to constitute learning of a strategic kind. By contrast, the market system encourages strategic learning and this means that whereas some firms may go under in the face of an economic crisis, others are likely to survive through making both relevant strategic and operational adjustments.

The argument here is that the hierarchical system has been non-adaptive because its centralized and closed nature led to information impactedness and discouraged incremental learning, and because its centralized control over the organizational population did not readily permit incremental or marginal adjustment through the selection dynamics of population ecology. The system on the whole has had to adjust through dramatic reactions to crises which are extremely costly and threatening to its survival.

There is a further consideration which casts doubt upon the survival capacity of the centralized hierarchical system. This stems from the tight coupling that reflects the attempts of its leaders to impose conformity and minimize "control-loss". The consideration is that once a social system reaches a critical state in terms of coping with a marginal additional load on its material, informational or political resources, the internal coupling of the system will determine whether that additional straw breaks the camel's back or merely strains one of its muscles.

Bak and Chen (1991) have advanced what they call "the theory of self-organized criticality", which provides a suggestive basis in this respect for comparing the ability of the two social systems to avoid catastrophic failure. The theory states, in their words, that:

> many composite systems ['those containing millions and millions of elements that interact over a short range'] naturally evolve to critical state in which a minor event starts a chain reaction that can affect any number of elements in the system (p. 26).

By reference to dominoes, Bak and Chen argue that the extent of the internal system collapse which occurs when a critical state is reached depends on the tightness of the internal coupling of that system:

> Dominoes demonstrate criticality, subcriticality and supercriticality. In the critical system, dominoes were randomly placed on about half the segments in a diamond grid. When the dominoes in the bottom row were tipped over, the critical system produced many sizes of chain reactions. The subcritical system – in which the density of dominoes was much less than the critical value – produced small chain reactions. The supercritical system in which the density was much greater than the critical value – exploded with activity [in other words, there was a major system collapse] (p. 27).

The theory of self-organized criticality could help to account for the resilience of market-based systems in coping with economic crises compared with the catastrophic economic reverses recently experienced by the centralized economies, especially the most centralized and tightly coupled of all – the former Soviet Union. In hierarchical systems, economic actors are tightly coupled through the absence of alternative resource sources and consequent resource dependencies, the absence of a clear boundary between enterprises and higher authorities, and the combined politico-economic power structure. So when this system reaches its critical stage, any failure to cope by one part of the system could start a chain reaction leading to progressive and widespread collapse. This is one possible reason why economic or ethnic crises could easily lead to a collapse of the system as a whole. The governments concerned therefore exert desperate efforts to localize the crises. They protect large loss-making state enterprises through subsidies in the attempt to avert the extensive chain reaction which could follow their failure, yet paradoxically this very protection prolongs the weakness of the system – its combination of tight coupling and inadequate performance.

In a market-based system, economic actors are more loosely coupled and the relationship between networks is not so tight. The bankruptcy of a firm, even a large one, does not endanger the whole system. Crises can therefore be localized and the flexibility of the system assists recovery even in the localized area. This is not, of course, to suggest in any Panglossian way that market-based systems are immune from crisis or that regions and sectors within them are not liable to collapse. But the system as a whole seems to have a better chance of self-sustained survival and recovery. There has been quite rapid recovery even from crises which have in the short term exploded through chain reactions along the tightly coupled channels of modern information technology. In the case of the 1987 stockmarket collapse, for example, the loose coupling between the financial and productive sectors of market economies protected the latter and therefore the economy as a whole was not seriously threatened.

A further behavioural contrast between the hierarchical and market-based systems concerns the prevalence, and indeed endemic necessity, of informal opportunistic behaviour. As Montias (1988) has argued, the centralized and vertical nature of the hierarchical system combined administrative resource distribution with mutual dependencies between its levels, and therefore set the conditions for firms to lobby and bargain with the resource redistributing authorities. As one Hungarian managing director said, "lobbying was the key requirement for a firm to succeed." (Spronz, 1991). Insofar as lobbying and bargaining were conducted within the closed confines of a bureaucratic system, they were not subject to the inhibitions common in a market-based system where both the process and the content of such deals would be open to scrutiny, especially if public funds were in question. Indeed, within the confines of bureaucratic coordination, the striking of deals which it might be difficult to justify on economic grounds were facilitated by the combination of roles across levels. Child and Loveridge (1990: 266) cite an example from pre-1989 Hungary in which investment allocation was influenced by the fact that the director of a resource-receiving organization had a seat on the resource-providing committee.

This combination of roles is another instance of tight coupling within the system. The opportunism it encouraged was directed towards the perceived mutual benefit of the related system levels, even though it often detracted from the efficient use of economic resources within the system as a whole. Thus the subordinate organization benefited from a soft budgetary constraint in terms of its growth or survival. The higher-level government authority benefited in terms of the political and administrative loyalty of its subordinate unit, including its willingness to follow government policy.

As already indicated, another reason for opportunistic behaviour under the hierarchical system lay in the fact that this was often the only way to meet the operational requirements of organizations under conditions of shortage and inefficient resource distribution. Enterprise managers had to strike deals with suppliers, the workforce and their counterparts in other enterprises, whether or not these were officially approved. The incapacity or unwillingness of the regulating authorities to recognize and cope with economic realities meant that enterprise managers had to resort to "alawful" practices, a term coined by Pearce et al. (1991) to refer to certain reward practices in Hungary. Alawful practices are here defined as those which transgress the letter of the law or government regulation, but which are socially accepted because they are seen to meet a functional requirement.

So one form of informal adaptation to the inefficiencies of the hierarchical system was to resort to alawful practices. Another way in which the system adapted informally, especially in Hungary, was through the development of a so-called "second economy" which was market-oriented in the supply of some consumer goods and of many services. This second economy is estimated to have accounted for as much as 25-30% of Hungary's GDP by 1990 (*The Economist*, 23 February 1991). Both types of informal adaptation helped to preserve the system by staving off economic collapse, and both were politically condoned.

The institutionalized interrelation between political and economic forces has now become evident from comparing the centralized hierarchical and market-based systems. This interrelation is evident in both systems, but the prime criterion in the hierarchical system is political acceptability whereas the prime criterion in the market system is the satisfaction of market requirements. The contrast is summarized by Figure 11.1.

In theoretical terms, it does not make sense to claim that considerations either of political power or of economic efficiency have primacy. Although the clear implication is that the market-based system enjoys considerable economic advantages and has delivered the goods, the hierarchical system persisted for many decades. It

Figure 11.1: Two Systems: Two Models

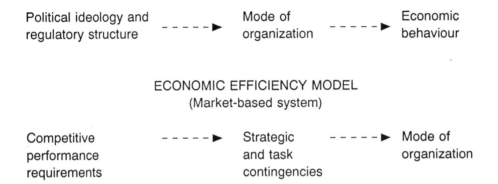

POLITICAL ACCEPTABILITY MODEL
(Centralized hierarchical system)

Political ideology and   Mode of   Economic
regulatory structure   ----▶ organization   ----▶ behaviour

ECONOMIC EFFICIENCY MODEL
(Market-based system)

Competitive   ----▶ Strategic   ----▶ Mode of
performance   and task   organization
requirements   contingencies

is also as yet unclear what kind of market or quasi-market system the former socialist countries will adopt, and this decision will of its very nature be political.

The title of this book applies to the societal level the paradigm of markets and hierarchies which Williamson developed for the governance of micro-economic transactions. The comparison which has been drawn between the centralized hierarchical and the market-based macro systems suggests (1) that the decision to opt for one or the other is primarily a political one which (2) carries direct consequences for the factors that Williamson (1975, 1985) sets up as contingencies determining the rational choice between hierarchical and market transaction modes at the micro level. This second observation requires some elaboration.

Williamson takes the criterion of efficiency to be the determinant of choice between a hierarchical and market mode for governing transactions, given certain contingent conditions. According to his argument, a preference for the hierarchical mode will be expressed under conditions where there is bounded rationality, information impactedness, asset specificity, a small numbers exchange condition (transactions with single or few buyers and sellers), and opportunism. In other words, the explanatory primacy given to the efficiency criterion leads Williamson to a position where he predicts preference for a mode of organization (a political phenomenon insofar as it establishes power, interest and reward differentials) by reference to how well it is likely to cope with contingencies in an economic and risk-reducing manner.

The comparison of hierarchical and market-based systems suggests that there is a reverse causal path to that mapped by Williamson. A hierarchical mode of organization may be imposed institutionally in some societies because the firm is taken to be an extension of higher-level agencies. That organizational mode, as we have seen, then tends to generate the very conditions which Williamson takes to be contextually contingent. By contrast and therefore relatively speaking, the market system tends to reduce the incidence of these conditions, so long as serious imperfections are not allowed to distort it. The conditions of bounded rationality, opportunism and so on are not, on the whole, conducive to economic efficiency, and this is why the centralized hierarchical systems tend towards eventual breakdown. They are, however, the products of an exercise of power which only *subsequently*, through their organizational dynamics, create conditions with economic consequences. These consequences may eventually undermine the legitimacy of their power base. Thus, as Williamson argues, the long-term survival of social systems may ultimately depend on their satisfying economic efficiency criteria, but both their creation and mode of operation in the intermediate term are more adequately explained in political terms.

The preceding analysis indicates that as societies transform from a hierarchical to a market basis, they become decentralized (with a consequent shift in the locus of risk), differentiated and information rich. These changes have important implications for enterprises, which can now be addressed.

3   Enterprises in their Economic Context between Market and Hierarchy

It will be helpful to consider for a moment how organization studies have progressed over the past few decades in their treatment of the relationship between organization and context in the Western world. The perspectives which have emerged in this progression can provide a framework that is useful for analysing the implications for enterprises of societal change in the socialist and former socialist countries.

From the early 1960s and for many years thereafter, organizational studies focused on ways in which contingencies in the so-called "task environment" helped to shape organizational forms and practices. For some, such as Donaldson (1985; 1991), this remains the most developed perspective within the subject area and the one from which the most reliable policy implications can be drawn.

Later on, from the mid-1970s, a more strategic view of organizational environment began to be adopted. Students of organization now came to regard the environment not simply as presenting a set of external conditions – in terms of available technology, labour skills, the rate and predictability of market change, and so on – to which management policies had to adjust. They began, instead, to view the relations between organizations and their environments in more dynamic and less deterministic terms, in which organization managers could engage actively with their contextual situation through the exercise of strategic choice (Child, 1972). The concept of strategic choice was compatible with a systems view of organizational effectiveness which defines this as the organization's "ability to exploit its environments in the acquisition of scarce and valued resources to sustain its functioning." (Yuchtman and Seashore, 1967: 393). This gave rise to a strategic perspective which viewed (senior) managers as strategists engaging both with resource providers and competitors, with the objective of ensuring a continued inflow of the resources necessary for survival, and indeed development, within the relevant population of organizations. This stage of thinking about organizations in their contexts encouraged an emphasis on the guiding role for structures and practices of strategic choice within a set of environmental possibilities, on the management of resource dependency and on the ability of organizations to adapt to the ecology of their populations (Miles and Snow, 1978; Pfeffer and Salancik, 1978; Hannan and Freeman, 1989). Various strands in this strategic view of the environment were comprehensively brought together by Aldrich (1979).

More recently still, though first signalled in the mid-1970s (e.g. Meyer and Rowan, 1977), the institutional perspective on organizations has come centre-stage into the discussion (Powell and DiMaggio, 1991). While this perspective takes many forms, it emphasizes how institutional norms (encompassing beliefs, structures and behaviours) are mapped onto organizations, or their constituent occupational groups, which for various reasons take the external institutions to be valid points of reference for guidance and emulation (Scott, 1987). The mechanisms by which that mapping or imprinting takes place, and the dynamic forces involved (be they the pursuit of perceived self-interest, the avoidance of normative uncertainty [anomie] or whatever) remain the subject of debate (cf. DiMaggio, 1988). The institutional perspective does not conceive of organization management as playing a strategic role but rather as accomodating to, and even internalizing, an external normative order and reflecting this in its own behaviour.

These three perspectives, in common with nearly all of organization theory, have been developed with reference to a Western capitalist context. If one regards them as offering complementary rather than mutually exclusive insights within that context, they provide a framework for analysing organizations within the market-based system towards which the hierarchically organized societies are moving. This framework comprises three levels, each corresponding to the focus of the three perspectives in reverse order, and which are depicted in Table 11.3.

The first level is institutional in context and normative in substance. At this level, societal values are projected into enterprises through the influence of relevant institutions, including those which educate and train staff, transmit social approval or disapproval through media coverage, and provide a legislative framework for business. Kornai (1985) identified the values which enterprises in socialist societies were expected to accept as social solidarity, economic security and priority of the general over the partial interest. Under a transformation to a capitalist market-based system, these values are likely to shift to competitiveness, risk in pursuit of profit, and ownership interest. Socialist values therefore tend towards maintenance of the

Table 11.3: Implications for Enterprises of Societal Change

HIERARCHICAL SYSTEM	MARKET SYSTEM
Two context levels:	Three context levels:
• *Normative institutional* • Task environment	• Institutional • *Strategic* • Task environment

Note: Italicized levels represent the critical environment under each system.

organizational status quo, and this is reinforced by the bureaucratic structure of the system, whereas the values of a market-based society tend towards innovation and change – as stereotyped by the "enterpreneur" – and this is reinforced by exposure to competition.

The normative institutional context provides the critical environment for state enterprises under the centralized hierarchical system (Markoczy, 1991). In market-based societies, neither the values nor the structures of external institutions are likely to map onto enterprises in anything like the same degree. The plurality of institutions in market-based societies means that no single one of them is in a position to impose itself fully. The state mostly adopts an arms-length role, even towards enterprises within its ownership. Moreover, the concomitant of the decentralization of policy-making and of risk to the enterprise in the market system is that it enjoys the right to decide on its own culture and it accepts responsibility for the consequences. Management is therefore able to make its own judgement as to how to strike a balance between the expectations of the various relevant institutions. In market systems, then, the normative force of the institutional context tends to be weaker.

The second level is the strategic. This concerns the managerial evaluation of the enterprise's positioning in its sector (strengths, weaknesses) and the competitive threats and opportunities open to it. If this evaluation is actually carried out and then acted on rationally, its logical consequence is a strategy which management believes to offer the prospect of securing the resources necessary for the enterprise's survival and indeed growth. Transformation from the hierarchical system requires enterprise managers to develop a strategic outlook and understanding which is consistent with the removal of bureaucratic paternalism, whereby there is a decentralization of the onus for survival to enterprises themselves and an exposure to competition. This strategic understanding takes the sector (or industry) as its primary point of reference and is conducive to the building of distinctive organizational cultures which reflect an evaluation of the enterprise's appropriate approach to competing within its sector. The strategic context constitutes the critical environment for enterprises under the market-based system, whereas it was not a significant context for enterprises under the hierarchical system.

The sector under the open market system is today typically competitive on an international scale, whereas in the state socialist system it often consisted of just one enterprise, like the *Ikarus* bus manufacturer in Hungary, producing for the whole COMECON market under government-to-government agreements. For this reason, large state-owned enterprises within socialist societies tended to be dependent for their strategic direction on their ministries or bureaux rather than developing their own strategies and cultures (cf. Czarniawska, 1986). The strategic context was in effect removed from the purview of enterprises and their managers.

The third level is the operational and has the task environment (Dill, 1958) as its contextual referent. This concerns the adoption of operational routines and techniques which are efficient in the light of the markets served, the technology employed, the competences and expectations of employees, and the size of the undertaking. The transformation towards a competitive market context will place enterprise managers under pressure to attend to the quality of their company's operations and to ensure that the configuration and organization of these operations fit the task environment in which the enterprise is located or which it seeks to enter.

The main difference between the hierarchical and market-based systems in their configuration of organizations and context lies in the way the state controls the strategic level in the former case. As a result, the normative and strategic levels of decision and action were combined giving rise to the situation analysed by Markoczy (1991) for Hungary in terms of an industrial governance system that linked the granting of institutional legitimacy to conforming enterprises with a distribution of resources in their favour. This gave rise to considerable isomorphism between the state and its enterprises, and indeed in many respects such enterprises had to be regarded as arms of the state.

As Tsoukas (1994) has pointed out, isomorphism between the state and enterprises can take a structural and a politically-induced form. Structural isomorphism occurs in both capitalist and socialist economies through a number of channels, such as the responsibility of the state for the creation, maintenance and certification of skills. However,

> What is qualitatively different in the case of socialist economies is the additional presence of politically-induced isomorphism. The all-pervasive presence of a socialist moral vision of society ... in combination with the socialist claims to a 'holistic' economic rationality and the consequent subordination of economic activities to broader societal goals, imply that the socialist political blueprint is invariably and unproblematically transposed at the formal organizational level. The organization becomes a political-cum-ideological miniature of the state (pp. 25-26 *mss.*).

In socialist societies, the enterprise carried out a number of crucial functions of the central authorities, such as maintaining employment. The enterprise was thus closely coupled to the state through an institutional linkage. In capitalist market-based societies, the state is part of the enterprise's environment, of relevance to (but not normally the determinant of) its managerial decisions. The monolithic and hierarchical system of industrial governance under state socialism meant that the normative and strategic levels of the organization-context relationship were integrated. The priorities for enterprises were significantly influenced by political criteria which expressed "socialist values" in regard to the balance between financial and social returns from investment. Studies of investment decision-making in Chinese and Hungarian enterprises during the 1980s clearly illustrate this phenomenon (cf. Markoczy, 1990; Child and Lu, 1992).

The structure of firms, their procedures and appointments to leading positions were determined under this system not so much by considerations of how well they suited the situation of the particular enterprise and the requirements for it to succeed economically in its sector, as by the criterion of acceptability to higher authorities. For a long time, enterprises were organized according to a model approved by these authorities. Procedures for collecting and reporting information reflected the requirements of the authorities rather than being oriented to the needs of the business for market information, financial control and so forth. The legacy of an institutional determination of enterprise design is one of the major problems which the foreign managers of joint ventures in China and Hungary have to tackle (Child and Markoczy, 1993). In effect, the imposition of institutional priorities on strategic decision-making meant that an understanding of the specificities of enterprise's sector and the strategic "recipe" (Spender, 1989) for operating successfully within it, was being subsumed to a uniformity guided by the concept of a monolithic tightly-coupled system.

Whereas in the market-based system enterprises are primarily dependent on market strategies that appeal to customers for ensuring a current and future income stream, rather than on social and governmental institutions that convey normative approval, in the hierarchical system this separation is not clear-cut. In China, even today, access to markets can depend significantly on products securing official recognition of their quality, a consideration which continues to render decision-making on new product development subject to the approval of higher authorities, even though this category of decision has now nominally been decentralized to the enterprise (Lu, 1991). Resources, including access to subsidies and other funds under the "soft budget constraint" (Kornai, 1980), tended to be allocated according to the goodwill and connection which enterprise leaders enjoyed with the resource-distributing higher authorities, rather than according to the economic value of the use to which they would be put. These same authorities were the purveyors of the political normative order which they were clearly in a strong position to impose on enterprises, especially those larger state-owned ones which were tightly coupled to them. The redistribution of resources in the form of tax liabilities, access to foreign exchange rights and COMECON export markets, was also in the hands of the normative state institutions.

In the hierarchical system, enterprise managers had to de-couple the operational level from the normative (Markoczy, 1991). In a highly institutionalized context, managers had to be seen to conform to the plans laid down by higher authorities, or if these no longer applied, to the preferences expressed by such authorities. Such conformity was, however, often in conflict with efficiency criteria; plans frequently failed to reflect customer requirements, or to provide the required supplies, or to match real production capabilities. Managers were obliged to decouple actual organizational practices from the formal ones, which became an appearance necessary to satisfy the normative state institutions.

In the market-based system, as already noted, there is only a loose coupling between the society's institutional norms and the strategies pursued in relation to the sector by individual firms. The main pressure on management in the market-based system is to couple operations to strategies – hence the considerable attention given to "manufacturing strategy" (Skinner, 1978). If the enterprise cannot deliver to its market, it cannot rely on the cushion of subsidies (though these are not unknown); rather, it is unlikely to survive.

The implication of this analysis is that the chief area of adaptation and new learning for enterprise managers experiencing the societal transformation towards a market economy is that of developing a strategic understanding. They have to learn to function without the protective paternalism of the centralized hierarchical system and instead to understand the nature of doing business competitively in a relevant domain. The chief difficulties in the way of acquiring this understanding and making the change in practices are posed by the uncertainty created by transformation itself in terms of the provisional limbo which accompanies it and the carry-over of institutional influence in its cultural and structural forms respectively. Paradoxically, the uncertainty generated by provisionality itself encourages managers to cling to both paradigms and practices with which they are familiar.

4   Problems of Transition: Provisionality and Institutional Lag

Social transition in a socialist country will create uncertainty among economic actors for two reasons. First, while the socialist system is being dismantled, economic decision-makers are left for a while without any certain guidelines for action. For example, the old channels of distribution through government middlemen are dissolved, but to be replaced by what? Second, if the system is only partially reformed and/or there is a discordance between political and economic policy statements as in China, then economic actors will be uncertain whether new rules of the game are really going to emerge and will feel it safer to stick to the old ones (especially if, as in China, adventurists have been punished in the past). When faced with uncertainty, people are in any case inclined to follow the routines on which they have previously relied, even though these may now be non-functional. In societies transforming away from centralized hierarchical social systems, this inclination to retain previous patterns of action is likely to be reinforced by what may be termed institutional lag.

The rulers of centralized hierarchical systems enlisted the support of a legitimizing socialist ideology and the system became institutionalized into a mutually reinforcing culture and governance structure. Some two generations of enterprise managers were exposed to the culture and worked within the structure. It is predictable that many internalized the norms of the culture and will now exhibit difficulty and/or reluctance in discarding it and the way of thinking, or paradigm (Johnson, 1990), that it engendered, even if the old governance structure is largely dismantled. In terms of the Argyris and Schon (1978) model of learning, the single-loop learning of acquiring new techniques from foreign sources is therefore likely to present far less of a challenge to former socialist managers than will the double-loop learning of understanding and accepting a new cognitive framework for doing business and conducting the task of managing. Evidence of the persistence of managerial adherence to the former paradigm has emerged from Chinese and Hungarian joint ventures, where the issue has often been highlighted by the desire of foreign partners to change local managerial understanding as well as behaviour. For example, Chinese managers have often found it difficult to appreciate the competitive significance of high quality standards, especially in relation to products destined for the international market (e.g. Mann, 1989). In the Sino-foreign joint ventures which the author and his colleagues studied, quality control was frequently mentioned as a problem by foreign managers but never by their Chinese counterparts (Child et al., 1990). Chinese managers had great difficulty conceptualizing their product market in an analytical manner, so that strategic decisions could be made on segmentation and other aspects of marketing policy.

The concept of linking personnel policies and practices – on hiring, firing, rewards and development – in a planned and systematic manner to the operational needs and performance of the enterprise was alien to both Chinese and Hungarian managers. They also continued to behave opportunistically and alawfully, even when dealing with foreigners who clearly expected that internationally accepted conventions should be followed with regard to agreements and contracts (for Hungarian examples see Markoczy, 1991). They found it difficult to accept the necessary assumptions for teamwork, such as treating information as a shared resource rather than as a personal property. They also exhibited considerable dependence on the authority of foreign managers and a reluctance to assume delegated decision responsibility (Child and Markoczy, 1993). These examples of non-adaptation to new expectations, even in situations where the authority of the foreign partner was legitimated by acknowledged expertise as well as equity ownership, point to a considerable cultural lag.

Cultural lag continues to be reinforced by a structural institutional lag, especially in China where the administrative structures of the hierarchical system have been retained. The main structural feature of the Chinese economic reform has been the decentralization of regulation over all but some strategic industries from the central government to provincial and municipal governments. Regulations issued under the reform also gave enterprise managements new decision rights over a range of issues, including the use of surplus funds, internal reorganization and personnel management. However, as Lu (1991) has shown in his detailed studies of decision-making in state enterprises, the maintenance of a structure of regulating higher authorities (now operating primarily at the local level) has meant that a platform still exists from which bureaucrats can exercise a strong influence over managerial actions. They can dominate the strategic development of enterprises through several channels: their role as co-signatories of responsibility contracts for enterprises; their control over investment funds; and their granting of official product quality classifications which can carry great influence with a poorly informed buying public. They have to approve the appointment of enterprise directors; they continue to have a major say on internal enterprise organization; they still control access to much technical and market information.

The persistence of the old structure of industrial governance in China and the continuation in post of many incumbent officials and managers had often frustrated the proclaimed intention of the economic reform to decentralize initiative to enterprises. This problem was surfacing in the official press before the events of 1989 and might have led to some eventual structural change if the reform process had not been halted and enterprise managers criticized for allowing ideological orthodoxy to take a back seat. The Chinese situation clearly illustrates how enterprises remain under the control of superior governance authorities when a structural decentralization of resource provision is not implemented. This retention of administrative influence restricts the ability of enterprises to engage in market transactions as autonomous decision-making players.

Even in Hungary, where there has been a political transformation, this has not been followed yet by much significant structural transformation. It is estimated that in 1991 about 75% of Hungarian national wealth remained in the ownership of state and cooperative firms. This high public ownership of enterprises, almost all of which are facing severe economic difficulties, means that the degree of state control over them remains very large despite the shift to a market economy (Tihanyi, 1991). Privatization in Hungary is in fact now decelerating, still a long way from the government's goal of releasing half of the economy from state ownership by

1994 (Denton, 1992). Indeed, the statistics of industrial restructuring in Hungary exaggerate the rate of change and mask the real situation. Thus some 22,000 small firms were established in 1990, but about 21,000 of these were the result simply of reorganization in state-owned firms, whereby unitary organizations were divided up. They stayed state-owned and the existing managers kept their positions.

5   Conclusion

This paper has made a number of points. The instigation of societal change in Eastern Europe and its arrest in China betray a combination of economic and political forces that requires a political economy analysis in the full sense of that term. At both societal and organizational levels, there is an interdependency between considerations of power and efficiency.

The experience of hierarchical systems does not support the assumption of many Western theories, that modes of organization are selected primarily because they appear to offer the most efficient way of governing economic transactions under certain contingent conditions. They may be selected for political reasons and create contingencies (such as information impactedness) which bear upon the conduct of economic transactions. However, the inherent characteristics of centralized hierarchical systems make them more vulnerable to collapse than market-based systems.

The transformation from hierarchical to market-based systems means that the context of enterprises changes from a two-level to a three-level phenomenon, in which the strategic significance of competitive sectors emerges as the critical environment for enterprise performance. This change implies that the biggest challenge facing enterprise managers is one of strategic learning, including the need to take autonomous initiatives in order to promote their firms' chances in a competitive context.

Institutional lag, in both its cultural and structural forms, poses a serious constraint on the willingness and the ability of managers to embark on this learning. Its conservative effect is reinforced by the uncertainty associated by the provisional nature of transitory arrangements, and the doubts in some post-socialist countries as to whether a successful transition will be achieved. The presence of institutional lag indicates that, in some degree, institutional factors *per se* account for enterprise behaviour over and above the political and economic forces which in turn contribute to the development and reproduction of institutions.

References

Aldrich, Howard E. (1979) *Organizations and Environments*. Englewood Cliffs, NJ: Prentice-Hall.

Argyris, Chris/Schon, Donald A. (1978) *Organizational Learning*. Reading, MA: Addison-Wesley.

Bak, Per /Chen, Kan (1991) 'Self-organized Criticality', *Scientific American* 264 (1): 26-33.

Balaton, Karoly/Dilova, Julia/Dobak, Miklos/March, James G. (1990) 'Some Fragmentary, Preliminary Throughts about Research on Organizational Change in Eastern Europe'. Unpublished manuscript. Budapest University of Economics.

Biggart, Nicole W. (1991) 'Explaining Asian Economic Organization: Toward a Weberian Institutional Perspective', *Theory and Society* 20: 199-232.

Boisot, Max (1986) 'Markets and Hierarchies in a Cultural Perspective', *Organization Studies* 7: 135-158.

Child, John (1972) 'Organizational Structure, Environment and Performance: The Role of Strategic Choice', *Sociology* 6: 1-22.

Child, John et al. (1990) *The Management of Joint Ventures in China*. Beijing: China-EC Management Institute.

Child, John/Loveridge, Ray (1990) *Information Technology in European Services*. Oxford: Blackwell.

Child, John /Lu, Yuan (1992) 'Institutional Constraints on Economic Reform: The Case of Investment Decisions in China', *Management Studies Research Paper* 8/92, University of Cambridge.

Child, John/Markoczy, Livia (1993) 'Host Country Managerial Behaviour and Learning in Chinese and Hungarian Joint Ventures', *Journal of Management Studies* 30 (forthcoming).

Cooper, Robert/Burrell, Gibson (1988) 'Modernism, Postmodernism and Organizational Analysis: An Introduction', *Organization Studies* 9 (1): 91-112.

Czarniawska, Barbara (1986) 'The Management of Meaning in the Polish Crisis', *Journal of Management Studies* 23: 313-331.

Davis, Howard/Scase, Richard (1985) *Western Capitalism and State Socialism*. Oxford: Blackwell.

Denton, N. (1992) "Running into Resistance", *Financial Times Survey on Hungary*, 29 October: 33.

Dill, William R. (1958) 'Environment as an Influence on Managerial Autonomy'. *Administrative Science Quarterly* 2: 409-443.

DiMaggio, Paul J. (1988) 'Interest and Agency in Institutional Theory' pp. 3-21 in Zucker, L.G. (ed.) *Institutional Patterns and Organizations*. Cambridge, MA: Ballinger.

Donaldson, Lex (1985) *In Defence of Organization Theory*. Cambridge: Cambridge University Press.

Donaldson, Lex (1991) 'The Liberal Revolution and Organization Theory'. Paper given to the Conference on 'Towards a New Theory of Organizations', University of Keele, April.

The Economist (1991) 'Reform in Eastern Europe: Hungary – Italy on the Danube'. 23 February: 58-59.

Featherstone, Mike (1988) 'In Pursuit of the Postmodern: An Introduction', *Theory, Culture and Society* 5: 195-215.

Hannan, Michael T./Freeman, John (1989) *Organizational Ecology*. Cambridge, MA: Harvard University Press.

Johnson, Gerry (1990) 'Managing Strategic Change: The Role of Symbolic Action', *British Journal of Management* 1: 183-200.

Kornai, Janos (1980) *The Economics of Shortage*. Amsterdam: North-Holland.

Kornai, Janos (1985) *Contradictions and Dilemmas*. Budapest: Corvina.

Kornai, Janos (1986) 'The Hungarian Reform Process: Visions, Hopes and Reality', *Journal of Economic Literature* 24: 1687-1737.

Littler, Craig R. (1983) 'A Comparative Analysis of Managerial Structures and Strategies' pp. 171-196 in Howard F. Gospel/Littler, Craig R. (eds.) *Managerial Strategies and Industrial Relations*. London: Heinemann.

Lu, Yuan (1991) *A Longitudinal Study of Chinese Managerial Behaviour: An Inside View of Decision Making under the Economic Reform*. Unpublished PhD thesis, Aston University.

Mann, Jim (1989) *Beijing Jeep*. New York: Simon and Schuster.

Markoczy, Livia (1990) 'Case Study of the IE Bank'. Case Study, International Management Centre, Budapest.

Markoczy, Livia (1991) 'Institutional Changes in Hungary and Modes of Organizational Learning'. Working Paper 3, Budapest University of Economics.

Meyer, John W./Rowan, Brian (1977) Institutional Organizations: Formal Structure as Myth and Ceremony', *American Journal of Sociology* 83: 340-363.

Miles, Raymond E./Snow, Charles C. (1978) *Organizational Strategy, Structure, and Process*. New York: McGraw-Hill.

Montias, J.M. (1988) 'On Hierarchies and Economic Reforms', *Journal of Institutional and Theoretical Economics* 144: 832-838.

Pearce, Jone L./Branyiczky, Imre/Bakacsi, Gyula (1991) 'Alawful Reward Systems: A Theory of Organizational Reward Practices in Reform-communist Organizations'. Working paper OB 91003, Graduate School of Management, University of California, Irvine.

Pfeffer, Jeffrey/Salancik, Gerald R. (1978) *The External Control of Organizations*. New York: Harper and Row.

Powell, Walter W./DiMaggio, Paul J. (eds.) (1991) *The New Institutionalism in Organizational Analysis*. Chicago: University of Chicago Press.

Reed, Michael I. (1991) 'Organizations and Modernity: Continuity and Discontinuity in Organization Theory'. Paper given to the conference on 'Towards a New Theory of Organizations', University of Keele, April.

Scott, W. Richard (1987) 'The Adolescence of Institutional Theory', *Administrative Science Quarterly* 32: 493-511.

Skinner, Wickham (1978) *Manufacturing in the Corporate Strategy*. New York: Wiley.

Soros, Gyorgy (1991) 'Conception of the Open Societies'. Lecture given at the Budapest University of Economics, May 14th.

Spender, J.-C. (1989) *Industry Recipes*. Oxford: Blackwell.

Spronz, Imre (1991) Contribution to Round-Table on 'Governance Issues in East-West Business Collaborations', organized by the Centre for Organizational Studies, Mondralin, Poland.

Tihanyi, Laszlo (1991) 'Business Strategies in the Emerging Eastern European Market: The Case of Hungary'. Paper given to the International Conference on Strategies for Players in a Larger World, Odense, Denmark.

Tsoukas, Haridimos (1994) 'Socio-economic Systems and Organizational Management: An Institutional Perspective on the Socialist Firm', *Organization Studies* 15 (forthcoming).

Weber, Max (1922) *Wirtschaft und Gesellschaft*. (Part I translated by A.M. Henderson and Talcott Parsons and edited by Talcott Parsons as The Theory of Social and Economic Organization, New York: Free Press 1964).

Williamson, Oliver E. (1975) *Markets and Hierarchies*. New York: Free Press.

Williamson, Oliver E. (1985) *The Economic Institutions of Capitalism*. New York: Free Press.

Yuchtman, E./Seashore, S. (1967) 'A System Resource Approach to Organizational Effectiveness', *American Sociological Review* 32: 891-903.

List of Contributors

Hans Berger, School of Management and Organization at the University of Groningen, The Netherlands

Max Boisot, Professor at the Escuela Superior de Administración y Dirección de Empresas, Barcelona, Spain

Cyril F. Chang, Professor of Economics at the Department of Economics, The Fogelman College of Business and Economics, Memphis State University, Memphis, USA

John Child, Guinness Professor of Management Studies, Director of The Judge Institute of Management Studies of the University of Cambridge, United Kingdom

Michel Crozier, President of the Centre de Sociologie des Organisations, Director of Research at the Centre National de la Recherche Scientifique, Paris, France

Paul du Gay, Research Fellow at the Department of Sociology of The Open University, Milton Keynes, United Kingdom

Silvia Gherardi, Researcher at the Department of Social Policy of the Università Degli Studi di Trento, Italy

Renate Mayntz, Director at the Max-Planck-Institut für Gesellschaftsforschung, Cologne, Germany

Bertrand Moingeon, Assistant-Professor at the Department of Strategy and Business Policy, HEC, Graduate School of Management, Jouy-en-Josas, France

Niels Noorderhaven, Faculty of Economics of the Catholic University of Brabant, Tilburg, The Netherlands

Bart Nooteboom, School of Management and Organization at the University of Groningen, The Netherlands

Roger Penn, Reader in Economic Sociology at the Department of Sociology of Lancaster University, United Kingdom

Bartjan Pennink, School of Management and Organization at the University of Groningen, The Netherlands

Bernard Ramanantsoa, Professor at the Department of Strategy and Business Policy, HEC, Graduate School of Management, Jouy-en-Josas, France

Ota Šik, Professor for System Comparisons at the St. Gallen University for Economic and Social Sciences, Switzerland

Howard P. Tuckmann, Distinguished Professor of Economics at the Department of Economics, The Fogelman College of Business and Economics, Memphis State University, Memphis, USA